Lecture Notes in Computer Science 16261

The series Lecture Notes in Computer Science (LNCS), including its subseries Lecture Notes in Artificial Intelligence (LNAI) and Lecture Notes in Bioinformatics (LNBI), has established itself as a medium for the publication of new developments in computer science and information technology research, teaching, and education.

LNCS enjoys close cooperation with the computer science R & D community, the series counts many renowned academics among its volume editors and paper authors, and collaborates with prestigious societies. Its mission is to serve this international community by providing an invaluable service, mainly focused on the publication of conference and workshop proceedings and postproceedings. LNCS commenced publication in 1973.

Raghunath Nambiar · Meikel Poess
Editors

Performance Evaluation and Benchmarking

17th TPC Technology Conference, TPCTC 2025
London, UK, September 1, 2025
Revised Selected Papers

Editors
Raghunath Nambiar
Advanced Micro Devices
Santa Clara, CA, USA

Meikel Poess
Server Technologies
Oracle Corporation
Redwood City, CA, USA

ISSN 0302-9743 ISSN 1611-3349 (electronic)
Lecture Notes in Computer Science
ISBN 978-3-032-18069-8 ISBN 978-3-032-18070-4 (eBook)
https://doi.org/10.1007/978-3-032-18070-4

This Springer imprint is published by the registered company Springer Nature Switzerland AG
The registered company address is: Gewerbestrasse 11, 6330 Cham, Switzerland

Preface

Established in August 1988, the Transaction Processing Performance Council (TPC) has played a pivotal role in shaping the computing industry through standardized benchmarks for more than 37 years. These benchmarks enable vendors to demonstrate the performance of their solutions and guide improvements in products under development. They also serve as trusted indicators for purchasers evaluating new computing systems, whether deployed on-premises or in the cloud.

This volume presents the proceedings of the 17th TPC Technology Conference on Performance Evaluation and Benchmarking (TPCTC 2025), held alongside the 50th International Conference on Very Large Data Bases (VLDB 2025) in London, UK, on September 1, 2025.

This year's conference accepted 10 of the 18 submitted papers, each peer reviewed (single blind) by an average of four experts. The proceedings also feature two invited papers and a panel discussion led by industry and academic leaders. The accepted papers span the following subject areas:

Core Database Benchmarking: Representing the largest category, these papers focus on creating or refining benchmarks for diverse data systems. Topics include new benchmarks for databases with varying value lengths, JSON data analytics (CH2++), and transactional key-value stores (Tectonic). Additionally, one study proposes a benchmark specifically for Role-Based Access Control.

AI/LLM-Related Benchmarking: This group addresses the emerging necessity of benchmarking AI workloads. Submissions cover flexible LLM inference benchmarking across different hardware (ScaleBench_AI), the evaluation of distilled language models, and reports on achieving leadership performance in MLPerf submissions.

Data Generation and Augmentation: These papers focus on the creation of realistic test data. Highlights include a system for generating synthetic relational data from SQL schemas (DataGenX) and an examination of tabular data augmentation using medical insurance claims for scalability testing.

System/Hardware Optimization and Sustainability: This section addresses system-level performance considerations beyond core data structures. Notable work includes a study on DiStash, a disaggregated, multi-stash architecture for transactional key-value stores.

TPCTC 2025 arrived at a transformative moment for performance evaluation as computing systems evolve under the influence of Artificial Intelligence, cloud-native architectures, and heterogeneous platforms.

By fostering collaboration between academia and industry, TPCTC 2025 aimed to advance scalable, accurate, and relevant methodologies for a rapidly changing technological landscape.

We extend our sincere gratitude to all authors, reviewers, VLDB organizers, volunteers, and TPC members whose efforts made this conference a cornerstone for progress in benchmarking and performance evaluation.

December 2025

Raghunath Nambiar
Meikel Poess

Organization

General Chairs

Raghunath Nambiar	AMD, USA
Meikel Poess	Oracle, USA

Publication Chair

Rodrigo D. Escobar	University of Texas at San Antonio, USA

Program Committee

Ahmad Ghazal	PingCAP, USA
Ajay Dholakia	Lenovo, USA
Andrew Bond	Red Hat, USA
Hans-Arno Jacobsen	University of Toronto, Canada
Hanumath Rao Maduri	Workday, USA
Harry Le	University of Houston, USA
John Poelman	IBM, USA
Karthik Krishna	InfobellIT Solutions, India
Klaus-Dieter Lange	Hewlett Packard Enterprise, USA
Michael Brey	Oracle, USA
Miro Hodak	AMD, USA
Nicholas Wakou	Dell, USA
Paul Cao	Hewlett Packard Enterprise, USA
Pratyush Agnihotri	Technical University of Darmstadt, Germany
Rodrigo D. Escobar	University of Texas at San Antonio, USA
Shahram Ghandeharizadeh	University of Southern California, USA
Tariq Magdon-Ismail	VMware, USA
Tilmann Rabl	Hasso Plattner Institute, Germany

Publicity Committee

Meikel Poess	Oracle, USA
Paul Cao	HPE, USA

About the TPC

Introduction to the TPC

The Transaction Processing Performance Council (TPC) is a non-profit organization with a primary objective of spearheading the development of industry standards tailored for data-centric workloads. Committed to promoting fairness and transparency in performance evaluation, the TPC diligently collects and disseminates vendor-neutral performance data across the industry. With a vision to foster collaboration and drive innovation, the TPC serves as a pivotal platform for industry stakeholders to benchmark and assess the efficiency of their technologies.

For further insights into the TPC's initiatives, standards, and resources, and for information on memberships and on ordering TPC materials, visit the official website at http://www.tpc.org/

Full Members

Alibaba
AMD
Boray Data
Cisco
Dell Technologies
Hewlett Packard Enterprise
Hitachi
Huawei
IEIT Systems
Inspur-Cloud
Intel
Lenovo
Microsoft
Nutanix
Nvidia
Oracle
Red Hat
Timecho
Transwarp
TTA
VMware

Associate Members

Tsinghua University, China
University of Coimbra, Portugal
Imec

Professional Affiliates

Hotea Solutions
Infobell IT Solutions
InfoSizing
Metrology
Performance Dynamics Company
Performance Tuning Corporation
SBI Association Management

TPC 2025 Organization

Steering Committee

Michael Brey (Chair)	Oracle
Paul Cao	HPE
Jamie Reding	Microsoft
Ken Rule	Intel
Nicholas Wakou	Dell EMC

Public Relations Committee

Meikel Poess (Chair)	Oracle
Paul Cao	HPE
Gary Little	Nutanix
Rodrigo Escobar	Intel
Nirmala Sundararajan	Dell Technologies

Technical Advisory Board

Jamie Reding (Chair)	Microsoft
Paul Cao	HPE
Gary Little	Nutanix
Mike Brey	Oracle
Ken Rul	Intel
Nicholas Wakou	Dell EMC

Technical Subcommittees and Chairs

Transaction Processing

- TPC-C: Jamie Reding (Microsoft)
- TPC-E: Jamie Reding (Microsoft)

Decision Support

- TPC-H: Meikel Poess (Oracle)
- TPC-DS: Meikel Poess (Oracle)
- TPC-DI: Meikel Poess (Oracle)

Virtualization

- TPCx-V Tariq Magdon-Ismail (VMware)
- TPCx-HCI Tariq Magdon-Ismail (VMware)

Big Data

- TPCx-HS: Tariq Magdon-Ismail (VMware)
- TPCx-BB: Rodrigo Escobar (Intel)

Internet of Things

- TPCx-IoT: Meikel Poess (Oracle)

Artificial Intelligence

- TPCx-AI: Hamesh Patel (Intel)

Open Source

- TPC-OSS: Andy Bond (Red Hat)

Common Benchmark Specifications

- TPC-Pricing: Jamie Reding (Microsoft)
- TPC-Energy: Paul Cao (HPE)

Contents

A Benchmark for Databases with Varying Value Lengths

Danushka Liyanage[1(✉)], Shubham Pandey[2], Joshua Goldstein[3], Michael Cahill[1], Akon Dey[4], Alan Fekete[1], and Uwe Röhm[1]

[1] University of Sydney, Sydney, Australia
{danushka.liyanage,michael.cahill,alan.fekete,uwe.roehm}@sydney.edu.au
[2] Austin, TX, USA
[3] Texas A&M University, College Station, TX, USA
[4] Predictable Labs, Inc., Foster City, CA, USA

Abstract. The performance of database management systems (DBMS) is traditionally evaluated using benchmarks that focus on workloads with (almost) fixed record lengths. However, some real-world workloads in key/value stores, document databases, and graph databases exhibit significant variability in value lengths, which can lead to performance anomalies, particularly when popular records grow disproportionately large. Existing benchmarks fail to account for this variability, leaving an important aspect of DBMS behavior underexplored.

In this paper, we address this gap by extending the Yahoo! Cloud Serving Benchmark (YCSB) to include an "extend" operation, which appends data to record fields, simulating the growth of values over time. Using this modified benchmark, we have measured the performance of three popular DBMS backends: MongoDB, MariaDB with the InnoDB storage engine, and MariaDB with the MyRocks storage engine. Our experiments alternate between extending values and executing query workloads, revealing significant performance differences driven by storage engine design and their handling of variable-sized values.

Our key contribution is the introduction of a novel benchmarking approach to evaluate the impact of growing value sizes and isolate the effect of querying data with a distribution of data sizes from any cost associated with accessing data after a history of updates. This highlights the need for more representative benchmarks that capture the dynamic nature of real-world workloads, providing valuable guidance for both practitioners and researchers.

Keywords: Key-value stores · Benchmarking · Throughput · Latency

1 Introduction

Benchmarks, such as the TPC suite, have served the database field well; they have helped practitioners with system and configuration choice, and have been

S. Pandey—Independent Researcher.

R. Nambiar and M. Poess (Eds.): TPCTC 2025, LNCS 16261, pp. 1–19, 2026.
https://doi.org/10.1007/978-3-032-18070-4_1

a spur for researchers to improve platform design. In this paper, we consider a gap in prior work on benchmarking: the neglect of cases where some data items (records in tables, documents in a document store, values in a key value store) get longer and longer as the system evolves, eventually becoming quite long (say megabyte size). This can happen particularly when an item has an attribute whose type is array and where the application uses this array to store information about the item's history. In that case, some operations of the application append extra information to that attribute; if the item is a popular one and the database lasts a long time, the item may grow very long. This situation has not been well covered in previous benchmarks. Some (e.g., YCSB) have fixed size for all items; while TPC-C does include some variation in record size (due to VARCHAR fields such as C_DATA), this variation is limited, with no record longer than 1KB.

The existence in real applications of items that grow in size over time can impact the performance of the system, depending on choices made in the implementation of the storage layer. These situations can cause fragmentation of the data on disk or in memory, or may lead to frequent re-arrangements if the storage uses an update-in-place approach. Some systems store deltas to optimize the case where only a small part of an item is modified in an update. If these design aspects are not exercised in a benchmark, we will not know how well the choices work in practice. Thus, the focus of this paper is to propose a benchmark that examines what happens when items have lengths that increase significantly over time.

When the data includes some items that are growing steadily, there are several consequential changes to the data, and we aim to disentangle the performance impact of these. One impact of some records growing longer through history is that at any given time, the data items in the database will vary in length among themselves. Another consequence is that the total volume of data in the database will grow. YCSB-IVS is designed to measure performance with a database where some items keep growing, but we also compare this with performance when the item sizes vary, but not as a result of a history of growth. Also, we look at the performance of two baselines with the same total volume and items of uniform size: one baseline has many small records, and the other has fewer records, which are all equally long.

We propose a benchmark called YCSB-IVS which builds on the framework provided by Yahoo! Cloud Serving Benchmark (YCSB), a widely used benchmarking tool originally for key/value stores, but also with bindings for a wide variety of platforms including SQL ones. While the original YCSB workload has fixed size items (by default, 1000 bytes exactly), which can be read, updated, etc., we introduce an "extend" operation that appends data to one or more fields of a record, causing the length to grow over time. In contrast to the original YCSB, where data is loaded initially, and then a single measured run executes a mix of read, update, etc. operations, YCSB-IVS loads data, and then proceeds in a sequence of epochs, each of which performs some number of extend operations applied to keys randomly chosen according to some distribution, and then we measure the metrics (throughput, latency, etc.) for standard YCSB workloads against the state at the end of the extension phase. As we run successive epochs, some of the data items become longer and longer, and the standard measurements show the slowdown that this causes. For comparison, we also measure for each epoch the read performance on a database with the same logical state (and thus the same distribution of item lengths) but no history of increase. We report the performance metrics for each epoch, and also report on two baselines which execute the queries against two datasets with equal-sized items and the same total volume as the given epoch; one baseline has the same number of items as in our benchmark (and so each item has length, which is the average length found after extensions). In the other baseline, all records have the unextended length, and so there are many more items than in the benchmark execution.

We have applied YCSB-IVS to measure the performance of several popular DBMS platforms - MongoDB, MariaDB with the InnoDB storage engine, and MariaDB with the MyRocks storage engine. Here we show a few examples of the results; full details are in our YCSB-IVS Tech Report.

Our findings reveal significant performance differences between systems, driven by their storage engines and handling of large, variable-sized values. For example, some systems demonstrate robust performance even as values grow, while others exhibit surprising slowdowns. These results underscore the importance of incorporating varying value sizes into benchmarking methodologies to uncover hidden performance characteristics and better inform DBMS design and optimization.

In Sect. 2 we discuss in more detail some real-world cases where items grow in length substantially over time. Section 3 provides a critical analysis of prior work relevant to this research domain. In Sect. 4 we describe the detailed operation of our new benchmark. In Sect. 5 we illustrate its use by reporting some measurements.

Our key contribution is to propose a novel benchmarking approach for databases/key-value stores. We extend YCSB to simulate realistic scenarios where value sizes grow over time, reflecting issues that occur in real-world workload patterns but have not been effectively benchmarked before. Through this work, we aim to broaden the scope of DBMS performance evaluation, expanding from the current focus on fixed-size data items to include workloads where some items can grow to be quite large. In doing so, we hope to contribute to a deeper understanding of how modern DBMS systems perform under conditions that are more closely aligned with real-world applications. The source code of YCSB-IVS and data from our experiments are provided at https://github.com/dliyanage/YCSB-IVS

2 Motivation

In numerous applications, array-valued attributes are a common feature within data records, playing an essential role despite not fitting the strict criteria of the first normal form (1NF) in traditional relational database models. These array attributes enable rich representations of complex data relationships and historical changes within the records. Despite their departure from conventional normalization principles, many relational databases (RDBMS) and modern NoSQL databases, such as document stores and graph databases, offer support for storing such multi-valued fields.

In practical applications, these array-type fields often serve critical functions. For example, an e-commerce platform might maintain a product record, complete with an array field that lists all previous prices at which the product was marketed. Each time the product is listed with a new price, the list of prices within the array attribute expands with the addition of the latest offered price. Similarly, a social media site keeps track of posts and tags. Over time, additional tags are appended to the existing list of tags for each post.

In long-term database usage, array-valued fields in popular items can experience significant growth, reaching megabytes in length, while entries in less popular items may only reach kilobyte ranges. This stark divergence in item size within a single collection or table is characteristic of data that has grown incrementally over time. The potential for such wide variations in record size can have implications for database performance. It underscores the need to understand and benchmark how the gradual expansion of array fields influences the overall performance of the DBMS.

We describe real-world situations from the industrial experience of some authors.

Record Growth in Dgraph. Dgraph is a distributed graph database platform optimized for high-throughput workloads. It stores graph-structured data by decomposing it into individual facts, called predicates. Each fact represented as a key-value pair is stored in Badger[1], an LSM-tree-based key-value store. Alongside this data, Dgraph also stores metadata, including type definitions and lists of unique identifiers (*uids*) for each type [20]. As the database matures and contains more data, the length of the values for a small number of keys, such as the types, scales in proportion to the overall growth of the application's data. This issue became particularly evident at Dgraph Labs, where it contributed to extended support calls, production outages at high-profile customer sites, and numerous sleepless nights.

Compounding the issue, record deletions provide little relief due to the underlying storage mechanisms. Even with garbage collection in place, large record sizes remain a persistent challenge, exacerbating storage inefficiencies and operational complexity over time.

Document Growth in MongoDB. MongoDB is a platform that directly supports a document data model. Certain application patterns with MongoDB can lead to documents expanding over time, such as maintaining an exhaustive history of events or tracking changes to a value across multiple iterations. In these scenarios, what begins as small increments to a document's size can compound

[1] https://github.com/hypermodeinc/badger.

over time, leading to substantial increases in document size after numerous updates.

This growth pattern is particularly concerning when each update causes the document to swell incrementally; without careful design, such expansion can precipitate memory and storage fragmentation. MongoDB addresses this challenge by delaying when small updates to large documents are persisted to storage[2]. Instead, they are cached and consolidated into fewer and larger updates upon subsequent write operations. This strategy mitigates the quadratic increase in work associated with handling numerous tiny updates and reduces the incidence of fragmentation.

The impact of this design choice is twofold: first, it alleviates the memory and storage overhead that would otherwise result from frequent small updates. Second, certain workloads experience considerable performance enhancement due to this optimization.

3 Related Work

Databases Value/Object Sizes. The size of values or objects in databases plays a crucial role in query execution, as larger sizes impose greater processing demands, thereby slowing down performance. Consequently, object size has been a central consideration in numerous query optimization cost models [11,14], often serving as a critical factor in addressing scalability challenges. For instance, Shapiro et al. [27] evaluated the performance of databases utilizing Binary Large Objects (BLOBs) and observed that increases in both database size and average object size significantly degrade transaction efficiency.

It is evident that database developers have long recognized the trade-offs associated with value sizes, particularly the efficiency gains achieved by keeping value sizes small. This understanding has made data *compression* a fundamental feature in modern databases and key-value stores [18,19,31]. A quantitative assessment by Hurson et al. [17] in the early 1990s demonstrated that smaller object sizes significantly improve the efficiency of object clustering, reducing I/O operations and achieving cost improvements ranging from a factor of 2 to 15.

Although efforts are often made to keep value or object sizes as small as possible, there are numerous scenarios in which value sizes naturally grow over time. Pelekis et al. [25] highlighted that size plays a critical role in spatio-temporal database models, especially in databases that undergo continuous changes.

Database Benchmarking. The 'Wisconsin' benchmarks [5], introduced in the early 1980s, were among the first systematic attempts to benchmark relational database systems, evaluating platforms like DIRECT, INGRES, ORACLE, and IDM500. Soon after, the TP1 benchmark (1985) emerged, measuring transaction throughput through components such as *transaction (DebitCredit)*, *OS and I/O*

[2] https://www.mongodb.com/community/forums/t/in-place-partial-updates/240487.

(Sort), and *file system (Copy)*. Jim Gray's benchmarking handbook [15] formalizes database benchmarking practices, leading to the expansion of benchmarks from the Transaction Processing Performance Council (TPC) [29].

The TPC benchmarks became influential, and *DebitCredit* evolved into TPC-A and then TPC-C for OLTP[3] workloads. To address both OLTP and OLAP[4] systems, the hybrid TPC-CH benchmark was introduced [13], bridging TPC-C (OLTP) and TPC-H (OLAP). Building on TPC-H, the *Star Schema Benchmark (SSB)* was developed to measure database performance in traditional warehousing applications [24].

Over time, specialized benchmarking tools emerged to evaluate diverse database architectures. Examples include a variety of benchmarks inspired by social network graph structures including LinkBench [1] and TAOBench [8], *Jackpine* for spatial databases [26], SmartBench [16] for IoT support. LDBC is a consortium which has defined a family of benchmarks for graph data, eg [12]. YCSB was introduced to measure performance of cloud-based key-value platforms [9], and because it offers an extensible framework, later work used YCSB as the basis to incorporate other aspects including transactions [10], geospatial data [21]. Recently, [3] focused on the danger of systems becoming tuned for widely-used benchmarks, and advocates for introducing new "surprise" aspects each year.

Value Size in Benchmarking. Large object sizes have been considered in database benchmarking due to their direct impact on overall database size. Biliris [4] analyzed the performance of large object management across three database systems from 1992—EXODUS [7], Starburst, and EOS—focusing on length-changing updates. The study proposed strategies for segment size adjustments to enhance operational efficiency while noting the trade-off between performance gains and reduced storage utilization with large fixed-size segments.

In past decades, the main relational database benchmarks have predominantly employed fixed (or only slightly varying) item sizes in their setups [2]. While scaling the total database volume has been a traditional benchmarking consideration (e.g. "scale factor" in the TPC benchmarks), the dynamic nature of individual value sizes and their distribution over time have received less attention.

Cao et al. demonstrated in RocksDB-based production systems such as UDB, ZippyDB, and UP2X at Facebook that the distribution of key and value sizes is closely tied to specific use cases and applications [6]. A recent study considered space-optimising storage structures in Neo4j under real application loads, and found little impact on overall performance, ascribed perhaps to the limited importance of indexing in that platform [28].

[3] OLTP - Online Transaction Processing.

[4] OLAP - Online Analytical Processing.

4 YCSB-IVS Benchmark Description and Design

The main contribution of this paper is a new benchmark called YCSB-IVS for *YCSB - Increasing Value Sizes*, which can assess the impact on database performance as the size of data items grows over time. We work within the framework of Yahoo! Cloud Serving Benchmark (YCSB[5]) [9]. This is a widely used framework to evaluate the performance of NoSQL and SQL databases and other cloud-based data delivery systems. Designed to facilitate comparative analysis, YCSB provides a set of core workloads that simulate varied real-world database use cases, including read-heavy, write-heavy, and balanced scenarios. The workloads are mixes of Read, Update, Insert, Delete and Scan operations, with configuration parameters that control the distribution of the keys involved as well as the proportion of the operation types. The framework enables us to measure crucial performance metrics, such as throughput and latency (average and tail), under different configurations. YCSB's extensibility allows for customisation of workloads, database bindings, and distributions, making it a versatile tool for assessing various aspects of data serving systems under controlled conditions. As YCSB is a benchmark that assumes only a key-value logical data model, we implement a *value-length extension* functionality, which increases the length of the value associated with a key; due to the generality of this logical data model, we can apply the benchmark to platforms with richer data models, including relations or JSON documents.

Extend Operation. To see the impact of growing value sizes on database performance, we implemented an extra operation, which will increase the length of value for a key chosen according to a specific distribution; this is similar to the original Update of YCSB, in that a key is chosen from a distribution, and the associated value is replaced by a new one; unlike the provided Update, our Extend associates to this key a new value which is longer than the previous one by the amount specified in the workload configuration as the `extendfieldlength` parameter (we have a default increase of 100 bytes). Since YCSB data model is multiple (default ten) string-valued fields as the value for each key, each extend operation randomly chooses one field uniformly and replaces the contents of that field by a longer string.

4.1 Benchmark Methodology

The original YCSB framework begins with a *load* phase where data is generated and loaded to the data store being evaluated, and then performance is measured during a *run* phase, where simulated clients submit operations (such as Read, Update, etc.) against the data store. In the original framework default configuration, the data is a collection of items all exactly 1000 bytes long. In our YCSB-IVS, we have a more complex experimental approach to capture performance when data items can grow; the initial data load is followed by a succession of *epochs*; each epoch has two phases, first an *extend* phase in which the

[5] YCSB: https://github.com/brianfrankcooper/YCSB.git.

Extend operation is performed many times, thus growing the length of some of the records, and then the epoch has a *run* phase where we measure throughput and latency for a mix of operations, against the data that resulted from the extend phase of this epoch. Then the next epoch begins, with further extending record lengths and then another measured run phase. In fact, we use the YCSB framework's run capability for both our extend and run phases in each epoch: our extend phase is simply a YCSB run of a workload containing 100% Extend operations, and our run phase can be an arbitrary mix of operations specified in the workload configuration. We make sure that the measurements we capture in our run phase of a given epoch are all against a data set with a particular distribution of item lengths, which grows from epoch to epoch due to the extend phases. Our experiment results display the way the metrics (throughput and latency) change as the epochs progress.

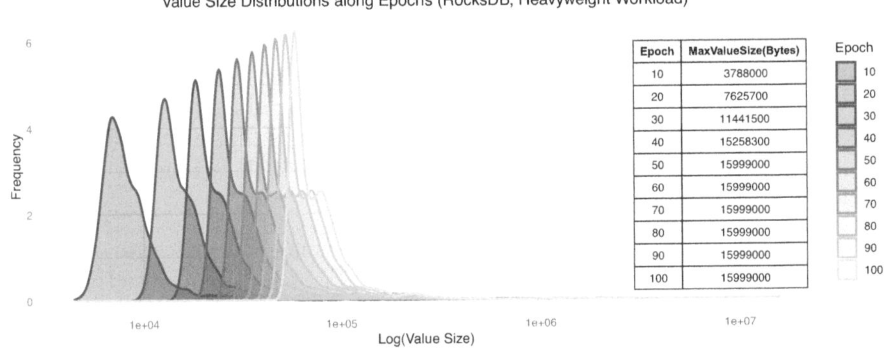

Fig. 1. Record size distribution and maximum value size change along the epochs with Zipfian distribution of extends.

Maximum Record Size. There is a pragmatic issue that arises from restrictions in the platforms with which we work and leads to some subtlety in the way we configure YCSB-IVS. Many database systems impose restrictions on the maximum size of individual records, stemming from both design considerations and practical limitations. For example, MongoDB restricts documents to a maximum size of 16MB, as detailed in their official documentation[6]. MariaDB, while more flexible, adheres to its own constraints: the LONGTEXT data type must be used for fields exceeding 64KB[7]. However, with MariaDB's default settings, a client application can create a row larger than 16MB, yet that row cannot be successfully read due to an underlying limit on the packet size.

Given these constraints, we designed YCSB-IVS to incorporate a cap on record sizes by limiting the size of individual fields. When an "extend" operation

[6] https://www.mongodb.com/docs/manual/reference/limits/#bson-documents.

[7] https://mariadb.com/kb/en/text/.

encounters a case that, if extended, would exceed its maximum allowable size, it is bypassed entirely, and no update is applied. In YCSB-IVS, the default field size limit is set at 1.6MB, which, in consequence, sets a record's upper boundary on length at just below the 16MB threshold to circumvent these platform-specific limitations. This choice affords us several advantages: it provides a workable solution that sidesteps platform constraints while having minimal impact on the workload's execution.

Our experiments, with the Zipfian request distribution for extend operations, target a small set of records to be extended most often. As shown in Fig. 1, the Zipfian distribution of extend operations both grows the typical record length *and* makes record lengths increasingly skewed as the epochs advance. Yet, we found that no more than two records reached this maximum limit. This validates our design decision, demonstrating that even under stringent conditions, the limit is sufficient to prevent record expansion beyond what the database systems can handle while minimizing the impact of the limit on ordinary operation of the workload. This limitation serves as a protective measure, ensuring the robustness and reliability of YCSB-IVS against the backdrop of real-world database constraints.

Extend Phase. This phase involves submitting Extend operations against the database, with keys chosen according to the `requestdistribution` parameter which is specified in the configuration. In our experiments, we consider both Uniform and Zipfian distributions for the keys to be extended (these distributions are in the default YCSB codebase). For the Zipfian distribution, we use the YCSB default parameter 0.99. Extending keys chosen as a Zipfian distribution means that a few data items will be extended much more frequently than others, and these popular items will therefore grow quite long as the epochs pass. An item which is chosen in an extend operation grows in length by the amount given as the `extendfieldlength` configuration parameter, defaulting to 100 bytes (this default is used for all the experiments we report here). We also use the data platform's backup capability to take a complete dump of the logical data state at the end of each *extend phase*, for use in the *clean-run* we describe later.

Run Phase. A workload comprising any arbitrary mix of Read, Scan, Insert, Update, or Delete operations can be performed within the *run phase* of an epoch in YCSB-IVS. Workloads involving Insert and Update operations may cause the value size distribution to change during the *run phase*. To mitigate this deviation, we configure YCSB to use a value size histogram that is calculated at the beginning of the run phase with a bin size of 100 by setting the parameter `fieldlengthdistribution=histogram`.

The number of operations in an epoch is controlled by the `operationcount` configuration parameter and is chosen to be large enough so that any startup effects from running the YCSB client are amortized. The experiments we report here use 100,000 operations per run phase. For this phase, the keys are chosen by the uniform distribution regardless of which distribution is used for the extend phase. Using a uniform distribution means that operations during a workload will be evenly distributed across value sizes. This ensures that the logical work done during the run phase depends on the total data volume but not the distribution of value sizes. In each epoch's run phase, we use the YCSB facility to capture the throughput and latency metrics (average or 99th percentile).

Experiment Modes. As described above, the ***main-run*** epochs in our experimental methodology involve iteratively executing *extend* and *run* phases following the initial data loading, to show how performance changes as some data items grow in length over time due to Extend operations. This is a simplified version of what we have seen in real-world scenarios. However, one might consider whether the performance is based on the history of growth in some records over time, or instead is just a consequence of having records of different sizes in the database state, without any change through time. So, for better understanding, we have included in our benchmark methodology another set of epoch-based measurements that aim to disentangle these issues.

In YCSB-IVS, we measure the ***clean-run*** mode, in which, in each epoch, the logical data backup taken at the end of the extend phase of *main-run* is restored to a fresh instance of the data platform, and then the run operations are submitted to this clean copy of the data. That is, in any epoch of *clean-run*, we have a database state which is logically the same as that in the corresponding epoch of *main-run*, but without any history of change over time, so the physical structures will likely be simpler. Any difference between *main-run* and *clean-run* reveals an effect that is due specifically to change in record lengths through an execution.

The baselines use only prior YCSB functionality (that is, there are no Extend operations, and all records have uniform length). They are measured separately, rather than after each extend phase, to show the impact of simple impacts of the scale of data volume, separate from non-uniformity. We perform the baselines for a range of scales corresponding to the data volume seen in the dump at the end of an epoch (this can in fact be calculated from the number of extend operations performed in the epochs up until then and the extra length added in each operation). ***spread-baseline*** measures the effect of having many items of a fixed size, and ***average-baseline*** measures the effect of a fixed set of long data items. In *average-baseline*, the data volume is distributed equally among the same number of records as in *main-run*; this ensures uniform item lengths which are quite long, and longer at increasing scale. The data with this uniform length is loaded into a fresh instance of the platform, and the read-only operations are run against that. In contrast *spread-baseline* for a given data volume has all records with the same length as those in the initial load of *main-run*, before any extensions; and thus the scale in data volume is achieved by having a very large number of records in *spread-baseline* (far more than in *main-run*).

As expected (and mostly confirmed in our measurements), the performance of *spread-baseline* is mostly independent of the scale of the data volume; the indexing in each platform is effective and so the reads are not much affected when there are many more records to choose from. In contrast, each platform shows substantial slowdown with long records, though the details vary. This is expected since each read operation accesses and outputs the whole record. In our charts, we will show the metrics for *main-run* and *clean-run* at each epoch, and also for comparison the metrics from *average-baseline* at the appropriate data volume.

Any substantial difference between the metrics in *clean-run* for an epoch, and *average-baseline* for the data volume at the end of that epoch, indicates that the platform is affected by variations in item lengths. In contrast, any difference between *clean-run* and *main-run* can be attributed specifically to the gradual growth of item lengths over time and its impact on physical storage structures. If all three modes yield similar metrics, then the determining factor is simply the total record length, rather than variations in individual item sizes.

Each result chart shows curves for a performance metric against the epoch number.

Performance Evaluation Matrices. We utilize *latency* and *throughput* as the primary metrics for evaluating system performance, reflecting their widespread adoption in performance analysis [30]. The YCSB framework provides overall throughput, and several measures of the distribution of latencies for each type of operation (Read, Update, etc.). We capture them during both the *extend* and *run* phases of our experiments, though our charts here focus on the measurements of the run phases, and we mostly report throughput, average latency for each operation type, and 99-percentile latency for each operation type. We often perform several (say, five) complete runs of the benchmark, and show the average value for a metric, and also a spread (from the mean to plus/minus 1.96 time standard error among the measured runs, all at the given epoch).

4.2 Scale of Benchmark

In Table 1 we describe the default settings for YCSB-IVS. We use these settings for the results reported in Sect. 5.

Table 1. Experiment default configuration.

record count	10000
field count per record	10
initial field length	100
extend operations during extend phase, per epoch	100000
added length in one extend operation	100
operations in run phase, per epoch	100000

Since there are 10000 records, which start at 1000 bytes, and each extend operation adds 100 bytes to a record, the database starts with about 10MB of data and grows to approximately 1GB. While this volume of data isn't enough to stress the caching or I/O of each system, our focus is on the cost to access records of varied lengths in cached data. By the time we have completed 100 epochs, one experiment run has performed 10 million operations in its run phases.

We have also performed some experiments (not reported here) with a smaller-scale "lightweight" workload, with 1000 records, and 10,000 extend operations in each extend phase, and 10,000 other operations in each run phase. However, these runs were sensitive to startup effects.

5 Case Studies of the Benchmark

To illustrate the use of the benchmark, we present here a selection from the results when using the benchmark with a range of platforms. More of the results are discussed in YCSB-IVS Tech Report. Data for all the experiments is at https://github.com/dliyanage/YCSB-IVS.

5.1 Experimental Setup

Platforms. We apply the benchmark with three widely used database platforms. These DBMSs, summarized in Table 2, represent a cross section of logical data models and physical storage structures. MongoDB and MariaDB+MyRocks were run with default settings [22,23]. MariaDB+InnoDB was run with the buffer pool size adjusted by setting `innodb_buffer_pool_size` to 4GB[8].

Table 2. Utilized DBMSs and their characteristics.

	Database	Version	Logical Model	Storage Structure
1	MariaDB+MyRocks	10.6	Relational	LSM-tree
2	MariaDB+InnoDB	10.6	Relational	B-tree
3	MongoDB	6.0	Document	B-tree

Infrastructure. The experiments were conducted on an AWS EC2 `m7i.xlarge` instance running Ubuntu 24.04 LTS. The machine is equipped with a dual-core Intel Xeon Platinum 8488C processor (Sapphire Rapids architecture) with a 105 MB L3 cache and hyper-threading enabled. It includes 16 GB of RAM and a 30 GB NVMe-backed Elastic Block Store for storage. Networking is handled by an Elastic Network Adapter, and the instance is configured without a graphical interface to optimize for computational workloads.

[8] https://mariadb.com/docs/server/storage-engines/innodb/operations/configure-buffer-pool/.

5.2 Impact of Average Length of Values

In Fig. 2, we illustrate how one platform (MariaDB+MyRocks) performs for the two baselines. Note that here, the data is not formed using Extend operations; rather for each data volume on the x-axis, we apply the YCSB Workload C directly to a database where all records are initialised to have equal length. One baseline, *spread-baseline*, involves obtaining the indicated total volume of data through as many records as needed, all of which have the same size (1KB) corresponding to the initial size in our benchmark runs. In contrast, *average-baseline* has the given data volume through the same number of records as in the benchmark (10,000), with whatever equal size is then needed for the given volume. Here the x-axis is data volume (which correlates linearly with the epoch numbers in other charts).

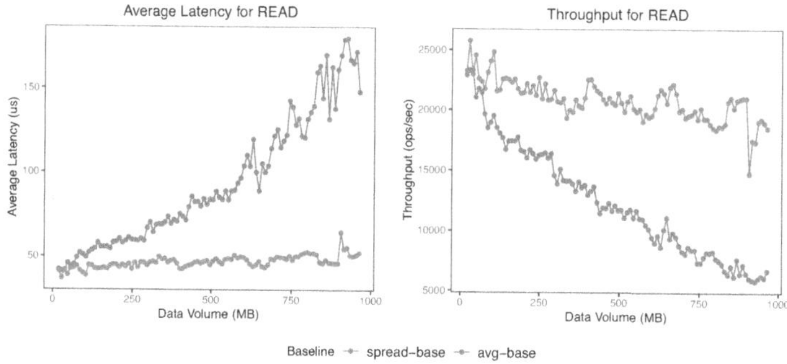

Fig. 2. Baselines for MariaDB+MyRocks, for YCSB Workload C.

As expected, due to an effective index on the key used for reads, *spread-baseline* shows that MariaDB+MyRocks experiences a slight gradual decline in read throughput, with some variance as the data volume scales through the presence of more records. However, the average read latency remains largely stable, suggesting that the addition of small records does not significantly impair MariaDB+MyRocks's ability to serve read operations efficiently.

In contrast, under *average-baseline*, we observe a clear degradation in throughput as record sizes increase, along with significant variance in latency. This is expected, since records become longer, and each read operation transfers the whole record.

The baselines for the other platforms similarly confirm that record size is an important influence on system performance. Long records generally slow performance compared to short ones when data volume is the same. Thus record length is worth examining when benchmarking.

5.3 Consistent Spread of Latencies

We applied YCSB-IVS to MongoDB. Here we found the platform seems well able to handle the situation we are examining, where some documents are growing

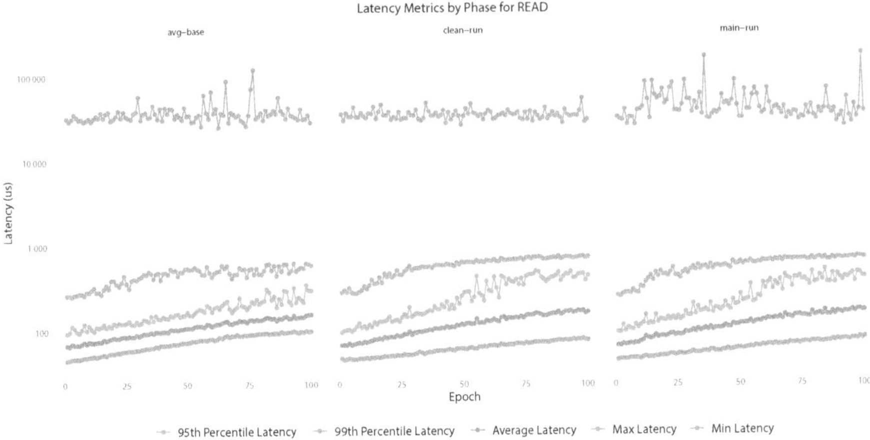

Fig. 3. Behavior of latency summary statistics for MongoDB *run* phases for YCSB workload C with Zipfian extensions.

in length. Overall, the results for *main-run* and *clean-run* are very close, and not much worse than *average-baseline*: through the epochs, latency grows and throughput drops, based largely on the impact from greater data transfer because of the record size. We show, in Fig. 3, charts for a variety of latency metrics on the run phases, taken in one execution of the benchmark with read-only YCSB workload C with Zipfian key distribution during the extend phase.

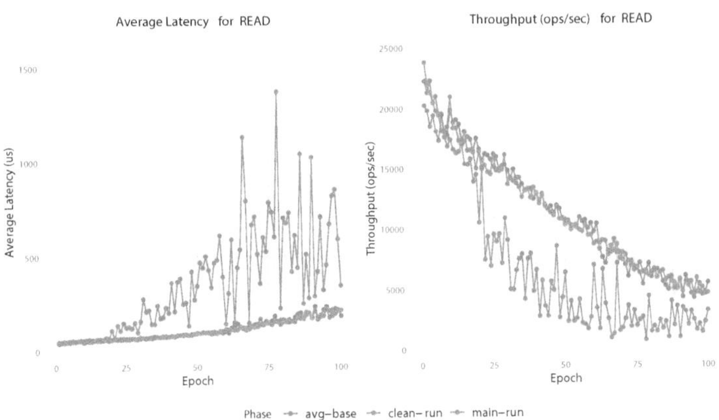

Fig. 4. YCSB Workload C performance in MariaDB+MyRocks with Zipfian request distribution for Extend operations and Uniform Reads.

5.4 Impact of Update History on Query Performance

Figure 4 shows the mean behavior of latency and throughput across five repetitions of the benchmark, with read-only YCSB workload C, and Zipfian distribution (parameter 0.99) for the Extend operations, applied to MariaDB+MyRocks. We also show a measure of spread around the data points, with shading for the range: mean plus or minus 1.96 times the standard error among the five runs. Here, the impact of a history of change is evident: results deviated significantly in *main-run* after 20 epochs. Beyond this point, the average read latency in *main-run* increased by more than an order of magnitude compared to its counterpart in *clean-run*, where a fresh copy of the data was queried. However, *clean-run* showed essentially the same performance as *average-baseline*, revealing that the variation in lengths between records was not impactful, only the average length of records matters.

5.5 Update Workload with a Distribution of Value Sizes

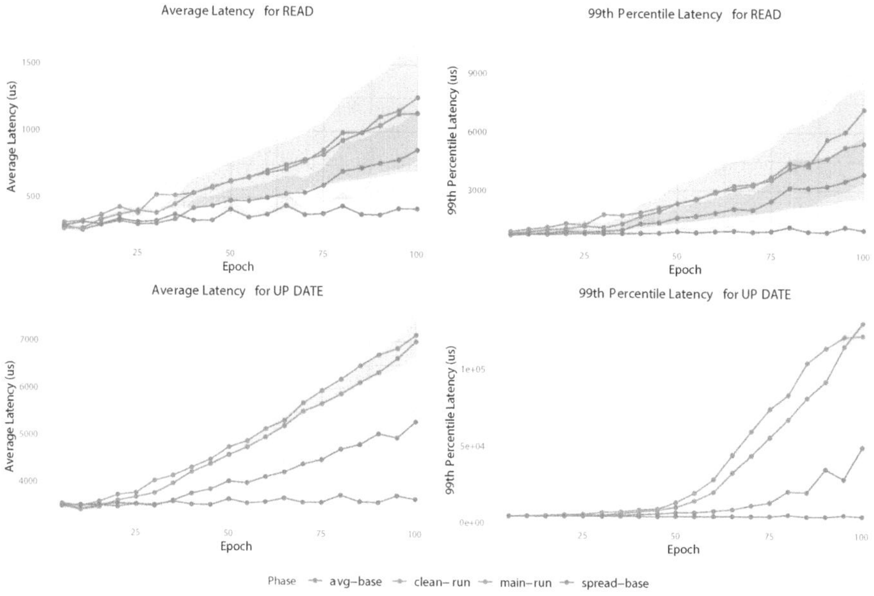

Fig. 5. YCSB Workload A in MariaDB+MyRocks with uniform extensions. Average and 99th percentile latency for Read and Update operations over 5 trials.

We further illustrate performance under YCSB workload A that includes 50% update operations. Figure 5 presents results for this workload comprising 50% reads and 50% updates, with Extend phase using uniform distribution of keys. Note that latency is shown separately for each operation type.

Both *main-run* and *clean-run* are noticeably slower for reads, and even more so for updates (especially in the tail of the distribution), compared to *average-baseline*, showing that variation in length between data items can be impactful. The spread of results from separate runs (shown by shading around the data

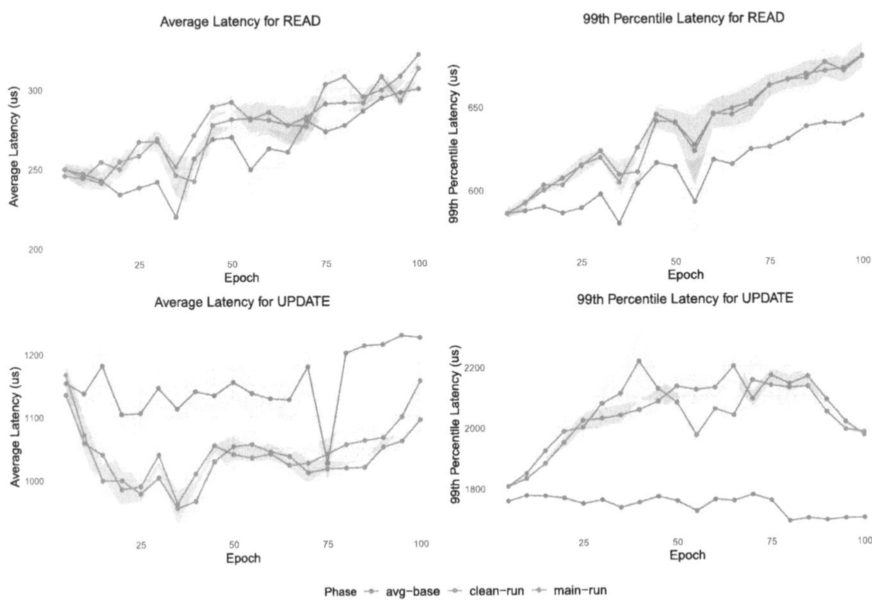

(a) Average and 99th percentile latency for Read and Update operations.

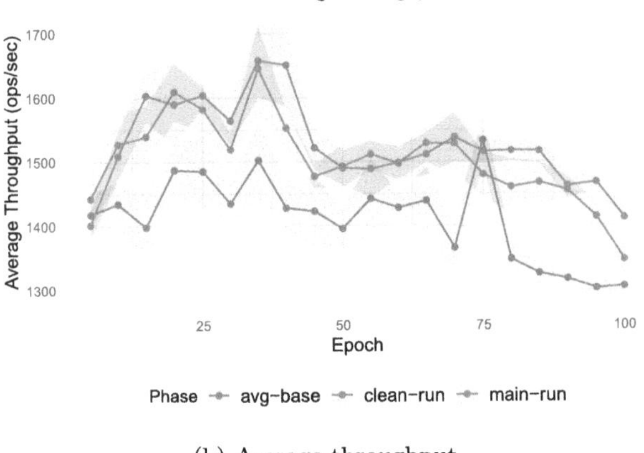

(b) Average throughput.

Fig. 6. YCSB workload A in MariaDB+InnoDB with Zipfian extensions.

points) further reveal that read operations, particularly in *main-run* and *clean-run*, show greater variance in latency than updates.

Although *main-run* and *clean-run* perform similarly, *clean-run* consistently shows slightly lower efficiency. This is surprising, with a freshly populated database less effective than one built over time.

5.6 Accessing Highly Skewed Value Sizes

We conducted multiple trials on MariaDB+InnoDB using YCSB workload A, as extend phases progressively increased value sizes with a Zipfian distribution for keys. Figure 6 presents the corresponding performance metrics. While the data seems very noisy, it does reveal that in most epochs, both *main-run* and *clean-run* perform similarly for average latency of reads and notably faster for updates, although with serious slowdown for tail latency. The throughput is mostly a bit better for *main-run* (with history) than *clean-run* (without history of extension), but both are generally higher than the *average-baseline* baseline.

6 Conclusion

We introduced a novel approach to capture the performance impact when some records become very long, distinguishing the influence of overall record length, variation in record length between items, and historic growth in length. We utilize the YCSB framework, but make substantial changes to the way runs are arranged, with four different modes of run, and a succession of epochs, showing performance under different length distributions.

Our benchmark, YCSB-IVS, has been applied to a variety of platforms. The code and all experiment data are available. Given the presence of such a pattern of growth in practical applications, using YCSB-IVS would not only help in making a wise choice for data management, but it will also aid platform implementers to cater to such use cases.

Acknowledgments. We thank the anonymous reviewers of TPCTC 2025 for their valuable feedback on the original version of this paper. This research was funded by Australian Research Council Discovery Project DP210101984.

References

1. Armstrong, T.G., Ponnekanti, V., Borthakur, D., Callaghan, M.: Linkbench: a database benchmark based on the Facebook social graph. In: Proceedings of the 2013 ACM SIGMOD International Conference on Management of Data, SIGMOD 2013, pp. 1185–1196. Association for Computing Machinery, New York (2013). https://doi.org/10.1145/2463676.2465296
2. Battle, L., et al.: Database benchmarking for supporting real-time interactive querying of large data. In: Proceedings of the 2020 ACM SIGMOD International Conference on Management of Data, SIGMOD 2020, pp. 1571–1587. Association for Computing Machinery, New York (2020). https://doi.org/10.1145/3318464.3389732
3. Benson, L., et al.: Surprise benchmarking: the why, what, and how. In: Proceedings of the Tenth International Workshop on Testing Database Systems, DBTest 2024, pp. 1–8. Association for Computing Machinery, New York (2024). https://doi.org/10.1145/3662165.3662763

4. Biliris, A.: The performance of three database storage structures for managing large objects. ACM SIGMOD Rec. **21**(2), 276–285 (1992)
5. Bitton, D., DeWitt, D.J., Turbyfill, C.: Benchmarking database systems-a systematic approach. Technical report, University of Wisconsin-Madison, Department of Computer Sciences (1983)
6. Cao, Z., Dong, S., Vemuri, S., Du, D.H.: Characterizing, modeling, and benchmarking {RocksDB} {Key-Value} workloads at Facebook. In: 18th USENIX Conference on File and Storage Technologies (FAST 2020), pp. 209–223. USENIX Association (2020)
7. Carey, M.J., DeWitt, D.J., Richardson, J.E., Shekita, E.J.: Object and file management in the exodus extensible database system. In: Proceedings of the 12th International Conference on Very Large Data Bases, VLDB 1986, pp. 91–100. Morgan Kaufmann Publishers Inc., San Francisco (1986)
8. Cheng, A., et al.: Taobench: an end-to-end benchmark for social network workloads. Proc. VLDB Endow. **15**(9), 1965–1977 (2022)
9. Cooper, B.F., Silberstein, A., Tam, E., Ramakrishnan, R., Sears, R.: Benchmarking cloud serving systems with YCSB. In: Proceedings of the 1st ACM Symposium on Cloud Computing, SoCC 2010, pp. 143–154. Association for Computing Machinery, New York (2010). https://doi.org/10.1145/1807128.1807152
10. Dey, A., Fekete, A.D., Nambiar, R., Röhm, U.: YCSB+T: benchmarking web-scale transactional databases. In: Workshops Proceedings of the 30th International Conference on Data Engineering Workshops, ICDE 2014, Chicago, IL, USA, 31 March–4 April 2014, pp. 223–230. IEEE Computer Society (2014). https://doi.org/10.1109/ICDEW.2014.6818330
11. Du, W., Krishnamurthy, R., Shan, M.C.: Query optimization in a heterogeneous DBMS. In: VLDB, vol. 92, pp. 277–291 (1992)
12. Erling, O., et al.: The LDBC social network benchmark: Interactive workload. In: Proceedings of the 2015 ACM SIGMOD International Conference on Management of Data, SIGMOD 2015, pp. 619–630. Association for Computing Machinery, New York (2015). https://doi.org/10.1145/2723372.2742786
13. Funke, F., Kemper, A., Neumann, T.: Benchmarking hybrid oltp&olap database systems. In: Datenbanksysteme für Business. Technologie und Web (BTW), pp. 390–409. Gesellschaft für Informatik eV, Bonn (2011)
14. Gardarin, G., Sha, F., Tang, Z.H.: Calibrating the query optimizer cost model of IRO-DB, an object-oriented federated database system. In: VLDB, vol. 96, pp. 3–6. Citeseer (1996)
15. Gray, J.: Database and transaction processing performance handbook (1993)
16. Gupta, P., Carey, M.J., Mehrotra, S., Yus, O.: Smartbench: a benchmark for data management in smart spaces. Proc. VLDB Endow. **13**(12), 1807–1820 (2020)
17. Hurson, A.R., Pakzad, S.H., Cheng, J.B.: Object-oriented database management systems: evolution and performance issues. Computer **26**(2), 48–58 (1993)
18. Idreos, S., Callaghan, M.: Key-value storage engines. In: Proceedings of the 2020 ACM SIGMOD International Conference on Management of Data, SIGMOD 2020, pp. 2667–2672. Association for Computing Machinery, New York (2020). https://doi.org/10.1145/3318464.3383133
19. Iyer, B.R., Wilhite, D.: Data compression support in databases. In: VLDB, vol. 94, pp. 695–704 (1994)
20. Jain, M.: Dgraph: synchronously replicated, transactional and distributed graph database (2021). https://github.com/hypermodeinc/dgraph/blob/master/paper/dgraph.pdf

21. Kim, S., Hoang, Y., Yu, T.T., Kanwar, Y.S.: GeoYCSB: a benchmark framework for the performance and scalability evaluation of geospatial NoSQL databases. Big Data Res. **31**, 100368 (2023). https://doi.org/10.1016/j.bdr.2023.100368
22. MariaDB: MariaDB: MyRocks System Variables (2025). https://mariadb.com/kb/en/myrocks-system-variables/. Accessed 30 May 2025
23. MongoDB: MongoDB Server Parameters for a Self-Managed Deployment (2025). https://www.mongodb.com/docs/manual/reference/parameters/. Accessed 02 June 2025
24. O'Neil, P., O'Neil, E., Chen, X., Revilak, S.: The star schema benchmark and augmented fact table indexing. In: Nambiar, R., Poess, M. (eds.) Performance Evaluation and Benchmarking, pp. 237–252. Springer, Heidelberg (2009)
25. Pelekis, N., Theodoulidis, B., Kopanakis, I., Theodoridis, Y.: Literature review of spatio-temporal database models. Knowl. Eng. Rev. **19**(3), 235–274 (2004)
26. Ray, S., Simion, B., Demke Brown, A.: Jackpine: a benchmark to evaluate spatial database performance. In: 2011 IEEE 27th International Conference on Data Engineering, pp. 1139–1150. IEEE (2011). https://doi.org/10.1109/ICDE.2011.5767929
27. Shapiro, M., Miller, E.: Managing databases with binary large objects. In: 16th IEEE Symposium on Mass Storage Systems in cooperation with the 7th NASA Goddard Conference on Mass Storage Systems and Technologies (Cat. No.99CB37098), pp. 185–193. IEEE (1999). https://doi.org/10.1109/MASS.1999.830036
28. Theodorakis, G., Clarkson, J., Webber, J.: An empirical evaluation of variable-length record B+trees on a modern graph database system. In: 40th International Conference on Data Engineering, ICDE 2024 - Workshops, Utrecht, Netherlands, 13–16 May 2024, pp. 343–349. IEEE (2024). https://doi.org/10.1109/ICDEW61823.2024.00051
29. (TPC), T.P.P.C.: TPC (2024). https://www.tpc.org/. Accessed 20 Dec 2024
30. Wang, X., Schulzrinne, H., Kandlur, D., Verma, D.: Measurement and analysis of LDAP performance. IEEE/ACM Trans. Netw. **16**(1), 232–243 (2008)
31. Westmann, T., Kossmann, D., Helmer, S., Moerkotte, G.: The implementation and performance of compressed databases. ACM SIGMOD Rec. **29**(3), 55–67 (2000)

Benchmarking Role-Based Access Control in Data Management Systems

Mads Cornelius Hansen, Pınar Tözün, and Martin Hentschel(✉)

IT University of Copenhagen, Copenhagen, Denmark
{coha,pito,mhent}@itu.dk

Abstract. Role-Based Access Control (RBAC) is a widely used method for controlling access to data in data management systems, offering a scalable approach to enforcing security policies. Despite its broad adoption, RBAC implementations vary significantly across different systems, leading to inconsistencies in performance. Currently, there is no standardized benchmark for evaluating RBAC performance. In this study, we propose a benchmark that focuses on two core components: the creation of role hierarchies with varying structures and the access to securable objects and role metadata through SQL queries. We evaluate three systems—PostgreSQL, MariaDB, and Snowflake—across on-premise and cloud deployments. Our findings reveal notable differences in RBAC performance, driven by I/O demand, caching behavior, and system architecture. These results highlight the diversity of RBAC implementations and the need for a systematic approach to evaluate RBAC at scale.

1 Introduction

Role-Based Access Control (RBAC) is a widely used method for controlling access to data in data management systems. By assigning privileges to roles instead of individuals, RBAC simplifies access management and provides a scalable mechanism for enforcing security policies. For example, in a corporate system, roles such as 'HR' or 'Management' can be defined with specific access rights to employee records. This ensures users access only the information necessary for their roles, thereby enhancing security and regulatory compliance. RBAC is an effective strategy for managing data access at scale and has been adopted in most modern data management systems.

Despite its broad adoption, RBAC is not implemented uniformly across data management systems. Each system tends to interpret and execute RBAC principles in slightly different ways, resulting in inconsistencies in functionality and performance. From our experience in the industry, customers with large RBAC setups may experience slow system behavior due to caching effects, for example. While the security of RBAC implementations has been extensively studied, research into how RBAC mechanisms affect system performance, such as latency

M. C. Hansen—Student at IT University of Copenhagen.

R. Nambiar and M. Poess (Eds.): TPCTC 2025, LNCS 16261, pp. 20–36, 2026.
https://doi.org/10.1007/978-3-032-18070-4_2

and resource utilization, is still lacking. Notably, there is no standardized benchmark for evaluating RBAC performance, especially under varying workloads, deployment configurations, and scales.

This study addresses these gaps by investigating the performance of RBAC across different data management systems. We examine how RBAC is implemented in three systems—PostgreSQL, MariaDB, and Snowflake—propose a benchmark for evaluating RBAC performance, and use this benchmark to conduct a performance assessment. These systems were selected for their widespread use and because they represent a diverse range of architectural differences: open-source vs. commercial, transactional vs. analytical, and on-premise vs. cloud-native. One of the goals of this study is to understand how these architectural differences influence the implementation and performance of RBAC.

Our results reveal a range of behaviors: PostgreSQL performs well locally but suffers in the cloud, MariaDB degrades at scale, and Snowflake exhibits constant yet high latency. These findings indicate that (a) there is no standard for RBAC implementation, as each system shows different performance characteristics; (b) there is a need for an accepted performance benchmark for RBAC; and (c) although RBAC metadata handling is not a primary performance focus of data management systems, all tested systems show potential for performance optimization, for example, improving I/O behavior, caches, and network traffic.

Overall, this study highlights the importance of understanding RBAC performance across different data management systems, particularly at scale. By proposing a first step towards an accepted benchmark and evaluating multiple systems, we provide insights into how RBAC implementations can vary significantly, affecting both local and cloud-based deployments. Our findings show the need for standardized benchmarks in the industry to facilitate comparisons and optimizations of RBAC performance.

The paper is organized as follows: Sect. 2 provides background on RBAC and the data management systems evaluated in this study. Section 3 reviews related work. Section 4 describes our benchmark proposal for evaluating RBAC performance. Section 5 presents the experimental setup and results of the performance evaluation. Finally, Sect. 6 concludes the paper and provides an outlook on future work.

2 Background

In this section, we provide background on role-based access control and the data management systems evaluated in this study.

2.1 Role-Based Access Control

Role-Based Access Control (RBAC) was introduced as a model for access control in data management systems in the 1990s [9,16] and proposed as a NIST standard in 2001 [10]. RBAC is more general than the two traditional access control models, Mandatory Access Control (MAC) and Discretionary Access Control

(DAC). In MAC, a central authority controls access. Users and documents are assigned security labels, and access is granted based on these labels. For example, in a military setting, documents might be labeled "Top Secret", "Secret", or "Confidential", and users with clearance levels matching these labels can access the documents. MAC is highly secure but can be complex to manage. DAC, on the other hand, allows users to control access to their own data. For example, DAC is used in Microsoft OneDrive or Google Docs, where users can choose who can view or edit their documents. DAC is flexible and easy to use but can be less secure if owners are not careful with privileges. RBAC combines the strengths of both models by assigning privileges to roles instead of individual users. This shifts access control from many user-specific decisions to a smaller number of role definitions, simplifying administration. At the same time, users only receive privileges relevant to their roles, which reduces the risk of accidental overexposure of sensitive data and thereby enhances security.

RBAC is defined by four key components: users, roles, privileges, and securable objects. *Users* are individuals or applications that access the data management system. *Roles* are abstract entities that hold a collection of privileges. *Privileges* define what actions can be performed on securable objects. *Securable objects* are the resources or data that users can access, such as databases, tables, functions, and views. In RBAC, privileges are granted from securable objects to roles, and roles are then granted to users. This means that users obtain access to resources indirectly through roles, rather than receiving individual privileges as in MAC and DAC.

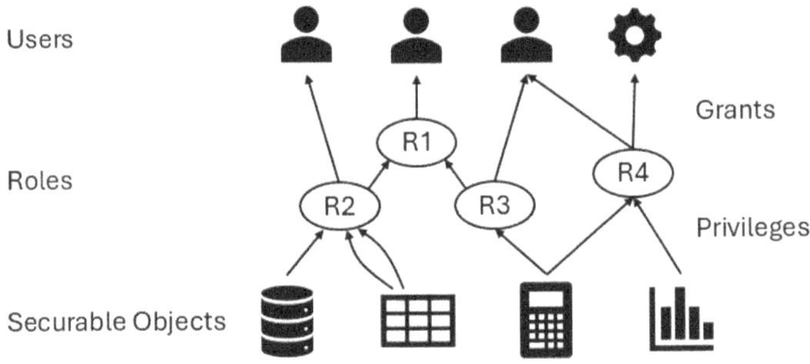

Fig. 1. The RBAC model consists of users, roles, privileges, and securable objects. Users can represent individuals or applications. Privileges are granted from securable objects to roles, and roles are granted to users or other roles.

Figure 1 illustrates the RBAC model. Privileges are granted from securable objects to roles, meaning roles obtain the rights to perform specific actions on those objects. Roles are then granted to users, which can represent either individuals or applications. A user may thus receive privileges indirectly through one or more roles. For example, read and write privileges on a database table might be granted to a role, and that role might then be granted to several users, allowing them to read from and write to that table.

Roles can also be granted to other roles, forming a role hierarchy. In Fig. 1, Role R1 is granted roles R2 and R3, which means R1 inherits all privileges granted to R2 and R3. Role hierarchies simplify privilege management by allowing roles to be structured in a way that reflects organizational needs. From our experience, role hierarchies with depths of up to 100 and overall hierarchy sizes of up to 100,000 roles are not uncommon.

Lastly, sessions are a key aspect of RBAC, representing the active instances of users accessing the system. A session is created when a user logs in and can include multiple roles assigned to that user. Typically, the user is assigned a primary role and can enable secondary roles. The combination of the primary role and secondary roles defines the privileges available to the user during that session.

2.2 Evaluated Data Management Systems

In this study, we focus on the implementation of RBAC in three popular data management systems: PostgreSQL [17], MariaDB [13], and Snowflake [7]. PostgreSQL and MariaDB are open-source database management systems that represent the class of online transactional processing (OLTP) systems, designed to support interactive applications requiring low-latency query responses and high-throughput transactions. While OLTP systems are typically deployed on-premises, they can also be hosted in the cloud, for example, on Amazon Web Services, as analyzed in this study.

Snowflake, on the other hand, is a commercial, cloud-native data management system that represents the class of online analytical processing (OLAP) systems optimized for analytical workloads. OLAP systems are designed to handle large datasets, up to petabytes of data, at the cost of increased latency and reduced transactional throughput. Analytical data management systems like Snowflake are typically hosted exclusively in the cloud, with no on-premise deployment options.

As mentioned, the choice of these systems allows us to evaluate RBAC performance across a range of architectures and deployment models from open-source to commercial, transactional to analytical, and on-premise to cloud-native. For MariaDB and PostgreSQL, we conduct the study on both on-premise and cloud deployments, while Snowflake is evaluated exclusively in the cloud. Details on the RBAC implementations of these systems appear in Sect. 5.2.

For the purposes of this study, we focus on RBAC features that are common across all three systems, such as role-to-role grants to create role hierarchies and `SHOW` queries to retrieve RBAC metadata. We exclude features that are not universally supported, such as privileges unique to a single system (e.g., PostgreSQL's `SUPERUSER` privilege or Snowflake's `OWNERSHIP` privilege) as well as features that are not relevant to our performance evaluation (e.g., row-level security policies or column-masking policies).

3 Related Work

Benchmarks around role-based access control in database systems have mostly focused on security aspects, such as the confidentiality and safety of data [21], as well as authentication, privileges, and encryption [22]. In a vision paper for benchmarking shared databases, the performance of verifiable transactions is considered [8]. YCSB++ [15] is an extension of the Yahoo! Cloud Serving Benchmark (YCSB) [6] that evaluates, among other features, the performance of authorization via access control lists.

Benchmarks for database and data management systems primarily focus on the performance of *data* management. Examples include TPC-C [18] for OLTP workloads; TPC-H [19], TPC-DS [20], and the Star Schema Benchmark [14] for OLAP workloads; and CH-benCHmark [5] for hybrid OLTP and OLAP workloads. In addition, there have been benchmarking standardization efforts for specialized data management scenarios, such as graph analytics [11], end-to-end data pipelines in AI [4], data correlations and skew [3], robustness [12], and dynamic or unexpected workloads [2]. However, these benchmarks do not address the performance of managing *metadata*, and specifically, RBAC metadata.

To the best of our knowledge, there is currently no benchmark that evaluates the performance of RBAC mechanisms, including role hierarchy creation and role hierarchy access, in data management systems. This study aims to take a first step toward filling this gap.

4 Benchmark Design

Based on our industry experience, operating on data protected by RBAC with large role hierarchies can result in high response times. To evaluate this, we designed a benchmark that measures the performance of creating role hierarchies with varying structures, as well as accessing securable objects and role metadata through SQL commands such as `SELECT` and `SHOW`. The primary goal is to assess how the structure and size of the role hierarchy impact query execution and metadata retrieval. The benchmark consists of two main components: Role Hierarchy Creation and Role Hierarchy Access, which are described in detail below. We have open sourced the benchmark on Github.[1]

4.1 Role Hierarchy Creation

In this component of the benchmark, we measure the performance of creating role hierarchies with varying structures. In general, role hierarchies can be of any graph structure, typically without including cycles. In this benchmark, we focus on tree structures because these are the most common based on our experience. The tree structures we consider are of the following types: deep linear hierarchies, wide linear hierarchies, and balanced hierarchies.

[1] https://github.com/MaCoHa/Study_of_Role-Based_Access_Control_Mechanisms.

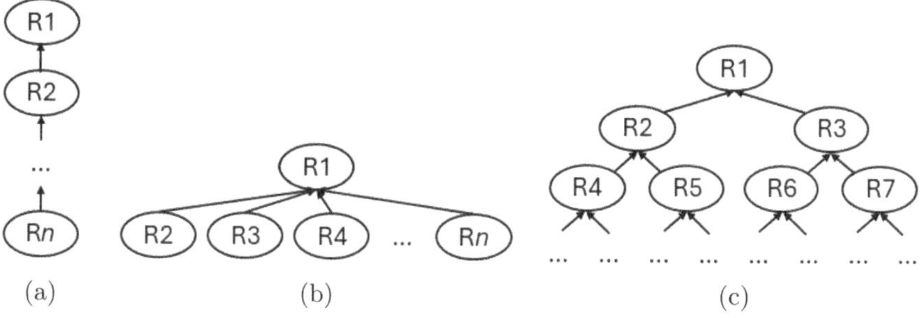

Fig. 2. Role hierarchy structures used in the benchmark: (a) deep linear, (b) wide linear, and (c) balanced.

Figure 2 illustrates the three types of hierarchies. *Deep linear hierarchies* (Fig. 2a) consist of a single path of roles, where each role has exactly one parent and one child, resulting in a long chain of roles (e.g., R1 $\leftarrow$ R2 $\leftarrow$ R3 up to Rn, where n is the final number of roles). *Wide linear hierarchies* (Fig. 2b) have a single root role with multiple child roles but no further descendants. *Balanced hierarchies* (Fig. 2c) combine both deep and wide structures, where roles have a fixed number of children (e.g., always two children in Fig. 2c) and can also be part of a deeper hierarchy.

We chose these structures for several reasons. Deep and wide linear hierarchies represent the two extremes of role hierarchy structures. With these structures, we aim to evaluate how well the systems handle both long chains of roles and wide role assignments. Balanced hierarchies represent a common structure in real-world applications. In one interesting example from the industry, a company has internal functionality where employees can "check out" projects consisting of databases and tables with sample data. Part of the check-out process is creating a subtree of roles that is added to the existing role hierarchy of the company. Over time, this leads to a role hierarchy that is large in size (up to 100,000 roles) and represents a wide hierarchy structure, however with subtrees of roles. It can be seen as a mix of a wide and a balanced hierarchy. The chosen structures in our benchmark therefore cover this scenario well.

The process for creating role hierarchies in this benchmark is as follows. Iteratively, the following commands are executed to create the role hierarchy:

1. Create a new role using the `CREATE ROLE` command.
2. Assign the new role to a parent role using the `GRANT` command, following the structure of the hierarchy (deep, wide, or balanced).
3. Repeat steps 1 and 2 until the desired number of roles is reached or until a time limit is reached.

For each command, we measure the execution time. After the time limit is reached, we also measure the total number of roles created.

4.2 Role Hierarchy Access

In the second component of the benchmark, we measure the performance of accessing securable objects and role metadata through SQL commands. The focus is on how the structure and size of the role hierarchy impact query execution and metadata retrieval. This component includes the following SQL operations: `SELECT * FROM table` and `SHOW ROLES`.

We selected these queries for several reasons. The `SELECT * FROM table` command is among the most common operations in data management systems. Measuring its performance allows us to assess how the size and structure of the role hierarchy affect authorization time when accessing a securable object. This query represents a broader class of "point access" operations, such as `ALTER`, `UPDATE`, `INSERT`, and `DELETE`, where a single securable object is accessed and authorization is performed.

The `SHOW ROLES` command is also widely used and is sometimes invoked automatically by third-party tools (e.g., graphical user interfaces or reporting systems). This command lists all roles within the role hierarchy, allowing us to evaluate how efficiently the metadata subsystem can retrieve role information.

The process for evaluating role hierarchy metadata access in this benchmark is as follows:

1. Create an empty table using the `CREATE TABLE` command.
2. Create a role hierarchy of size n using one of the three hierarchy structures, as defined in the Role Hierarchy Creation component.
3. Grant read access on the table to the last role (Role R_n) in the hierarchy using the `GRANT` command, and activate the root role (Role R_1) in the current session using either the `SET ROLE` or `USE ROLE` command.
4. Execute the `SELECT * FROM table` query to measure the performance of table access authorization.
5. Execute the `SHOW ROLES` command to measure the performance of role metadata retrieval.

For Steps 4 and 5, we record the execution time to evaluate system performance. These steps may be repeated multiple times after the role hierarchy has been created in Steps 1–3.

5 Experiments and Results

5.1 Experimental Setup

Hardware and Environment Configuration. The experiments were conducted in an on-premise setup and in the cloud. For the on-premise setup, the experiments were conducted on a local machine, which was used both to execute the benchmark script and to host the MariaDB and PostgreSQL databases. The machine was a MSI GF65 Thin 10SER laptop running Microsoft Windows 11. It featured an Intel i7-10750H CPU at 2.60 GHz with 6 physical cores, supported by 16 GB of DDR4 RAM and a 1 TB WDC PC SN730 NVMe SSD. GPU acceleration was not used in this study. The cache configuration included 64 KB of L1 cache and 256 KB of L2 cache per core, along with 12 MB of shared L3 cache.

For the cloud setup, we used the Amazon Relational Database Service (RDS) to deploy PostgreSQL and MariaDB. Both systems ran on Free Tier instances (db.t4g.micro), each configured with 2 vCPUs, 1 GiB of RAM, 2.085 Mbps of network throughput, and 20 GiB (gp2) of SSD storage. All instances were deployed in the AWS Oregon (us-west-2) region, with encryption disabled. The benchmark script was executed on an Amazon EC2 instance (t2.micro) in the same region, configured with 1 vCPU, 1 GiB of RAM, and 10 GiB of SSD storage, running Ubuntu Server 24.04 LTS.

Snowflake was evaluated using a cloud-native setup, with the experiments conducted on a Snowflake account in the AWS Oregon (us-west-2) region. The Snowflake instance was set up with a single virtual warehouse at the X-Small size, with all other settings left at their default values. To assess the impact of geographic proximity on performance, we conducted two sets of experiments: in one, the benchmark driver was run from the local laptop located in Europe (Denmark); in the other, the benchmark script was executed on the Amazon EC2 instance in the AWS Oregon region, co-located with the Snowflake deployment.

Snowflake is a natively distributed service that replicates data and metadata across multiple servers, resulting in multiple additional network round trips. In contrast, the single-node setups of PostgreSQL and MariaDB exclude replication, avoiding this networking overhead. Benchmarking a replicated setup of PostgreSQL and MariaDB is left for future work.

System Configuration. The configurations of PostgreSQL, MariaDB, and Snowflake were as follows. For PostgreSQL, we used version 17.4 in the on-premise setup and version 17.2-R2 in the cloud setup (both on the free tier and paid tier instances of RDS). For MariaDB, we used version 11.4.4 in both on-premise and cloud setups.

For Snowflake, at the time of the experiments, we used release version 9.9[2]. Snowflake follows a weekly release cycle, with all customers automatically upgraded to the latest version. Therefore, repeating the experiments at a later date may yield different results due to system changes.

5.2 Experimental Results

Role Hierarchy Creation Performance. In this experiment, we executed the Role Hierarchy Creation component of the benchmark, measuring the performance of creating role hierarchies with varying structures (deep, wide, and balanced). The balanced hierarchy structure consisted of four children per node. We evaluated this component across the on-premise and cloud setups of PostgreSQL and MariaDB, as well as Snowflake accessed from both Europe and

[2] https://docs.snowflake.com/en/release-notes/2025/9_09.

an EC2 instance in the same AWS region. The benchmark was run with a 15-minute time limit, during which the benchmark script continuously executed `CREATE ROLE` and `GRANT` statements. We measured the execution time of each individual statement and the total number of roles created within the time limit. The experiment was repeated twice, and we report the average number of roles created across both runs.

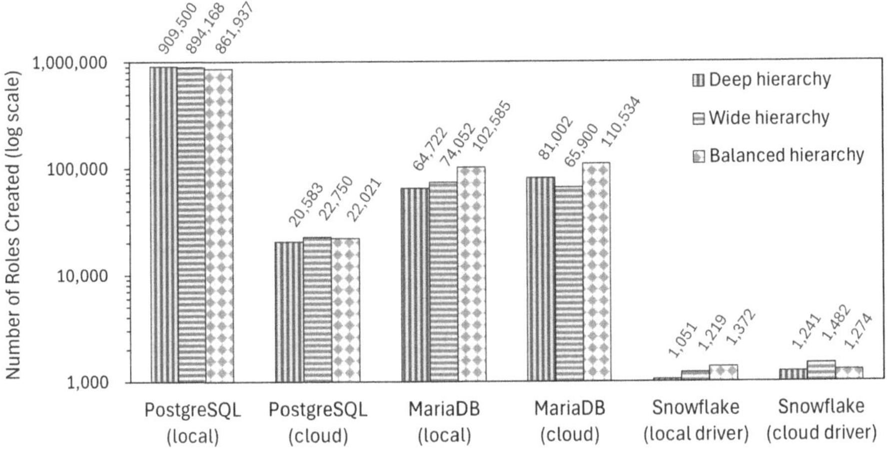

Fig. 3. Number of roles created within the 15-minute time limit.

Findings. Figure 3 shows the number of roles created within the 15-minute time limit for each system and hierarchy structure. Note the logarithmic scale of the y-axis. We observe the following findings: In the on-premise setup, PostgreSQL performed extremely well, creating hierarchies with around 900,000 roles within 15 min. However, in the cloud setup, PostgreSQL performed worse, creating hierarchies with only around 22,000 roles. MariaDB performed equally well in both the on-premise and cloud setups, creating around 65,000 to 110,000 roles within the time limit. Interestingly, MariaDB was able to create almost 50% more roles for the balanced hierarchy structure compared to the deep and wide structures. Snowflake was able to create around 1,000 to 1,500 roles within the time limit, regardless of the hierarchy structure or whether it was accessed from Europe or the EC2 instance in the AWS Oregon region.

Figure 4 shows the individual execution times of the `CREATE ROLE` and `GRANT` statements for PostgreSQL across all hierarchy structures. We show the execution times of the second benchmark run only. The x-axis represents the experiment time in minutes, up to the 15-minute time limit. The y-axis shows the measured latency in milliseconds. We observe the following findings: In the on-premise setup, execution times for all statements remain steady at around 0.22 milliseconds, even as the role hierarchy grows over time. The structure and size of

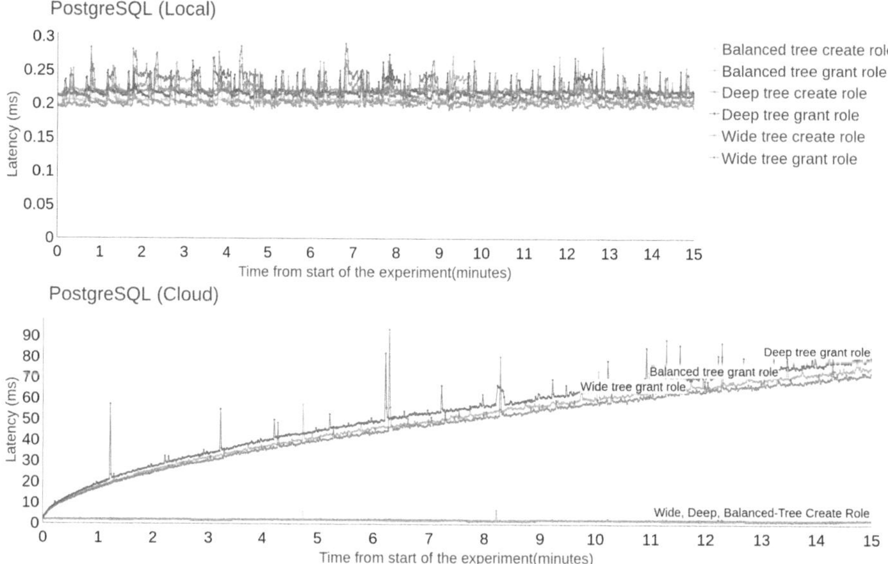

Fig. 4. Latency of `CREATE ROLE` and `GRANT` statements in PostgreSQL for all role hierarchies in the on-premise setup (top) and cloud setup (bottom).

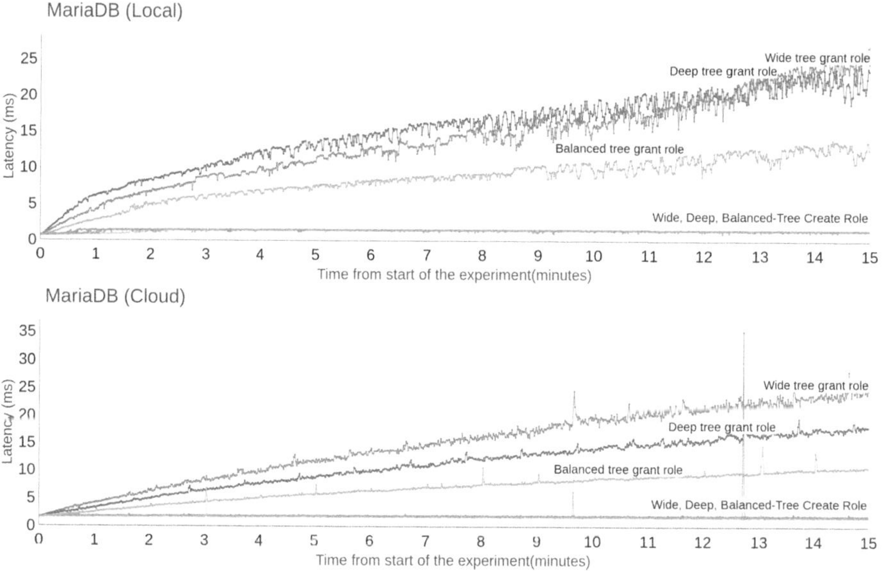

Fig. 5. Latency of `CREATE ROLE` and `GRANT` statements in MariaDB for all role hierarchies in the on-premise setup (top) and cloud setup (bottom).

the role hierarchy do not affect the execution time of the CREATE ROLE and GRANT statements. In the cloud setup, however, the execution time of GRANT statements increases significantly over time (up to 80 milliseconds per statement), while the execution time of CREATE ROLE statements remains constant.

Similar to Fig. 4, Fig. 5 shows the individual execution times of the CREATE ROLE and GRANT statements for MariaDB across all hierarchy structures. We observe the following findings: The execution times of GRANT statements increase over time, while the execution times of CREATE ROLE statements remain fairly constant. Interestingly, the execution time of GRANT statements for the balanced hierarchy structure is significantly lower than for the deep and wide structures, capping at around 12 milliseconds instead of 25 milliseconds. The execution time of CREATE ROLE statements for the wide hierarchy structure is the highest in the cloud setup.

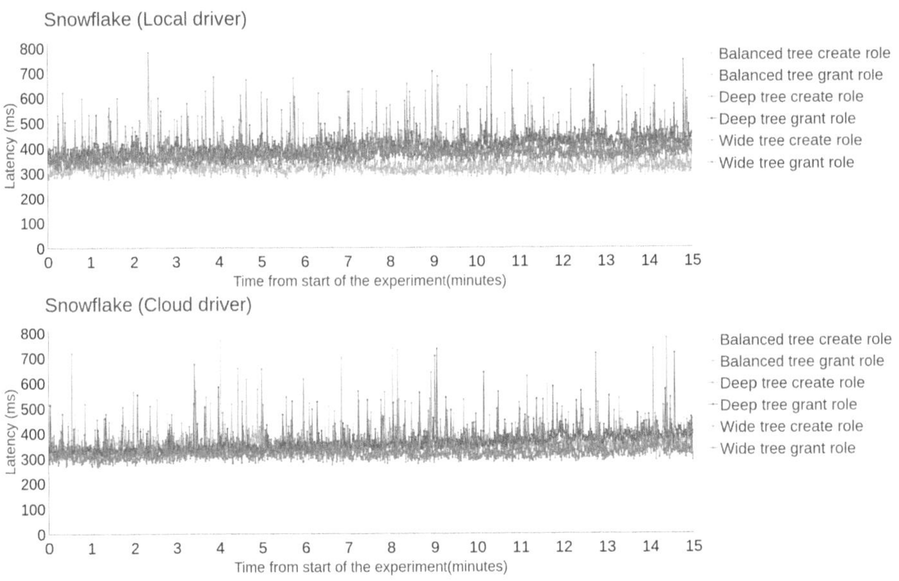

Fig. 6. Latency of CREATE ROLE and GRANT statements in Snowflake for all role hierarchies in the local-driver setup (top) and cloud-driver setup (bottom).

Figure 6 shows the individual execution times of the CREATE ROLE and GRANT statements for Snowflake across all hierarchy structures. We observe that the execution times fluctuate between 300 and 450 milliseconds, with frequent spikes up to 800 milliseconds. The execution times remain constant over time, with no significant differences between the hierarchy structures and statement types (GRANT vs. CREATE ROLE).

Explanation of Findings. The results of the Role Hierarchy Creation experiment show significant differences in performance across the evaluated systems and setups. In the following, we try to explain the observed findings.

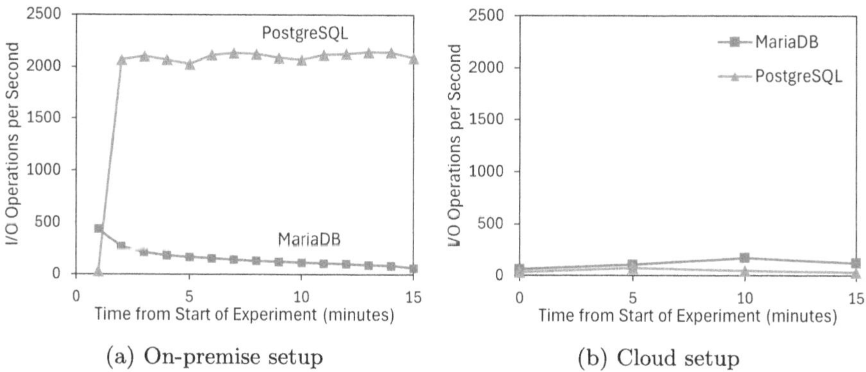

(a) On-premise setup

(b) Cloud setup

Fig. 7. I/O operations per second for PostgreSQL and MariaDB in the on-premise setup and the cloud setup.

PostgreSQL's drastic performance difference between the on-premise and cloud setups can be attributed to its high number of I/O operations per second (IOPS)—that is, the number of read and write operations performed on the storage device—when executing `GRANT` statements. This is illustrated in Fig. 7, which shows the number of IOPS for PostgreSQL and MariaDB in the on-premise setup (Fig. 7a) and the cloud setup (Fig. 7b). IOPS were measured every minute using Windows Performance Monitor in the on-premise setup, and every five minutes using AWS CloudWatch in the cloud setup. In the on-premise setup, PostgreSQL uses approximately 2,000 IOPS, whereas in the cloud setup, it drops to a maximum of 70 IOPS. AWS imposes limits on IOPS: GP2 storage devices, as used in our experiment, are allowed to perform 3 IOPS per GiB with a minimum of 100 IOPS [1]. Actual performance may fall short of provisioned IOPS [1], which likely occurred in our experiment. We attribute the high IOPS demand to the `GRANT` statements rather than the `CREATE ROLE` statements, based on the elevated latencies observed in Fig. 4.

MariaDB does not use the same I/O-intensive approach for grants as PostgreSQL and generally performs well in both on-premise and cloud environments. However, the performance of `GRANT` statements in MariaDB can degrade depending on the structure of the role hierarchy. This is due to the way MariaDB manages and caches privilege data at each role in the hierarchy. When a role is added or modified, MariaDB invalidates the privilege cache of that role and recursively invalidates all ancestor roles up to the root. Then, for each invalidated role, MariaDB traverses its subtree to rebuild the privilege cache, descending only into subtrees with invalidated caches.[3] In deep linear hierarchies, this results in high latency because every parent in the chain is invalidated and must be traversed again (complexity of $O(N)$). In wide hierarchies, any modification to a role causes the root's cache to be invalidated, requiring traversal of all its children during cache reconstruction (also $O(N)$). By contrast, balanced hierarchies are more efficient: only $O(\log N)$ ancestor roles are invalidated, and most subtrees retain valid caches, leading to lower latency when modifying a balanced role hierarchy.

Finally, Snowflake's high latency of around 300 to 450 milliseconds for `CREATE ROLE` and `GRANT` statements is due to its distributed architecture, which prioritizes large-scale data processing over low-latency operations. Snowflake's architecture consists of three layers: a service layer, a compute layer, and a storage layer [7]. Requests arrive at the service layer, which is a distributed mesh of nodes, and are forwarded to the compute and storage layers if necessary. Metadata in Snowflake is stored in a key-value store within the service layer. This key-value store is itself a distributed service in which metadata is replicated for durability. Modifying metadata, such as creating roles or granting privileges, therefore requires coordination across multiple nodes in the service layer. This coordination involves network communication, which results in higher latency compared to database systems like PostgreSQL and MariaDB. In our setup, these systems were installed as single-node instances without replication and additional network round trips.

Role Hierarchy Access Performance. In this experiment, we executed the Role Hierarchy Access component of the benchmark, measuring the performance of accessing securable objects and role metadata through SQL commands (`SELECT` and `SHOW` queries). We created role hierarchies of varying sizes (1,000, 10,000, and 100,000 roles) using three hierarchy structures: deep, wide, and balanced. The `SELECT * FROM table` and `SHOW ROLES` queries were each executed five times, and we report the median execution time. We measured the end-to-end round-trip time from the benchmark driver, which includes network latency from the driver to the database system.

Table 1 shows the execution times for the `SELECT * FROM table` and `SHOW ROLES` queries across the evaluated systems and hierarchy structures, with results reported in milliseconds. For role hierarchies that took more than 15 min to create, the experiment was aborted and the corresponding table entries are left blank.

For the `SELECT` query, we make the following observations: On-premise setups for PostgreSQL and MariaDB generally perform better than their cloud counterparts, which is expected due to the absence of network latency. Snowflake exhibits higher latency, which we speculate may be due to inefficient caching and the overhead of loading roles and privileges from its key-value store. A clear distinction can be seen between the local driver in Europe and the cloud driver

[3] The source code for this process can be found in https://github.com/MariaDB/server/blob/main/sql/sql_acl.cc, beginning at line 6359 (accessed: 2025-05-28).

Table 1. Median execution time (ms) for `SELECT * FROM table` and `SHOW ROLES` across systems. Blank cells indicate timeouts of hierarchy creation (>15 min).

	`SELECT * FROM table`			`SHOW ROLES`		
	Role Hierarchy Size			**Role Hierarchy Size**		
	1,000	**10,000**	**100,000**	**1,000**	**10,000**	**100,000**
PostgreSQL						
Local, Deep	0.28	0.22	0.24	1.41	7.53	69.57
Local, Wide	0.18	0.27	0.28	0.95	7.08	71.16
Local, Balanced	0.26	0.24	0.23	1.39	7.73	71.56
Cloud, Deep	0.46	0.50		1.74	9.28	
Cloud, Wide	0.68	0.46		1.75	9.16	
Cloud, Balanced	0.79	0.53		1.56	9.26	
MariaDB						
Local, Deep	0.13	0.16		1.47	7.22	
Local, Wide	0.22	0.16		1.35	6.87	
Local, Balanced	0.22	0.12	0.16	1.18	6.87	68.85
Cloud, Deep	0.44	0.53		2.08	11.19	
Cloud, Wide	0.46	0.40		1.85	9.81	
Cloud, Balanced	0.28	0.28	0.28	1.82	9.49	84.45
Snowflake						
Local driver, Deep	618			2354		
Local driver, Wide	456			2044		
Local driver, Balanced	571			2719		
Cloud driver, Deep	441			2580		
Cloud driver, Wide	391			559		
Cloud driver, Balanced	253			374		

in the same AWS region, due to the overhead of end-to-end network traffic. Overall, the performance of the `SELECT` query is not significantly affected by the structure of the role hierarchy, except in MariaDB's cloud setup, where the balanced structure outperforms the deep and wide variants. We currently have no clear explanation for this anomaly, and there are no noticeable differences or outliers between the five query repetitions in MariaDB's cloud setup.

For the `SHOW ROLES` query, we observe that PostgreSQL performs equally well in both the on-premise and cloud setups, with the `SHOW ROLES` command taking roughly 10 times longer as the role hierarchy increases in size, which is expected. MariaDB's performance is similar to PostgreSQL's. Snowflake's performance is considerably slower, in the range of 1–2 s. The outliers of 559 ms and 374 ms for the "cloud driver, wide" and "cloud driver, balanced" cases, may likely be explained by caching effects. Examining the individual execution times across the five runs, we recorded the following for "cloud driver, wide": 3359 ms, 344 ms,

2713 ms, 357 ms, and 559 ms (in that order). For "cloud driver, balanced": 3163 ms, 2724 ms, 365 ms, 351 ms, and 374 ms. Snowflake, being a distributed system, routes query requests to different nodes in the service layer, which can lead to varying latencies due to potentially different hardware characteristics and warm or stale caches.

6 Conclusion

In this study, we investigated the performance of Role-Based Access Control (RBAC) across three data management systems: PostgreSQL, MariaDB, and Snowflake. We designed a benchmark to evaluate the performance of RBAC mechanisms, focusing on the role hierarchy creation and access. The benchmark measures the performance of creating role hierarchies with varying structures (deep, wide, and balanced) and accessing securable objects and role metadata through SQL commands. The experiments were conducted in both on-premise and cloud setups.

Our results show significant differences in performance characteristics across the systems and deployment configurations. PostgreSQL performs well in the on-premise setup, creating large role hierarchies efficiently, but suffers in the cloud due to IOPS limitations. MariaDB shows consistent performance across both setups, with balanced hierarchies performing better than deep and wide hierarchies due to how MariaDB invalidates and rebuilds caches. Snowflake exhibits high latency for role hierarchy creation and access operations, due to its distributed architecture in which metadata is managed in a key-value store within one of its architectural layers. PostgreSQL and MariaDB were not set up in a distributed manner, so direct comparisons between these systems and Snowflake should be made with caution.

These findings reveal that each system exhibits different performance characteristics, and all tested systems show potential for optimization. PostgreSQL could be improved with respect to I/O operations when executing `GRANT` statements. MariaDB could benefit from optimizing the invalidation mechanism of its role hierarchy cache. Snowflake's RBAC performance will improve if Snowflake optimizes network patterns within its architecture.

Our study also highlights the need for a standardized benchmark for RBAC performance in data management systems. This is important as organizations increasingly centralize their data management and provide access to a growing number of users and applications, regulated via RBAC. This leads to increasingly large role hierarchies, which can impact performance. The benchmark we designed provides a first step toward evaluating RBAC performance, specifically focusing on the role hierarchy component at scale.

Future work includes extending the benchmark to cover additional RBAC features, such as granting different privileges, scaling the number of securable objects accessed via the role hierarchy, and evaluating more complex hierarchy structures such as DAGs and disjoint graphs. Furthermore, various other queries to access RBAC metadata can be considered, for example, `INFORMATION SCHEMA` queries. Finally, we plan to evaluate RBAC performance in additional data management systems as well as in replicated setups of PostgreSQL and MariaDB, and to investigate data governance performance in open-source metadata catalogs, such as Apache Polaris and Unity Catalog.

References

1. Amazon Web Services: Amazon RDS DB instance storage. https://docs.aws.amazon.com/AmazonRDS/latest/UserGuide/CHAP_Storage.html. Accessed 28 May 2025
2. Benson, L., et al.: Surprise benchmarking: the why, what, and how. In: DBTest, pp. 1–8 (2024)
3. Boncz, P., Anatiotis, A.-C., Kläbe, S.: JCC-H: adding join crossing correlations with skew to TPC-H. In: Nambiar, R., Poess, M. (eds.) TPCTC 2017. LNCS, vol. 10661, pp. 103–119. Springer, Cham (2018). https://doi.org/10.1007/978-3-319-72401-0_8
4. Brücke, C., Härtling, P., Palacios, R.E., Patel, H., Rabl, T.: TPCx-AI - an industry standard benchmark for artificial intelligence and machine learning systems. Proc. VLDB Endow. **16**(12), 3649–3661 (2023)
5. Cole, R., et al.: The mixed workload CH-benCHmark. In: DBTest, pp. 1–6 (2011)
6. Cooper, B.F., Silberstein, A., Tam, E., Ramakrishnan, R., Sears, R.: Benchmarking cloud serving systems with YCSB. In: Proceedings of the 1st ACM Symposium on Cloud Computing, pp. 143–154 (2010)
7. Dageville, B., et al.: The Snowflake elastic data warehouse. In: Proceedings of the 2016 International Conference on Management of Data, pp. 215–226 (2016)
8. El-Hindi, M., Arora, A., Karrer, S., Binnig, C.: Towards a benchmark for shared databases [vision paper]. Datenbank-Spektrum **22**(3), 227–239 (2022)
9. Ferraiolo, D., Kuhn, R.: Role-based access controls. In: Proceedings of the 15th National Computer Security Conference, pp. 554–563 (1992)
10. Ferraiolo, D.F., Sandhu, R., Gavrila, S., Kuhn, D.R., Chandramouli, R.: Proposed NIST standard for role-based access control. ACM Trans. Inf. Syst. Secur. (TISSEC) **4**(3), 224–274 (2001)
11. Iosup, A., et al.: LDBC graphalytics: a benchmark for large-scale graph analysis on parallel and distributed platforms. Proc. VLDB Endow. **9**(13), 1317–1328 (2016)
12. Kersten, M.L., Kemper, A., Markl, V., Nica, A., Poess, M., Sattler, K.U.: Tractor pulling on data warehouses. In: DBTest, pp. 1–6 (2011)
13. MariaDB Foundation: MariaDB server. https://mariadb.com. Accessed 28 May 2025
14. O'Neil, P.E., O'Neil, E.J., Chen, X.: The star schema benchmark (SSB). https://www.cs.umb.edu/~poneil/StarSchemaB.pdf. Accessed 28 May 2025
15. Patil, S., et al.: YCSB++ benchmarking and performance debugging advanced features in scalable table stores. In: Proceedings of the 2nd ACM Symposium on Cloud Computing, pp. 1–14 (2011)
16. Sanhu, R.S., Coyne, E.J., Feinstein, H.L., Youman, C.E.: Role-based access control models. IEEE Comput. **29**(2), 38–47 (1996)
17. Stonebraker, M., Rowe, L.A.: The design of Postgres. ACM SIGMOD Rec. **15**(2), 340–355 (1986)
18. Transaction Processing Performance Council (TPC): TPC Benchmark™ C (2010). http://www.tpc.org/tpcc/

19. Transaction Processing Performance Council (TPC): TPC Benchmark™ H (2022). http://www.tpc.org/tpch/
20. Transaction Processing Performance Council (TPC): TPC Benchmark™ DS (2024). http://www.tpc.org/tpcds/
21. Vieira, M., Madeira, H.: A dependability benchmark for OLTP application environments. In: Proceedings 2003 VLDB Conference, pp. 742–753. Elsevier (2003)
22. Vieira, M., Madeira, H.: Towards a security benchmark for database management systems. In: International Conference on Dependable Systems and Networks, pp. 592–601. IEEE (2005)

CH2++: New HOAP for Benchmarking JSON Data Analytics

M. J. Carey(✉), V. Sarathy, D. Nagy, B.-C. Wang, K. Murthy, M. Muralikrishna, P. Gupta, and T. Westmann

Couchbase, Inc., San Jose, CA, USA
mike.carey@couchbase.com

Abstract. Database systems with hybrid data management support, referred to as HTAP or HOAP architectures, have gained popularity for performing near-real-time data analytics. Such systems first emerged in the relational world, and the CH-benCHmark (CH) was proposed in 2011 to evaluate such relational systems. A decade later, with NoSQL database systems gaining traction for new application development, we proposed a first document-oriented variant of CH – called CH2 – that was aimed at evaluating hybrid data platforms in the document database space. Here, we introduce CH2++, a major revision of CH2 that is significantly more suitable for evaluating systems that support JSON analytics.

Like CH and CH2, this new CH2++ benchmark borrows from and extends both TPC-C and TPC-H. Differences from CH2 include a much more document-oriented schema, the inclusion of additional fields to exercise analytical systems' column-oriented features, and a corresponding JSON "do over" of the CH2 queries. The paper also includes preliminary performance isolation and scaling results from running CH2++ against Capella Operational and Capella Columnar, which are Couchbase's DBaaS cloud service offerings. The results highlight the value of CH2++ for evaluating JSON-targeted HOAP and HTAP platforms.

Keywords: Benchmarks · NoSQL · JSON · HTAP · HOAP

1 Introduction

In today's world, organizations are becoming ever more reliant on real-time information and its analysis to steer and optimize their operations. Historically, operational (OLTP) and analytical (OLAP) processing were two separate activities, each running on their own separate infrastructures. Periodic ETL processes served to bridge these worlds in the overall IT architecture of a typical enterprise [22]. Today, database management systems with hybrid data management support – known as HTAP (Hybrid Transactional/Analytical Processing [33]) or HOAP (Hybrid Operational/Analytical Processing [1]) support – have appeared on the scene and gotten traction in both industry and research in order to address the pressing needs for timely analytics. Born in the relational world, these hybrid

R. Nambiar and M. Poess (Eds.): TPCTC 2025, LNCS 16261, pp. 37–57, 2026.
https://doi.org/10.1007/978-3-032-18070-4_3

platforms are often associated with other concurrent high-end server technology trends. Columnar storage and main memory data management are two technologies that are often assumed to be part of that picture.

While relational databases still dominate the IT landscape, today's applications demand support for millions of interactions with end-users via the Web and mobile devices. Relational database systems were initially built to target hundreds or perhaps thousands of users and were designed for strict consistency and strict data control. About 15 years ago, developers of applications like those of today began to feel that relational database systems were falling short of their agility, flexibility, and scalability demands. This led to the emergence of a new category of data management systems known as NoSQL systems [30]; our focus here will be on the NoSQL subcategory of document databases. Examples of such systems include Couchbase Server [4] and MongoDB [16]. NoSQL systems aim to provide incremental and horizontal scalability on clusters of computers as well as to eliminate the mismatch between an application's view of data and its persisted form, thus enabling players, ranging from application developers to DBAs and data analysts, to work with their data in its natural form.

Given these developments, one might wonder if the NoSQL world is HOAP-less[1], particularly the world of document databases. The answer is no; the need to combine operational and analytical capabilities for up-to-the-minute analytics exists there as well. NoSQL vendors have begun to provide enterprise customers with HOAP and to include HOAP-ful messaging in their marketing materials. One such vendor, whose document data management capabilities we will benchmark here, is Couchbase. The Couchbase Server platform introduced HOAP when it added Couchbase Analytics [2]. Today, the Couchbase Capella DBaaS cloud offering provides HOAP via its Operational and Columnar services. We propose a benchmark for evaluating HOAPfulness in the world of document data management, a world where JSON is the dominant data model and where the elimination of the ETL requires analytical query support for JSON data. However, our benchmark is not Couchbase-specific; it can be applied to HOAP-ful configurations of other NoSQL databases, which is one goal of its design.

In the relational world, the problem of evaluating database system performance under hybrid OLTP/OLAP workloads has attracted attention. Perhaps the most prominent example is the mixed workload CH-benCHmark [12] (CH). CH was proposed by a gathering of database query processing and performance experts and has since been used to evaluate the performance of new HTAP systems [29]. The same is not yet the case in the NoSQL world; a truly successful benchmark to assess HOAP for scalable NoSQL systems has yet to appear. We offered a first NoSQL HOAP benchmark called CH2 [8] based on extending and improving CH in several important ways, but it has not enjoyed significant uptake outside of Couchbase. In this paper we propose take two – namely CH2++, a derivative of CH2. Major differences include a much more document-oriented schema (involving the use of natural nesting and arrays), the inclusion

[1] We prefer the term HOAP over HTAP for NoSQL, as the term HTAP seems more tied to strict ACID transactions and main-memory technology presumptions.

of additional fields to exercise the tested platforms' handling of narrow analytical queries, and a corresponding JSON "do over" of all of the CH2 queries. The complete CH2 and CH2++ schemas and query sets are available at https://github.com/couchbaselabs/ch2. Other contributions of the paper include preliminary performance isolation and scaling results from running CH2++ against Capella Operational and Capella Columnar, which are Couchbase's DBaaS cloud service offerings. The results highlight the value of CH2++ for evaluating JSON-targeted HOAP and HTAP platforms.

The rest of this paper is organized as follows: Sect. 2 surveys work on HTAP and on prior SQL and NoSQL benchmarks. Section 3 describes CH2++, our proposed HOAP-for-NoSQL benchmark, explaining how it differs from CH and CH2. As a HOAPful document platform example, Sect. 4 provides an overview of Couchbase's Capella cloud DBaaS offering and its approach to HOAP. To demonstrate CH2++'s potential to be an effective hybrid workload benchmark for NoSQL, Sect. 5 presents a set of results from running CH2++ on Capella under different service configurations. Section 6 summarizes the CH2++ proposal and invites others to take CH2++ for a test drive of their own.

2 Related Work

We first review related work on HTAP/HOAP and database benchmarks.

2.1 HTAP (HOAP)

The relational database world has seen the emergence of HTAP (a.k.a. HOAP) capabilities in a number of commercial systems as well as growing research interest related to HTAP. Notable HTAP offerings include HyPer [17], born in research but now owned and used by Salesforce in Tableau, and SAP-HANA [21]. Other relational HTAP offerings include IBM's DB2 BLU [28], Oracle's dual-engine main-memory database [18], and the real-time analytical processing capabilities in Microsoft's SQL Server [19]. As an example on the research side, a relatively recent paper introduced and explored the concept of adaptive HTAP and how to manage the CPU core and memory resources of a powerful (scale-up) many-core NUMA server for handling a mixed main-memory workload [29].

HTAP in the relational world has focused mainly on in-memory scenarios involving modestly sized operational databases. With the availability of multi-core servers with very large main memories, and compression from columnar storage, it is now possible for main memory to hold much or all of an enterprises' operational data. This is why most current HTAP offerings have focused on main-memory database technology. And, as might be expected, their focus has been on single-server architectures, i.e., on scale-up rather than scale-out.

Bringing HOAP to the world of document data management involves different problems that need different solutions. To scale document databases while providing HOAP, the focus needs to be on Big Data, i.e. large volumes of flexible, schemaless data. Also, NoSQL systems and their applications tend to have different transactional consistency requirements [30]. Data timeliness is important in the NoSQL world, but there is less of a need to focus on reducing or eliminating ACID transaction interference and a greater need to focus on providing strong performance isolation at the level of a cluster's physical resources.

2.2 Benchmarks

There are many benchmarks for evaluating the performance of relational database systems in various application scenarios [15]. The most notable benchmarks are the Transaction Processing Council (TPC) TPC-x benchmarks, including TPC-C [27] for transaction processing, as well as TPC-H [25] and TPC-DS [26] for decision support and analytics. There have also been various benchmarks proposed and used in the NoSQL world, including YCSB [13] for key-value stores, BigFUN [23] for Big Data management platform performance, MongoDB's adaptation of TPC-C to evaluate NoSQL transactional performance [16], and a similar NoSQL adaptation [24] of TPC-H to evaluate Big Data analytics performance, to name a sample of the NoSQL and Big Data benchmarks.

A recent survey examined HTAP databases and benchmarks [20]. An especially notable HTAP benchmark is the CH benCHmark for mixed workloads [12]. CH-benCHmark (CH) came from a Dagstuhl workshop attended by database query processing and performance experts from both industry and academia. CH combined the schemas and database operations of TPC-C and TPC-H to bridge the divide between the established single-workload benchmark suites of TPC-C for OLTP and TPC-H for OLAP, thereby providing a foundation for mixed-workload performance evaluation. The original CH paper included results from running CH on PostgreSQL with all data in memory and a read-committed isolation level. CH gained traction for HTAP evaluation, including being used to assess the performance of an adaptive HTAP system and its scheduling ideas [29]. Several other HTAP benchmarks have appeared subsequently, including HTAPBench [11] and HyBench [34]. HTAPBench is a descendent of CH; it proposed setting a fixed transaction performance target and increasing the analytical query workload until measurable transaction interference is observed relative to the target. HyBench is based on a different application scenario and it also added interactive transactions (OLXP) to the workload mix. Both of those benchmarks were still focused on the evaluation of relational HTAP systems.

To our knowledge, our CH2 [8] extension of CH, discussed in more detail next, was the first mixed workload benchmark intended to evaluate HOAP for scalable NoSQL (JSON-based) systems. An earlier exploratory step was [32], where performance isolation in Couchbase Server was studied for a simple scenario with lightly nested TPC-C data and a mix of NewOrder transactions and a stream of join/group-by/top-K analytical queries. Our subsequent CH2 effort was suggested as future work at the end of that earlier article. As was the case for CH2, the aim of the CH2++ benchmark in this paper is to evaluate HOAPful platforms and services in the document database space.

3 CH2++ Benchmark Design

When we started the CH2 effort that preceded this work, our goal was to explore HOAP support on NoSQL platforms, including (1) their delivery of performance isolation for mixed OLTP and OLAP workloads, and (2) their query performance for OLAP-style queries. These points were of particular interest because most NoSQL systems were designed to scale horizontally and their query engines have been OLTP-oriented, so NoSQL systems have generally aimed to support high-concurrency/low-latency operational workloads rather than richer analytics.

As discussed in [8], while reviewing relational HTAP benchmarks, we came across the CH benchmark [12]. We were pleased to find that it adopted and merged data, operations, and queries from TPC-C and TPC-H. Having had very similar thoughts, we decided for CH2 to adapt the CH schema and operations to the JSON world by re-modeling orders as objects with embedded line items (rather than as two separate tables), as was done in [16] and [24]. While doing so, we also encountered and fixed a number of problems with the original CH design that required more extensive changes to CH's data and query predicate generation. In the remainder of this section we describe CH2++, our recent re-work of CH2, including its reason(s) for being and its differences from CH2.

3.1 CH2++ Database Schema

Figure 1 summarizes the schema of the CH2++ benchmark, including its eleven collections and their relationships. We borrow the optionally typed collection DDL from Apache AsterixDB [6] to convey the structure of the JSON objects in each collection, with solid black links to indicate the N:1 relationships between them. The numerical annotations on the links show the number of child objects per parent (e.g., 10 districts per warehouse, 3000 customers per district). Like CH and CH2, the CH2++ database is scalable by varying the number of warehouses (W). Sizes for three of the collections, supplier (10K objects), region (5 objects), and nation (62 objects), are fixed instead of scaling with W. CH and CH2 borrowed those collections from TPC-H; the other eight are either taken from TPC-C or from both (using TPC-C's naming conventions).

To relate objects in the TPC-H inspired collections to objects in TPC-C, CH2++ does what CH (and then CH2) did: An entry in stock is associated with its supplier through the functional relationship `stock.s_i_id * stock.s_w_id mod 10,000 = supplier.su_suppkey`. Customer nations are identified by the first character of `customer.c_state`. In TPC-C this character can take any of 62 different values (upper- and lower-case letters and numbers), so CH chose 62 nations (vs. 25 in TPC-H) to populate the nation collection. The values for `nation.n_nationkey` are chosen so their associated ASCII values are letters or numbers. The region collection then contains five regions for these nations. Linkages between these collections are modeled via the foreign key fields `nation.n_regionkey` and `supplier.su_nationkey`. These functional linkages (stitching) are denoted by the dotted links and formulae shown in Fig. 1.

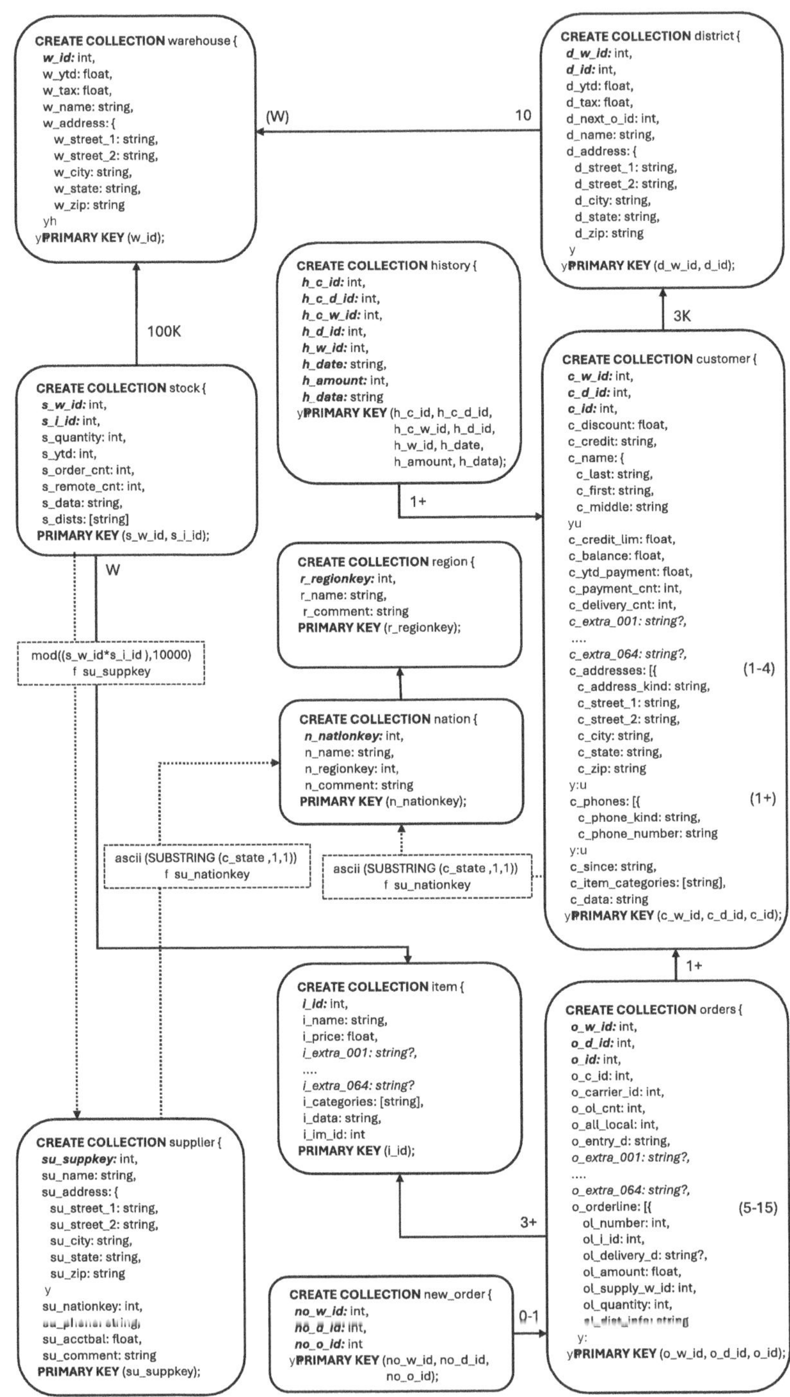

Fig. 1. CH2++ Schema

As mentioned above, the design goal for CH2++ was to create an effective benchmark for HOAP workloads involving JSON analytics. CH was a modest relational melding of TPC-C and TPC-H, and the original CH2 was a minimal JSON-ification of CH that simply nested orderlines within orders. In contrast, CH2++ is a modern-day update of CH2 that we arrived at by asking the question "what might TPC-C and TPC-H have looked like, schema-wise, if they were designed today for document-based applications?" We answered this question by following current best practices for JSON database design [5]. As a result, CH2++'s schema is much more JSON-ic in nature than that of CH2:

- Addresses and names are now modeled as nested objects wherever they appear in any of the collections.
- Customers now have an array of 1–4 addresses (shipping, home, work, and/or billing) with a shipping address being mandatory and the others each occurring with 1/3 probability.
- Customers now have an array of 1–4 phones (contact, home, work, mobile) with a contact phone being mandatory and the others each occurring with 1/3 probability.
- Customers now have an additional array of 0–15 category names (drawn from 128 possibilities) to capture the kinds of items of particular interest to them.
- Items now have an additional array of 1–3 categories (drawn from the 128 possibilities) to indicate what kind(s) of item they are.
- Stock entries now have a 10-element array of inventory levels instead of having ten separate, numerically named fields.
- Several of the collections (customer, item, orders) now have 64 extra fields to simulate the modern-day reality that typical data objects in 2025 can be much wider than those in the 1990s (when TPC-C and TPC-H were born).

Table 1 lists the CH2++ collections with an example of their scaling, showing cardinalities for a 1000-warehouse benchmark instance. As in CH2, orders have a nested orderline array with an average of 10 line items. The line separates the 8 borrowed TPC-C collections from the 3 borrowed TPC-H collections.

3.2 CH2++ Database Data

As mentioned above, when initially generating the database for CH2, we found that the CH (and TPC-C) data generators had issues in generating data suitable for the analytical queries. The biggest problem can be described as the TPC-C "big bang" – all date fields in the initial CH database had the current date (i.e. the date of a benchmark run) as their value, so there were no useful date ranges in the data for analytical queries. (TPC-H's queries operate on a 7-year history.) Thus, while CH's queries were based in principle on TPC-H, many predicates returned nothing, everything, or a run-date-dependent result.

To address this in CH2 [8], we created a new data generator using the TPC-C data generator from CMU's py-tpcc benchmarking package to (i) generate orders with nested items and (ii) carefully generate values for fields used in the predicates of the analytical queries. For (ii) we introduced a RUN_DATE parameter to

Table 1. CH2++ Collections and Cardinalities for 1,000 Warehouses

Collection	Cardinality (W = 1000)
warehouse	1,000
district	10,000
history	30,000,000
neworder	9,000,000
stock	100,000,000
customer	30,000,000
orders (orderline)	30,000,000 (300,000,000)
item	100,000
supplier	10,000
nation	62
region	5

drive data generation; RUN_DATE led to derivative parameters START_DATE and END_DATE that are similar to TPC-H's date range. RUN_DATE controls the historical characteristics of the data by determining when the benchmark's past should end and when its operational life should begin, i.e., START_DATE = RUN_DATE - 7 years and END_DATE = RUN_DATE - 1 day. We also adjusted the dates in the data generator based on TPC-H, added the supplier, nation, and region collections, and adjusted the dates and ranges in the analytical queries to conform to TPC-H's predicate selectivities and business semantics [8].

In addition to these changes, to transition from CH2 to the now richer CH2++ schema, we modified our CH2 generator to create nested objects for the nested names and addresses, to use array-based modeling of customer addresses and phones (with the mandatory shipping address and mandatory contact phone carrying the address and phone values that CH2 had before the additional kinds of addresses and phones were added), to add category arrays to customers and items, and to add 64 extra fields to customers, orders, and items. (Note: Although 64 is the setting used in this paper, it is a tuneable CH2++ parameter.) None of the extra fields are actually accessed in the benchmark's queries, as their role is to test an analytical system's ability to avoid touching unused data.

3.3 CH2++ Transactional Operations

The operational workload of TPC-C models transactions for a typical order processing scenario. The transactions are a mix of five read-only and update-intensive business transactions: NewOrder, Payment, OrderStatus, Delivery, and StockLevel. CH2++, like CH and CH2, uses this mix as its operational workload. Like its predecessors, CH2++'s operational performance reporting focuses on NewOrder, a transaction that enters a new order (containing multiple orderlines) into the database. NewOrder touches most of the TPC-C tables, and consists of both read-only queries and updates against them. Details of the five TPC-C transactions as well as the prescribed mix can be found in [27]. One change that CH2 and CH2++ made to py-tpcc's TPC-C implementation is to chop Delivery, which does delivery processing for ten orders, into ten per-order transactions rather than grouping them as one transaction. This is more in line with what the TPC-C specification prescribes (Sect. 2.7 in [27]) and follows best practices for selecting transaction boundaries [31]. Also, py-tpcc deviates from the TPC-C Delivery specification, which says that Delivery should be processed as an asynchronous request. We kept that deviation of the py-tpcc implementation, so CH2 and CH2++ are non-compliant (by design) in that they process Delivery operations synchronously. CH2++'s operational performance is reported in terms of throughput and response times for NewOrder operations.

```
SELECT ol_number,
  SUM(ol_quantity) AS sum_qty,
  SUM(ol_amount) AS sum_amount,
  SUM(ol_quantity) AS avg_qty,
  AVG(ol_amount) AS avg_amount,
  COUNT(*) AS count_order
FROM orderline
WHERE ol_delivery_d >
  '2007-01-02 00:00:00.000000'
GROUP BY ol_number
ORDER BY ol_number
```

```
SELECT ol.ol_number,
  SUM(ol.ol_quantity) AS sum_qty,
  SUM(ol.ol_amount) AS sum_amount,
  AVG(ol.ol_quantity) AS avg_qty,
  AVG(ol.ol_amount) AS avg_amount,
  COUNT(*) AS count_order
FROM orders o, o.o_orderline ol
WHERE ol.ol_delivery_d >
  DATE_ADD_STR('[START_DATE]',[DAYS],'day')
GROUP BY ol.ol_number
ORDER BY ol.ol_number;
```

Fig. 2. Query 1 – CH (left) vs. CH2/CH2++ (right)

3.4 CH2++ Analytical Queries

When we designed CH2's analytical workload, we started with CH's 22 queries, which were inspired by TPC-H's 22 queries. We modified the CH queries to work meaningfully against the historical data discussed in Sect. 3.2 with selectivities like those of TPC-H: We replaced baked-in constants with randomly generated controlled values and examined and modified their query predicates to produce 22 queries that were better aligned with TPC-H [8]. The queries were expressed in SQL++, a generalization of SQL that handles nested and schemaless data [7,10]. For CH2++, we reformulated the queries from CH2 to operate against CH2++'s JSON schema, which involved dealing with its nested objects and nested arrays. Here we will discuss three of the 22 queries to illustrate some of the key differences between CH2++'s queries and their CH and CH2 predecessors.

Figure 2 shows Query 1 of the CH2++ query set (on the right) along with the original relational CH query (on the left). For this first query, the CH2++ version is the same as CH2. The differences between the relational CH query and the CH2++ version are highlighted. The first difference is due to the JSON-ic nesting of orderlines in orders; the second difference is the replacement of a (non-meaningful) constant date with a parameterized date range.

```
SELECT o.o_id, o.o_w_id, o.o_d_id,
  SUM(ol.ol_amount) AS revenue,
  o.o_entry_d
FROM customer c,
  neworder no,
  orders o, o.o_orderline ol
WHERE c.c_state LIKE '[CSTATE]%'

  AND c.c_id = o.o_c_id
  AND c.c_w_id = o.o_w_id
  AND c.c_d_id = o.o_d_id
  AND no.no_w_id = o.o_w_id
  AND no.no_d_id = o.o_d_id
  AND no.no_o_id = o.o_id
  AND o.o_entry_d <
    '[O_YEAR]-[O_MONTH]-[O_DAY]' ||
    '00:00:00.000000'
GROUP BY o.o_id, o.o_w_id, o.o_d_id,
  o.o_entry_d
ORDER BY revenue DESC, o.o_entry_d;
```

```
SELECT o.o_id, o.o_w_id, o.o_d_id,
  SUM(ol.ol_amount) AS revenue,
  o.o_entry_d
FROM customer c, c.c_addresses ca,
  neworder no,
  orders o, o.o_orderline ol
WHERE ca.c_state LIKE '[CSTATE]%'
  AND ca.c_address_kind = 'shipping'
  AND c.c_id = o.o_c_id
  AND c.c_w_id = o.o_w_id
  AND c.c_d_id = o.o_d_id
  AND no.no_w_id = o.o_w_id
  AND no.no_d_id = o.o_d_id
  AND no.no_o_id = o.o_id
  AND o.o_entry_d <
    '[O_YEAR]-[O_MONTH]-[O_DAY]' ||
    '00:00:00.000000'
GROUP BY o.o_id, o.o_w_id, o.o_d_id,
  o.o_entry_d
ORDER BY revenue DESC, o.o_entry_d;
```

Fig. 3. Query 3 – CH2 (left) vs. CH2++ (right).

Figure 3 shows Query 3 from the new CH2++ query set (right) alongside the corresponding version from CH2 (left). In this query, one can see the impact of having the nested array of addresses for customers, with the shipping address being the one of interest: The CH2++ query unnests the array (as variable *ca*) and singles out the shipping address. This is the sort of complexity that can be expected to arise in non-1NF JSON analytics scenarios.

As a slightly more complex example, Fig. 4 offers a side-by-side comparison for Query 10. Since the CH2++ customers have nested arrays of phones as well as addresses, more unnesting and singling-out is needed to answer Query 10's business question using the shipping address and contact phone number. Similar changes were made for each of CH2's analytical queries in order to create CH2++'s analytical query set. Again, all 22 queries for both CH2 and CH2++ can be found at https://github.com/couchbaselabs/ch2.

The analytical performance of CH2++ is reported in terms of the geometric mean ("power") of the response times of the 22 queries when they are looped and run in a sequence. The order of execution for the 22 analytical queries follows the permutations specified at the end of the TPC-H specification [25].

4 A DBaaS Target: Couchbase Capella

To show the utility of CH2++, we apply it here to Couchbase Capella, a scalable and HOAP-ful document DBaaS offering [14]. Figure 5 gives a high-level overview of Couchbase Capella. As a managed cloud version of the scalable, shared-nothing Couchbase Server platform [4], the Capella Operational service includes a fast key-value store for sub-millisecond data operations, secondary indexing for fast querying, and a SQL++-based query engine. Its target workloads are online applications that need low query latency and high throughput. The complementary new Capella Columnar service [9] brings HOAP to Capella

```
SELECT c.c_id,
  c.c_last,
  SUM(ol.ol_amount) AS revenue,
  c.c_city, c.c_phone,
  n.n_name
FROM customer c,

  orders o, o.o_orderline ol,
  nation n
WHERE c.c_id = o.o_c_id
  AND c.c_w_id = o.o_w_id
  AND c.c_d_id = o.o_d_id
  AND  o.o_entry_d >=
    '[O_YEAR]-[O_MONTH]-[O_DAY]' ||
    '00:00:00.000000'
  AND o.o_entry_d <
    DATE_ADD_STR(
      '[O_YEAR]-[O_MONTH]-[O_DAY]' ||
    '00:00:00.000000', 3, 'month'
    )


  AND n.n_nationkey =
    string_to_codepoint(c.c_state)[0]
GROUP BY c.c_id,
  c.c_last,
  c.c_city, c.c_phone,
  n.n_name
ORDER BY revenue DESC
LIMIT 20;
```

```
SELECT c.c_id,
  c.c_name.c_last,
  SUM(ol.ol_amount) AS revenue,
  ca.c_city, cp.c_phone_number,
  n.n_name
FROM customer c,
  c.c_addresses ca, c.c_phones cp,
  orders o, o.o_orderline ol,
  nation n
WHERE c.c_id = o.o_c_id
  AND c.c_w_id = o.o_w_id
  AND c.c_d_id = o.o_d_id
  AND o.o_entry_d >=
    '[O_YEAR]-[O_MONTH]-[O_DAY]' ||
    '00:00:00.000000'
  AND o.o_entry_d <
    DATE_ADD_STR(
      '[O_YEAR]-[O_MONTH]-[O_DAY]' ||
    '00:00:00.000000', 3, 'month'
    )
  AND ca.c_address_kind = 'shipping'
  AND cp.c_phone_kind = 'contact'
  AND n.n_nationkey =
    string_to_codepoint(ca.c_state)[0]
GROUP BY c.c_id,
  c.c_name.c_last,
  ca.c_city, cp.c_phone_number,
  n.n_name
ORDER BY revenue DESC
LIMIT 20;
```

Fig. 4. Query 10 – CH2 (left) vs. CH2++ (right).

by providing a much-extended version of Couchbase Analytics [2] to support more complex analytical SQL++ queries against JSON data drawn from a variety of sources, including Capella Operational data, in a highly parallel manner.

Figure 6 shows the main components of the Couchbase Operational service. Internally, the Operational service is organized as a set of microservices deployed and managed on a Couchbase Operational cluster. Nodes can be added or removed via a rebalance process that redistributes data across all nodes to increase or decrease the CPU, memory, and/or storage capacity of a cluster. A homogeneous cluster of 6 nodes is shown, but applications with advanced performance needs can map the microservices to different numbers of nodes; this option is referred to as Multi-Dimensional Scaling. Internally, data changes are communicated across services via an internal Database Change Protocol (DCP) that notifies other services of changes to the documents managed by the Data Service.

The Data Service provides caching, persistence, and inter-node replication. The data model is JSON, and documents are stored in containers called buckets. There are no explicitly defined schemas, so the "schema" for documents is captured in the structure of each stored document. Developers can thus add new objects and properties at any time by deploying new application code that stores new JSON data without having to make and deploy changes to a static schema. Within a bucket, documents reside in collections (which are similar to tables

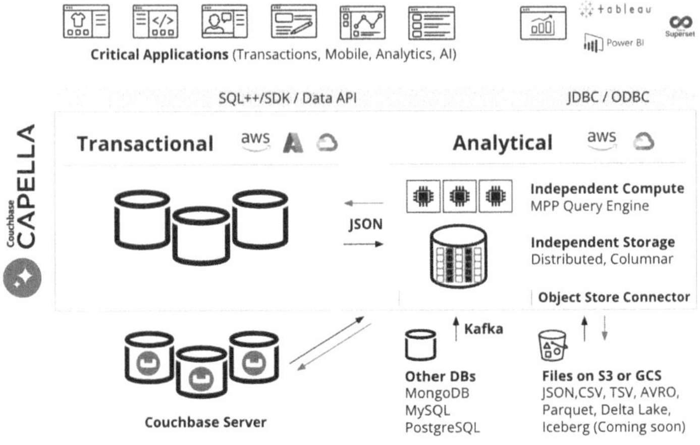

Fig. 5. Couchbase Cappella Service.

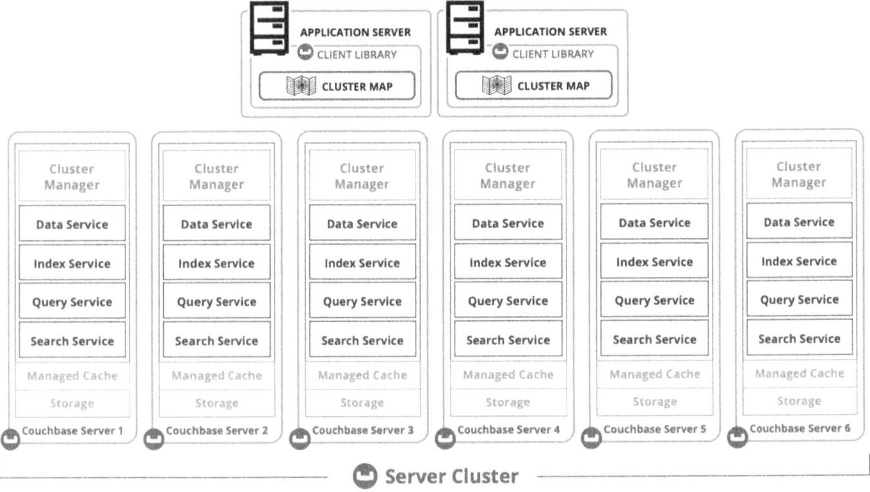

Fig. 6. Capella Operational Server Components

in an RDBMS) that can be grouped together logically using scopes (similar to RDBMS schemas).

The Indexing, Query, and Search Services work together to provide JSON database functionality. The Indexing Service provides global secondary indexing for data in the Data Service, and the Search service offers richer text indexing and search. The Query Service ties things together by exposing database functionality through SQL++, a declarative, SQL-based language that relaxes the 1NF and strong typing demands of SQL. It includes support for SQL-style transactions using a combination of optimistic and pessimistic concurrency control.

SQL++ statements can be grouped into atomic transactions whose effects span the Query, Indexing, and Data Services.

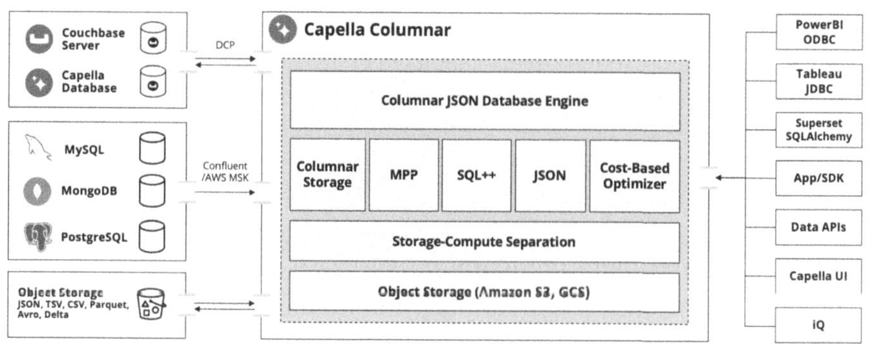

Fig. 7. Capella Columnar Service Overview

Figure 7 gives a high-level overview of the Capella Columnar service. It complements the Capella Operational service by supporting complex ad-hoc analytical queries (e.g. large joins, aggregations, windowing, etc.) over JSON document collections. Whereas Capella Operational supports many users making well-defined, programmatic requests that are smaller and inexpensive, Capella Columnar focuses on ad hoc and analytical requests, with fewer users posing larger, more expensive queries. As Fig. 5 indicated, Capella Columnar supports the real-time shadowing (i.e., continuous ingestion) of JSON data from Capella Operational, from on-prem Couchbase Server clusters, or from other databases, including MongoDB and relational sources. Under the hood, Capella Operational uses a largely point-to-point-based query execution model, whereas Capella Columnar utilizes partitioned-parallel processing (MPP) in order to bring all of its resources to bear on each query.

So – how does Couchbase Capella provide HOAP? Because the data in Capella Operational becomes available for analysis in Capella Columnar as soon as it is created or changed, analysts always see fresh application data (thanks to DCP). They can immediately pose queries about their operational data, in its natural JSON form (with no ETL), thereby lowering the time to insight from days or hours to seconds. A Capella Columnar cluster can be scaled both horizontally and independently from its data sources. In contrast to many relational HTAP offerings, Capella Columnar is not an in-memory solution. Rather, it is designed to handle large volumes of NoSQL documents – documents whose individual worth and access frequencies would not justify the cost of a memory-resident solution, but whose aggregated content can be invaluable for decision making. CH2++ provides a means to assess the HOAP-fulness of the Capella cloud offering via its hybrid operational/analytical workload, with the Capella Operational service providing the "O" in HOAP and the Capella Columnar service providing the "A".

5 Benchmark Results

Here we present some results from implementing and running the CH2++ benchmark on Capella's Operational and Columnar cloud services. In the future, we hope to see CH2++ being applied to other HOAP-ful JSON platforms as well. (Given the absence of NoSQL query language or API standards, the main effort to do so would involve reexpressing the CH2++ driver's operations and queries in terms of other target platforms' interfaces).

5.1 Benchmark Implementation

In the Capella Operational service, the CH2++ data was in a scope called *ch2pp* in a bucket called *bench*. Data Definition 1.1 shows the DDL statements for creating the benchmark's collections, and Data Definition 1.2 shows the DDL for creating their indexes. In Capella Columnar, a shadow collection was created for each Operational collection. Data Definition 1.3 shows the DDL statements to create the shadows and Data Definition 1.4 shows the DDL statements used to index them. Data Definition 1.5 shows the Columnar DDL statements used to create collection samples to enable cost-based query optimization (CBO).

```
CREATE SCOPE bench.ch2pp;
CREATE COLLECTION bench.ch2pp.customer;
CREATE COLLECTION bench.ch2pp.district;
... (etc.) ...
```

Data Definition 1.1. Capella Operational Collection DDL

```
CREATE INDEX cu_w_id_d_id_last
 ON bench.ch2pp.customer(c_w_id, c_d_id, c_last) USING GSI;
CREATE INDEX di_id_w_id
 ON bench.ch2pp.district(d_id, d_w_id) USING GSI;
CREATE INDEX no_o_id_d_id_w_id
 ON bench.ch2pp.neworder(no_o_id, no_d_id, no_w_id) USING GSI;
CREATE INDEX or_id_d_id_w_id_c_id
 ON bench.ch2pp.orders(o_id, o_d_id, o_w_id, o_c_id) USING GSI;
CREATE INDEX or_w_id_d_id_c_id
 ON bench.ch2pp.orders(o_w_id, o_d_id, o_c_id) USING GSI;
CREATE INDEX wh_id
 ON bench.ch2pp.warehouse(w_id) USING GSI;
```

Data Definition 1.2. Capella Operational Index DDL

To drive the benchmark's workload, we took py-tpcc from CMU, which has also been used by MongoDB [16], modified its data generator per earlier discussions, and added a CH2++ driver to meet our new schema and mixed workload requirements.[2] Operational and analytical users are simulated by threads running on a client driver node; each constantly sends requests to the system. Up to

[2] All of the software artifacts associated with this paper's benchmark can be found at `https://github.com/couchbaselabs/ch2`.

```
CREATE ANALYTICS COLLECTION customer ON bench.ch2pp.customer AT RemoteLink;
CREATE ANALYTICS COLLECTION district ON bench.ch2pp.district AT RemoteLink;
... (etc.) ...
```

Data Definition 1.3. Capella Columnar Collection DDL

```
CREATE INDEX customer_c_balance ON customer(c_balance:DOUBLE);
CREATE INDEX orders_entry_d ON orders(o_entry_d:STRING);
CREATE INDEX orderline_i_id
 ON orders(UNNEST o_orderline SELECT ol_i_id:BIGINT) EXCLUDE UNKNOWN KEY;
CREATE INDEX orderline_delivery_d
 ON orders(UNNEST o_orderline SELECT ol_delivery_d:STRING) EXCLUDE UNKNOWN KEY
```

Data Definition 1.4. Capella Columnar Index DDL

```
ANALYZE COLLECTION customer WITH { "sample": "high" };
ANALYZE COLLECTION district WITH { "sample": "high" };
... (etc,) ...
```

Data Definition 1.5. Capella Columnar Sampling DDL

160 threads send TPC-C operations to Capella Operational, with 0 or 1 threads issuing analytical queries to Capella Columnar. These thread counts simulate a scenario involving many front-end users and a few data analysts (in this case one). In the future we will investigate higher numbers on both sides of CH2++'s operational/analytical workload wall.

5.2 Benchmark Configuration(s)

Our objective is to use CH2++ to explore the characteristics of HOAP-ful platforms for NoSQL, including their effectiveness at providing OLTP/OLAP performance isolation for mixed workloads and their scalability when faced with a need to support more operational users or to deliver faster analytics.

We ran the CH2++ benchmark on a pair of clusters in Couchbase Capella in the AWS cloud. The Capella Operational cluster consisted of 4–8 nodes, each with 8 vCPUs, 32 GB of memory, and 1000 GB of gp3 storage. The Capella Columnar cluster consisted of 2–8 nodes with 8 vCPUs and 32 GB of memory; each one included a 474GB NVMe local disk. We used an AWS c5.24xlarge instance with 96 vCPUs, 192 GB of memory, 100 GB gp3 storage and up to 25 Gbps of network bandwidth to run the client driver. The Capella Operational nodes were configured to have a Data+Index+Query Service combination.

Similarly to what we did once for CH2 [8], we sized the two clusters in the different configurations shown in Table 2. We abbreviate the Capella Operational nodes as Query (Q) nodes since transactions are directed to its Query service. We abbreviate the Capella Columnar nodes as Analytics (A) nodes since they process (in parallel) the analytical queries. In the first configuration, 4Q+4A, 4 Operational nodes are configured with the Query, Index, and Data Services, and 4 Columnar nodes process the analytical queries. Operational requests from the client driver go to a Capella Operational API endpoint, while analytical requests go to a Capella Columnar endpoint. In the second configuration, 8Q+4A, the

Table 2. Couchbase Capella Cluster Sizing

Configuration	Operational Cluster Size	Columnar Cluster Size
4Q+4A	4 nodes	4 nodes
8Q+4A	8 nodes	4 nodes
4Q+8A	4 nodes	8 nodes
8Q+8A	8 nodes	8 nodes
8Q+2A	8 nodes	2 nodes

Operational cluster size is doubled. Symmetrically, in configuration 4Q+8A, the Columnar cluster size is instead doubled relative to its initial size. In configuration 8Q+8A, both clusters are twice their initial size. We also tried one more configuration, 8Q+2A, to test an environment with a scaled-up operational cluster feeding a scaled-down analytical cluster. The Operational and Columnar services run on disjoint cloud hardware, which in principle should ensure performance isolation for the operational workload. On each side, data is hash-partitioned across each cluster's nodes for scalability. The experiments that follow were done using a 1,000 warehouse instance of CH2++; the cardinalities of its collections are consistent with those shown earlier in Table 1.

5.3 Example Benchmark Results

We now review the findings from the 1000-warehouse mixed workload runs of CH2++. The operational and analytical clients were run concurrently until the client running the analytical queries completed one full loop through all 22 queries; the benchmark then ended and assembled its performance results.

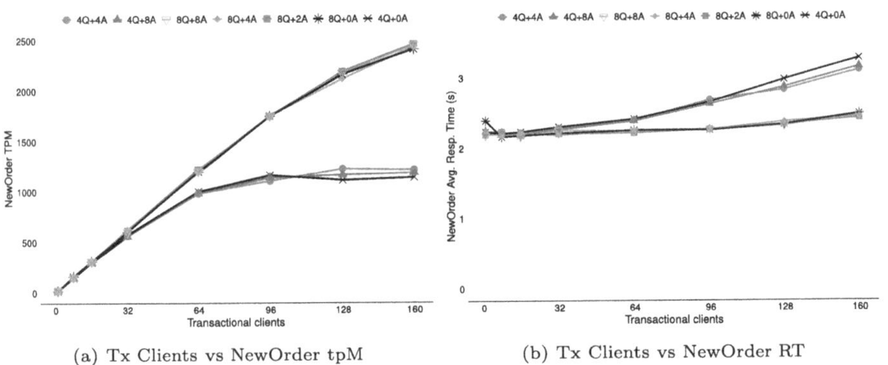

(a) Tx Clients vs NewOrder tpM

(b) Tx Clients vs NewOrder RT

Fig. 8. NewOrder tpM and NewOrder RT vs. Tx Clients.

Figure 8 shows the operational performance of CH2 ++ as a function of the number of operational client threads (4–160) for the different configurations of the cluster. In addition to the HOAPful configurations described earlier, results are shown for two configurations (8Q+0A and 4Q+0A) that have no Capella Columnar cluster (hence the 0A). Figure 8(a) shows the operational throughput in NewOrder transactions per minute. Figure 8(b) shows the corresponding average response times in seconds for the NewOrder transactions. We can make a number of important observations by examining their trends.

The first observation is that, for all configurations, Capella Operational delivers textbook performance in terms of the throughput expectations for a system with a closed workload: The throughput curves in Fig. 8(a) first increase linearly and then they plateau when the system's resources become saturated, so the Operational system is *well-behaved* and it exhibits no thrashing. The response time results in Fig. 8(b) reflect this as well: The average NewOrder response times are initially flat but then they gradually become linearly proportional to the number of client threads once the system becomes saturated.

The second observation is that, if we compare the throughput curves in Fig. 8(a) for a given Operational cluster size, we see *effective performance isolation.* The curves are essentially coincident despite the varying Columnar cluster sizes and presence or absence of an analytical workload. The response time results in Fig. 8(b) also reflect this: The average NewOrder response time curves for a given Operational cluster size are essentially pairwise identical.

The third observation is that, if we compare the NewOrder throughput results in Fig. 8(a) when the Operational cluster size is doubled (to 8Q from 4Q), the system can provide *linear transactional scaleup.* Thus, if you require twice the operational throughput, doubling your investment in "cloud hardware" can meet your requirement. In terms of the response times in Fig. 8(b), we see the average response time being constant as the number of clients increases – until the cluster resources become saturated. Beyond that, response times go up linearly, and, as one would hope, a larger Operational cluster is able to keep the average response time curve flat much longer since it saturates much later.

Let us now see what CH2++ can tell us about Couchbase Capella's analytical query performance. Figure 9 shows the geometric mean of the 22 queries' average response times (a.k.a. query power) for the different cluster configurations versus the number of operational client threads. Two key take-aways are evident. First, we see the analytical side of Couchbase Capella's successful delivery of performance isolation (HOAP) – the analytical workload's query performance is all but unaffected as the number of concurrent operational client threads increases. Queries are initially a little slower as the Operational cluster starts to generate updates to ingest, that is, as the number of clients first grows. This is because data ingestion uses some of the Columnar cluster's capacity, but query power is unaffected once the Operational cluster later becomes saturated. Second, we see the successful delivery of *linear query speedup* – when the number of nodes for the Columnar service is doubled, its (geometric) mean CH2++ query execution time is essentially cut in half. Thus, one can get one's analytical queries to run twice as fast by simply doubling the investment in the Capella Columnar cluster.

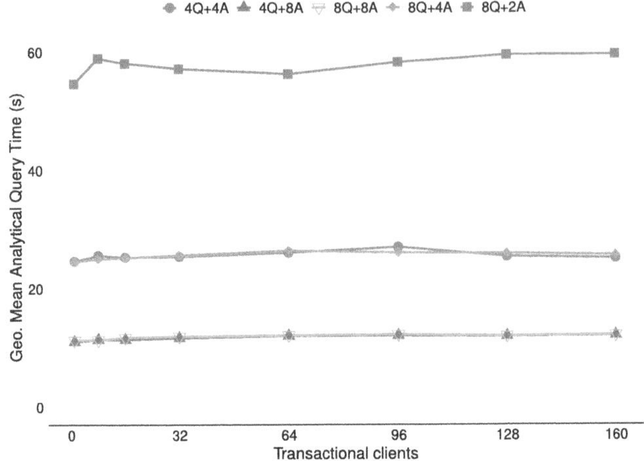

Fig. 9. Query Power (Geometric Mean of Analytical Query Times) vs. Tx Clients.

Space precludes the details, but we have also examined other analytical workload issues using CH2++. In one experiment, we doubled the size of the Columnar cluster from 4 to 8 nodes and simultaneously doubled the number of analytical query threads from 1 to 2. With 4 nodes and 1 analytical thread, the geometric mean query time was 26 s with a throughput of 107 queries/hour. With 8 nodes and 2 query threads, the geometric mean query time was 21.5 s with a throughput of 266 queries/hour. (The better than linear scaling is due to the additional aggregate memory provided by the additional nodes.) We also measured the time taken for operational (NewOrder) changes to propagate to the analytical side; we observed mean delays of under 400 milliseconds.

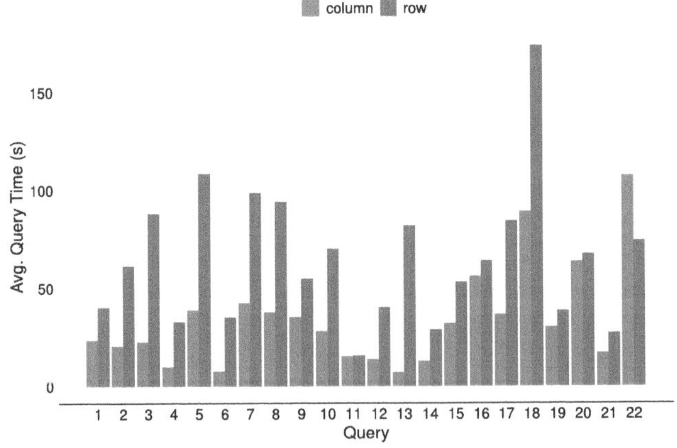

Fig. 10. Format Impact on Analytical Query Times (4Q+4A).

In addition to studying the hybrid workload handling capabilities of a NoSQL platform, CH2++ can also be more broadly useful. As one example, Capella Columnar is a descendent of Couchbase Analytics [2]. When our earlier CH2 benchmark was created, the underlying JSON storage format was a row-oriented, self-describing binary format. Fast forward to 2025, and Capella Columnar offers both a column-oriented binary JSON format [3] as well as the older row-oriented format. The newer column-oriented format is now the default format for Capella Columnar collections (hence the name). We can use CH2++ to explore the impact of storage formats on the performance of JSON analytical queries.

Figure 10 presents individual CH2++ query response times for both formats for the 4Q+4A configuration. We see significant format-related gains under the columnar format for most queries, with roughly equivalent performance in a few cases (e.g., Q11 and Q20) and a performance loss in just one case (Q22). Table 3 shows the overall 4Q+4A performance metrics for the two format options. (The ingestion rate measurement is based on the time required for Capella Columnar to ingest the initial set of 1000-warehouse-scale CH2++ collections from the corresponding Capella Operational collections.) We see that the data ingestion rate is slightly lower for the columnar format, as it has to tear apart and reformat the incoming objects as it persists them. However, we also see a factor of two improvement in overall query performance since the columnar format allows most queries to read less data (i.e., to avoid I/O for most unreferenced columns).

Table 3. Format Impact on Overall Columnar Performance (4Q+4A)

Storage Format	Avg. Data Ingestion Rate	Geo. Mean Query Time (Power)	Query Throughput
Column	200,633 items/sec	26.06 sec	106.85 queries/hr
Row	214,138 items/sec	55.81 sec	55.72 queries/hr

6 Conclusion

Systems that support hybrid workloads (HTAP or HOAP systems) first appeared in the relational world, often linked to technology trends like columnar storage and memory-rich, many-core, scale-up servers. In this paper, we introduced CH2++, a major revision of our earlier CH2 benchmark, which is well-suited to evaluate NoSQL systems that offer support for both JSON document management and JSON analytics. Like CH and CH2 before it, CH2++ borrows from and extends TPC-C and TPC-H. CH2++'s differences from CH2 include a much more document-oriented schema, the inclusion of additional fields to exercise analytical systems' column-oriented features, and a corresponding JSON "do over" of the CH2 queries. We have shared performance isolation and scaling results obtained by running a 1000-warehouse instance of CH2++ against the Capella Operational and Capella Columnar services, Couchbase's cloud service offerings. We also shared some results regarding Capella Columnar's row-vs. column-oriented JSON storage format choice. Our results have hopefully demonstrated the value of CH2++ for studying and evaluating the performance of JSON-oriented HOAP platforms. In the future, we would encourage others to try applying the CH2++ benchmark to other HOAP-ful NoSQL platforms.

References

1. 451 Research: Hybrid processing enables new use cases (business impact brief) (2018). https://www.intersystems.com/isc-resources/wp-content/uploads/sites/24/Hybrid_Processing_Enables_New_Use_Cases-451Research.pdf. Accessed 19 Oct 2020
2. Al Hubail, M., et al.: Couchbase analytics: NoETL for scalable NoSQL data analysis. PVLDB **12**(12) (2019)
3. Alkowaileet, W., Carey, M.: Columnar formats for schemaless LSM-based document stores. PVLDB **15**(10) (2022)
4. Borkar, D., et al.: Have your data and query it too: from key-value caching to big data management. In: Proceedings of the ACM SIGMOD Conference (2016)
5. Carey, M., Alkoalwaileet, W., DiGeronimo, N., Gupta, P., Smotra, S., Westmann, T.: Towards principled, practical document database design. PVLDB **18**(12) (2025)
6. Carey, M.: AsterixDB mid-flight: a case study in building systems in academia. In: 35th IEEE International Conference on Data Engineering, 8–11 April 2019 (2019)
7. Carey, M., et al.: SQL++: we can finally relax! In: 40th IEEE International Conference on Data Engineering, 13–16 May 2024 (2024)
8. Carey, M., Lychagin, D., Muralikrishna, M., Sarathy, V., Westmann, T.: CH2: a hybrid operational/analytical processing benchmark for NoSQL. In: Nambiar, R., Poess, M. (eds.) Performance Evaluation and Benchmarking. Springer, Cham (2022)
9. Carey, M., et al.: Cloudy with a chance of JSON. PVLDB **18**(12) (2025)
10. Chamberlin, D.: SQL++ for SQL Users: A Tutorial. Couchbase Inc. (2018)
11. Coelho, F., Paulo, J., Vilaca, R., Pereira, J., Oliveira, R.: HTAPBench: hybrid transactional and analytical processing benchmark. In: Proceedings of the 8th ACM/SPEC International Conference on Performance Engineering, ICPE 2017. ACM (2017)
12. Cole, R.L., et al.: The mixed workload CH-benCHmark. In: Proceedings of the Fourth International Workshop on Testing Database Systems, DBTest 2011, Athens, Greece, 13 June 2011. ACM (2011)
13. Cooper, B.F., et al.: Benchmarking cloud serving systems with YCSB. In: Proceedings of the 1st ACM Symposium on Cloud Computing (SoCC), 10–11 June 2010 (2010)
14. Couchbase Inc: Welcome to Couchbase Capella (2025). https://docs.couchbase.com/home/cloud.html. Accessed 07 June 2025
15. Gray, J. (ed.): The Benchmark Handbook for Database and Transaction Systems, 1st edn. Morgan Kaufmann (1991)
16. Kamsky, A.: Adapting TPC-C benchmark to measure performance of multi-document transactions in MongoDB. PVLDB **12**(12) (2019)
17. Kemper, A., Neumann, T.: Hyper: a hybrid OLTP&OLAP main memory database system based on virtual memory snapshots. In: 2011 IEEE 27th International Conference on Data Engineering, 11–16 April 2011 (2011)

18. Lahiri, T., et al.: Oracle database in-memory: a dual format in-memory database. In: 2015 IEEE 31st International Conference on Data Engineering, 13–17 April 2015 (2015)
19. Larson, P., et al.: Real-time analytical processing with SQL server. PVLDB **8**(12) (2015)
20. Li, G., Zhang, C.: HTAP databases: what is new and what is next. In: Proceedings of the ACM SIGMOD Conference. ACM (2022)
21. May, N., Böhm, A., Lehner, W.: SAP HANA - the evolution of an in-memory DBMS from pure OLAP processing towards mixed workloads. In: Proceedings of the BTW 2017, 17. Fachtagung des GI-Fachber. DBIS, März 2017, Stuttgart, Germany (2017)
22. Özsu, M.T., Valduriez, P.: Principles of Distributed Database Systems, 4th edn. Springer, Cham (2020)
23. Pirzadeh, P., Carey, M., Westmann, T.: BigFUN: a performance study of big data management system functionality. In: 2015 IEEE International Conference on Big Data (2015)
24. Pirzadeh, P., Carey, M., Westmann, T.: A performance study of big data analytics platforms. In: 2017 IEEE International Conference on Big Data (2017)
25. Pöss, M., Floyd, C.: New TPC benchmarks for decision support and web commerce. SIGMOD Rec. **29**(4) (2000)
26. Pöss, M., et al.: TPC-DS, taking decision support benchmarking to the next level. In: Proceedings of the ACM SIGMOD Conference (2002)
27. Raab, F.: TPC-C - the standard benchmark for online transaction processing (OLTP). In: Gray, J. (ed.) The Benchmark Handbook for Database and Transaction Systems, 2nd edn. Morgan Kaufmann (1993)
28. Raman, V., et al.: DB2 with BLU acceleration: so much more than just a column store. PVLDB **6**(11) (2013)
29. Raza, A., et al.: Adaptive HTAP through elastic resource scheduling. In: Proceedings of the ACM SIGMOD Conference (2020)
30. Sadalage, P.J., Fowler, M.: NoSQL Distilled: A Brief Guide to the Emerging World of Polyglot Persistence. Addison-Wesley, Upper Saddle River (2013)
31. Shasha, D.E.: Database Tuning - A Principled Approach. Prentice-Hall (1992)
32. Tian, Y., Carey, M., Maxon, I.: Benchmarking HOAP for scalable document data management: a first step. In: 2020 IEEE International Conference on Big Data (2020)
33. Wikipedia: Hybrid transactional/analytical processing. (2025). https://en.wikipedia.org/w/index.php?title=Hybrid_transactional/analytical_processing&oldid=981969658. Accessed 07 June 2025
34. Zhang, C., Li, G., Lv, T.: HyBench: a new benchmark for HTAP databases. PVLDB **17**(5) (2024)

ScaleBench_AI - Flexible LLM Inference Benchmarking Across Architectures and Environments

Karthik Krishna(✉), Sarthak Dwivedi, and Divya Singh

Infobell IT Solutions Pvt. Limited, 3rd Floor, The Cube-Karle Town Centre, 500ft, Nada Prabhu Kempe Gowda Main Rd, next to Nagavara, Bengaluru 560045, India
karthik@infobellit.com

Abstract. The demand for LLM inference is soaring, driven by widespread adoption of generative AI. Dr. Lisa Su recently projected the data center AI accelerator market to exceed $500B by 2028—with over 60% tied to LLM and AI inference workloads.

LLMs power a wide range of applications with their deep understanding and language generation capabilities. As their use grows, accurate benchmarking becomes essential for making infrastructure decisions and optimizing performance for throughput, latency, scalability, and cost.

MLPerf's LLM inference has become the industry benchmark for measuring LLM inference performance, especially among hardware vendors. While valuable for peak performance comparisons, this creates a gap for practitioners who need to evaluate diverse, real-world inference scenarios involving varying architectures, software stacks, and deployment models and different LLM models. What's needed is a flexible, open benchmark that can simulate realistic workloads and provide actionable insights for end users across a range of operational environments.

ScaleBench_AI addresses this gap with an open, extensible benchmarking framework built to address this need, enabling scenario-driven evaluation of LLM inference performance across architectures using real-world REST API loads.

Keywords: Large language models · LLM Inference · LLM Performance · AI Benchmarking

1 Introduction

Large Language Models (LLMs) have fundamentally reshaped how we approach language understanding and generation. As their integration into production environments becomes standard, the need to assess their real-time performance under varying workloads and infrastructure constraints is more pressing than ever.

While other benchmarking efforts often focused on specific models or were designed for rigid, predefined environments with limited extensibility, the landscape has evolved. Today, organizations are deploying a wide range of LLMs—from Meta's **Llama2**

R. Nambiar and M. Poess (Eds.): TPCTC 2025, LNCS 16261, pp. 58–68, 2026.
https://doi.org/10.1007/978-3-032-18070-4_4

and Llama3 series to newer contenders like **DeepSeek**—each with distinct architectural traits, parameter sizes, and quantization strategies (e.g., BF16, Int8, Int4). As the ecosystem grows more diverse, there is a clear need for a flexible, modular benchmarking framework that adapts to real-world deployment conditions across models and infrastructures.

To meet this challenge, we present **ScaleBench_AI**: a highly flexible and extensible benchmarking framework designed to test inference performance on any model running on any inference server and deployed on any system or scalable architecture. Building on the foundation of its predecessor, ScaleBench_AI is no longer limited to Llama-based models—it supports a growing ecosystem that includes DeepSeek, Mistral, Phi, and other state-of-the-art LLMs with varying inference servers Triton, vLLM, Text Generation Inference (TGI), SGLang or a custom backend. Models can also be deployed on a single instance or a system with CPU or GPU to multi-node architectures spanning many systems deployed with any software stack. ScaleBench_AI delivers a unified interface to evaluate latency, throughput, and time-to-first-token (TTFT) in real-time under realistic conditions. This benchmark is designed specifically for conversational AI inference workloads. While conversational systems are a critical and growing AI application, they represent only one of many possible domains, and results here should not be interpreted as representative of all AI tasks.

This publication introduces ScaleBench_AI and details how it empowers researchers and engineers to benchmark and optimize any LLM deployment on a scale.

2 ScaleBench_AI Overview

ScaleBench_AI addresses the limitations of MLPerf's LLM inference benchmarking test by offering an open, extensible framework built for AI developers, data center architects, and operations teams. It enables end-to-end benchmarking of LLM inference via REST APIs, tracking critical metrics like throughput (tokens/sec), token latency, and TTFT. These measurements align with community benchmarks of 200ms latency and 2000ms TTFT.

Unlike MLPerf's LLM Inference system-centric design, ScaleBench_AI [4] supports evaluation across diverse deployment scenarios—from single-node GPUs to distributed Kubernetes clusters, CPU-based systems, and cloud GPU instances and supports a variety of popular inference servers, including vLLM, Triton Inference Server, Text Generation Inference (TGI), SGLang, and others enabling users to evaluate LLM performance across diverse deployment environments. Its architecture-agnostic approach makes it ideal for real-world inference optimization beyond lab settings.

Building on the foundation of EchoSwift v1.0 [3], which introduced configuration discovery techniques and real-time telemetry, ScaleBench_AI [4] significantly expands capabilities. It introduces an intuitive CLI, broader inference server compatibility, and an enhanced dataset for realistic benchmarking. The framework captures per-token latency, TTFT, and throughput under customizable workloads, allowing for accurate simulation of production environments.

One major enhancement is the automated load threshold discovery mechanism, which identifies the maximum number of concurrent users that an inference server can support while maintaining TTFT below 2000ms and token latency under 200ms. Real-time progress indicators and detailed logs provide deep observability and facilitate troubleshooting.

3 Dataset

A conversational dataset is selected to stress-test low-latency, streaming generation, a scenario where user experience is highly sensitive to delay. This focus enables precise measurement of responsiveness, though alternative datasets can be considered based on the user requirements.

ScaleBench_AI introduces the Dataset-20k [5], an expansion from the earlier 8k set. This dataset comprises 20,000 queries curated for conversational benchmarking. This dataset is based on the ShareGPT [6], the dataset is refined for structure, prompt clarity, and real-world interaction patterns.

Inspired by MLPerf's LLM Inference use of the OpenOrca dataset [7], Dataset-20k incorporates structured prompts, realistic scenarios, and standardized formatting to ensure consistency and reproducibility in evaluation. The dataset is bucketed by token length to simulate varied workloads based on their input token size which are all below 1024 tokens:

- **Bucket-1 (10–63 tokens)**: 2,000 queries
- **Bucket-2 (65–128 tokens)**: 8,000 queries
- **Bucket-3 (129–256 tokens)**: 8,000 queries
- **Bucket-4 (257–1024 tokens)**: 2,000 queries

This structure aligns with MLPerf's LLM inference standards and supports benchmarking across diverse prompt lengths.

Figure 1 below shows the structured prompts used in **Dataset-20k**.

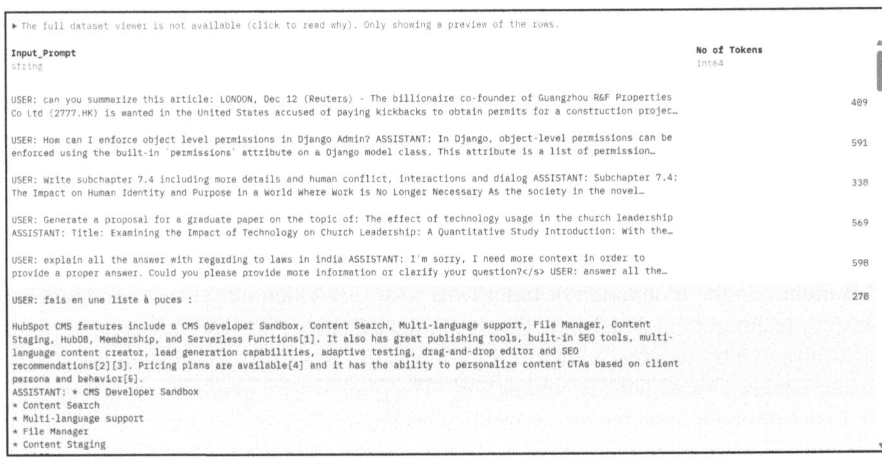

▸ The full dataset viewer is not available (click to read why). Only showing a preview of the rows.

Input_Prompt string	No of Tokens int64
USER: can you summarize this article: LONDON, Dec 12 (Reuters) - The billionaire co-founder of Guangzhou R&F Properties Co Ltd (2777.HK) is wanted in the United States accused of paying kickbacks to obtain permits for a construction projec…	409
USER: How can I enforce object level permissions in Django Admin? ASSISTANT: In Django, object-level permissions can be enforced using the built-in `permissions` attribute on a Django model class. This attribute is a list of permission…	591
USER: Write subchapter 7.4 including more details and human conflict, interactions and dialog ASSISTANT: Subchapter 7.4: The Impact on Human Identity and Purpose in a World Where Work is No Longer Necessary As the society in the novel…	338
USER: Generate a proposal for a graduate paper on the topic of: The effect of technology usage in the church leadership ASSISTANT: Title: Examining the Impact of Technology on Church Leadership: A Quantitative Study Introduction: With the…	569
USER: explain all the answer with regarding to laws in india ASSISTANT: I'm sorry, I need more context in order to provide a proper answer. Could you please provide more information or clarify your question?</s> USER: answer all the…	598
USER: fais en une liste à puces : HubSpot CMS features include a CMS Developer Sandbox, Content Search, Multi-language support, File Manager, Content Staging, HubDB, Membership, and Serverless Functions[1]. It also has great publishing tools, built-in SEO tools, multi-language content creator, lead generation capabilities, adaptive testing, drag-and-drop editor and SEO recommendations[2][3]. Pricing plans are available[4] and it has the ability to personalize content CTAs based on client persona and behavior[5]. ASSISTANT: * CMS Developer Sandbox * Content Search * Multi-language support * File Manager * Content Staging	278

Fig. 1. Dataset-20k

4 Traffic Pattern

Dataset-20k employs a structured traffic pattern designed to emulate real-world usage. It utilizes token-based bucketing to introduce controlled variability in prompt lengths, closely aligning with MLPerf's LLM inference traffic distribution methodology. This ensures that model evaluations remain standardized, realistic, and comparable across systems.

Each time a prompt is issued to the LLM, it is randomly selected from the Dataset-20k. Due to the uniform distribution of the random selection function, approximately 80% of the input prompts fall within Bucket-2 and Bucket-3—i.e., 16,000 out of the 20,000 prompts. This results in the input token distribution shown below.

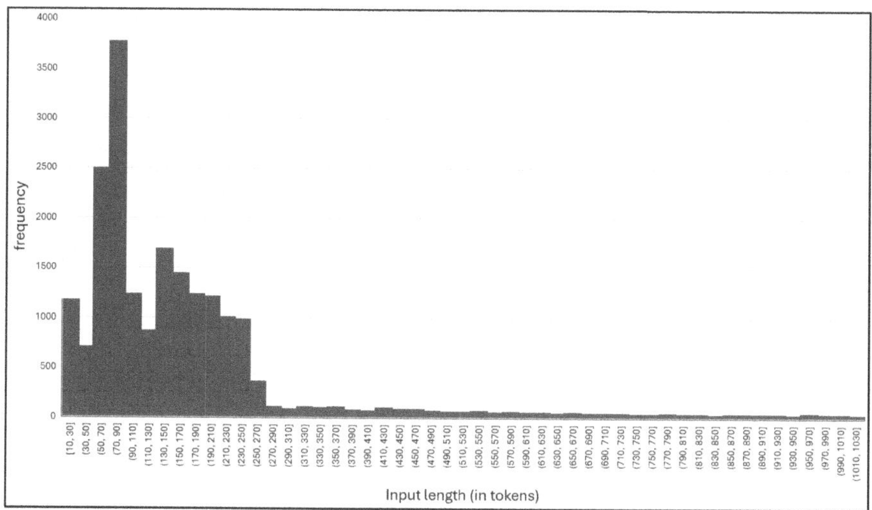

Fig. 2. Input Tokens Distribution of Prompts

Figure 2 illustrates the prompt length distribution, aligning the dataset with standardized evaluation practices while preserving EchoSwift's unique benchmarking goals.

This bucketing strategy reflects the methodology used in MLPerf's LLM inference benchmark, which evaluates prompts ranging from 3 to 1024 tokens. ScaleBench_AI adopts a similar distribution approach. The Datset-20k dataset enables robust benchmarking by maintaining realistic, industry-aligned input variability.

The length of output tokens for the response is kept at less than 1024 tokens.

5 Throughput Measurement (Tokens Per Second)

In **ScaleBench_AI**, the throughput calculation logic has been enhanced by including validation criteria for **Time to First Token (TTFT)** and **token latency**. This improvement allows the tool to identify the **maximum number of concurrent users** (also known as parallel requests) a large language model (LLM) can reliably serve while maintaining compliance with defined performance thresholds.

Throughput in ScaleBench_AI is defined as the total number of output tokens generated per second across all users (which is number of parallel requests), post warm-up phase.

This throughput calculates the average tokens/second per each parallel request and multiplies that with the total number of parallel requests.

Warm-up phase is where number of parallel requests starts from a low number increasing gradually to reach the maximum number of parallel requests which can server at a strict validation criteria:

- **TTFT < 2000 ms**
  Ensures the first output token is produced within 2000 ms (2 s) of request submission, maintaining conversational responsiveness. Delays beyond 2 s noticeably disrupt the user experience in interactive applications.
- **Token latency < 200 ms**
  Ensures each subsequent token is generated in < 200 ms, equivalent to a streaming rate of at least 5 tokens per second, preserving the perception of continuous output.

That is, the validation criteria are **TTFT** must be below **2000 ms** and **Latency per token** must be below **200 ms.** These thresholds prevent inflated throughput measurements from configurations that prioritize bulk processing over interactivity, ensuring reported results reflect real-time, user-facing performance.

Throughput(tokens/second)=Average throughput per Request * Total Number of Parallel Requests

Throughput per request (or per parallel request) is computed excluding the TTFT

Throughput per request=(Total tokens generated - 1)/(Total time - TTFT)

where:

- **Total tokens generated** is the sum of all output tokens from successful inference responses across all users.
- **Total time** is the complete duration between the first token request sent and the completion of the last response, excluding any setup or initialization latency.
- **TTFT** is the time to generate the first token.

These thresholds are continuously evaluated during the benchmarking process to ensure system responsiveness and scalability under load.

Optimal User Discovery Steps:

1. **Initial Load Generation:**
   The benchmarking process in **ScaleBench_AI** begins by generating concurrent requests based on an initial user count and input token mode (random or fixed) both of which are configurable parameters. The *random_prompt* flag (True for random, False for fixed) and *user_count* are defined in the configuration to control the input pattern and concurrency level for the load generation phase. Valid benchmark sets *random_prompt* to true as the test must exercise across prompts with random input tokens as discussed in traffic pattern.

2. **Metric Evaluation:**

   During each iteration, average performance metrics such as **throughput (tokens/second)**, **latency per token**, and **TTFT** are measured. If all observed performance metrics remain within the threshold, the user count will increase by a fixed step size (as specified in the configuration), and the process continues.

   Throughput here is calculated as the formula mentioned above by finding the average throughput or token/second of all the individual parallel request and then multiplied with total number of parallel requests.
3. **Threshold Violation Detection:**

   The incremental load-testing loop continues until one or more validation thresholds are breached—specifically, if **TTFT** exceeds 2000 ms or **token latency** surpasses 200 ms—indicating the system has reached or exceeded its sustainable capacity.
4. **Binary Search Backtracking:**

   When a threshold violation is detected, ScaleBench_AI initiates a binary search to efficiently identify the optimal user count the maximum number of concurrent users for which all performance criteria remain satisfied.

   The search begins by selecting the midpoint between the last valid user count (which met all thresholds) and the first failing user count (which breached a threshold). The benchmark is re-run at each midpoint, progressively narrowing the range until it pinpoints the highest concurrency level that still adheres to the validation criteria.

   After getting the optimal user count the benchmark repeats the parallel requests three times by incrementing the user count by 1. The validation criteria must be exceeded in all three iterations to conclusively determine that the threshold has been crossed.
5. **Stability Validation:**

   Once the optimal user count is identified, the benchmark establishes validity of the number by executing 10 additional test runs to establish statistical reliability.
6. **Result Qualification:**

   If at least 90% of these test runs confirm to the specified validation thresholds, the throughput corresponding to the average of the throughput of the test runs which satisfies the validation criteria is accepted as the throughput supported by the System under test under given model and system configurations.

The iterative load testing, combined with binary search optimization and multi-run validation, ensures that the identified user capacity is both performant and reliable. This enables developers and platform engineers to confidently deploy LLM-based models with predictable latency and throughput characteristics under production ready conditions.

ScaleBench_AI provides both **Total throughput** (across all users) and **per-user throughput**, allowing granular performance analysis. Additionally, throughput measurements are recorded for test runs that meet the TTFT and token latency thresholds, ensuring that reported values reflect production-viable performance levels.

6 Experimentation

We benchmarked the DeepSeek-R1-Distill-Qwen-32B model using the SGLang inference server with 8 Docker containers attached to GPUs and enabling *random_prompt* set to true. When the model is deployed using SGLang, this provides a RESTApi endpoint which ScaleBench_AI hits with load.

ScaleBench_AI identified the optimal user count through incremental testing and binary search, with the final result converging at 1293 concurrent users.

- Figure 3: User Discovery Results
- Figure 4: Throughput of Inference as measured by ScaleBench_AI
- Figure 5: TTFT Distribution of Inference as measured by ScaleBench_AI
- Figure 6: Token Latency of Inference as measured by ScaleBench_AI

Figure 3 shows the results for the tests. The Benchmark test initially starts with 100 users, and the step size (increment number of parallel requests if thresholds met) of 100 is defined. The test continues for the users until the validation criteria fail at 1300 users and ScaleBench_AI starts the binary search and gets the optimal user as 1293 after the Result Qualification.

As one can see with the number of parallel requests proceeding, line item 14 is the binary search enabled identifying the number of parallel requests.

At Line item 17 is where the threshold was met last at 1294 parallel requests and at line 20–22 were three iterations confirming that at 1294 parallel requests exceed the threshold. Once 1293 is established to be the maximum number of parallel requests, 10 iterations of requests are made at parallel requests (or concurrent requests) of 1293. Average of total throughput of all iterations which satisfy the criteria is taken as the final total throughput provided more than 90% of the 10 requests satisfy the threshold criteria.

Deepseek_32B_SGLang (Docker-compose 8 containers)							
Requests	concurrent_user	throughput(tokens/second)	latency(ms)	TTFT(ms)	latency_per_token(ms/token)	Total Throughput	
1	100	42.066	5868.424	659.560	24.198	4206.627	Initial load generation
2	200	41.310	5743.596	625.781	24.357	8261.962	
3	300	37.130	6822.325	776.259	29.605	11138.963	
4	400	34.289	7183.214	876.100	29.729	13715.506	
5	500	31.359	7861.827	999.216	32.591	15679.305	
6	600	28.801	8782.613	1205.310	35.512	17280.523	
7	700	27.402	9056.989	1318.507	37.629	19181.468	
8	800	25.463	9956.312	1475.403	40.244	20370.431	
9	900	24.069	10494.305	1545.906	42.606	21662.259	
10	1000	22.968	10796.696	1599.493	44.989	22967.817	
11	1100	21.007	11899.369	1810.233	50.702	23107.953	
12	1200	19.695	12510.165	1811.253	52.303	23634.246	
13	1300	18.247	13372.480	2035.591	56.923	23720.791	
14	1250	19.241	12702.487	1863.548	54.954	24051.582	Binary search backtracking and got 1293 as an optimal user count
15	1275	18.653	13034.126	1926.155	55.625	23783.140	
16	1288	18.431	13284.060	1882.976	56.803	23739.041	
17	1294	18.393	13361.975	2003.620	56.434	23800.998	
18	1291	18.637	13088.050	1975.516	55.831	24060.916	
19	1293	18.705	13232.194	1908.645	56.561	24106.940	
20	1294	18.265	13321.272	2001.876	56.750	23634.637	
21	1294	18.275	13758.713	2123.758	56.721	23647.292	
22	1294	18.226	13398.584	2012.569	56.868	23584.036	
23	1293	18.658	13235.271	1922.490	56.943	24124.748	Stability validation
24	1293	18.795	13251.785	1911.533	56.364	24301.387	
25	1293	18.746	13305.872	1948.872	56.345	24238.444	
26	1293	18.546	13311.249	1956.518	56.920	23979.844	
27	1293	18.569	13304.712	1951.479	56.853	24009.684	
28	1293	18.355	13481.515	2014.852	56.481	23732.877	
29	1293	18.778	13205.479	1945.255	56.252	24280.594	
30	1293	18.589	13321.255	1993.488	56.795	24035.892	
31	1293	18.785	13214.242	1985.478	56.235	24288.659	
32	1293	18.801	13253.274	1992.479	56.189	24309.996	

Fig. 3. Parallel Requests (users) Discovery Results

Figure 4 shows the Total Throughput for the different requests sent.

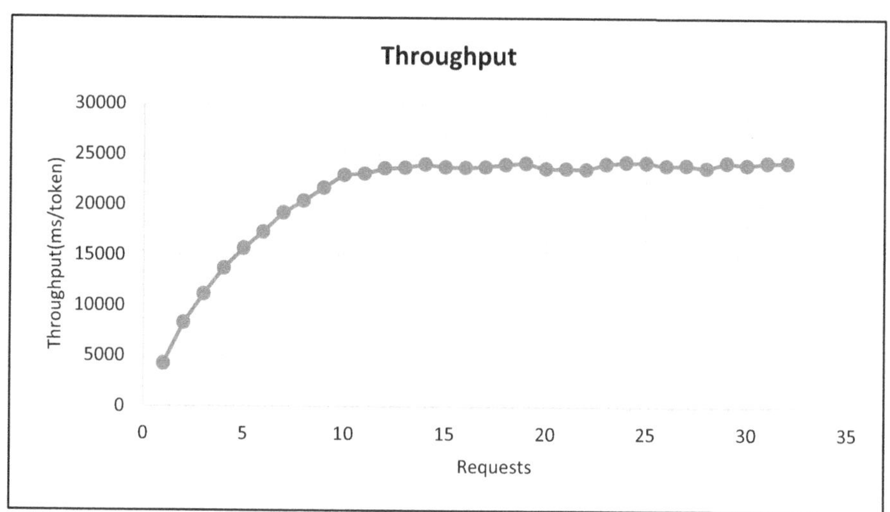

Fig. 4. Throughput of Inference as measured by ScaleBench_AI

Figure 5 shows TTFT for the different requests sent.

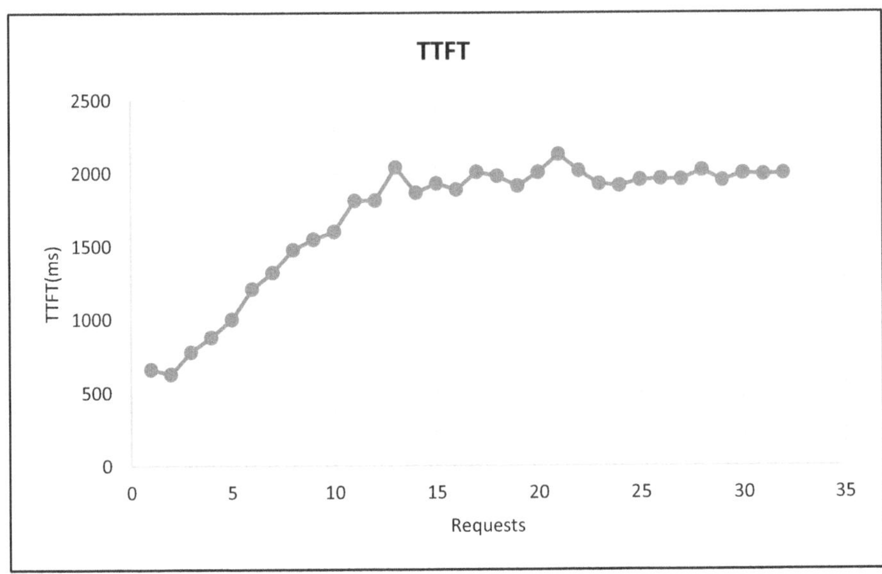

Fig. 5. TTFT Distribution of Inference as measured by ScaleBench_AI

Figure 6 shows Latency per token for the different requests sent.

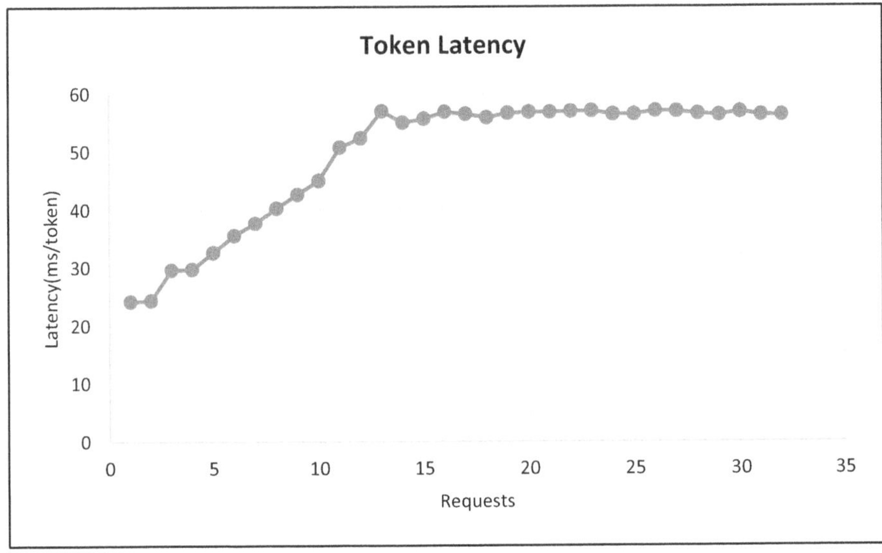

Fig. 6. Token Latency of Inference as measured by

7 Capacity Planning and Sizing with ScaleBench_AI

This methodology of measuring throughput—defined as tokens per second across parallel requests—provides actionable insights for sizing LLM inference deployments.

By simulating concurrent user load and dynamically adjusting the number of parallel requests, ScaleBench_AI helps determine the maximum sustainable throughput a system can achieve without violating critical latency thresholds (e.g., TTFT < 2000 ms, token latency < 200 ms).

This approach mirrors real-world usage where multiple users or applications access an inference endpoint concurrently. Unlike isolated single-thread benchmarks, ScaleBench_AI accounts for contention, queuing delays, and infrastructure saturation—capturing how inference systems behave under realistic, scaled conditions.

For end users, this enables precise **capacity planning**. For example:

- A model deployed on a given hardware stack (e.g., 1x A100 or 8x L4s) might sustain 1200 concurrent users while delivering acceptable latency and throughput.
- If each user generates an average of 10 tokens per second, the deployment supports a total of 12,000 tokens/sec throughput.
- Based on this, users can estimate how many API requests per minute their system can handle, or whether they need to scale out horizontally (add more containers) or vertically (upgrade hardware) to meet service-level objectives.

Furthermore, by capturing throughput only when validation thresholds are met, ScaleBench_AI ensures that the reported capacity reflects production-viable performance—not theoretical peak throughput under ideal conditions. This makes it a **trustworthy tool for deployment sizing**, especially in environments requiring deterministic latency behaviour (e.g., chatbots, copilots, or real-time assistants).

Overall, ScaleBench_AI bridges the gap between benchmark metrics and operational readiness, enabling developers, architects, and DevOps teams to make informed decisions about scaling strategies, autoscaling thresholds, cost-performance trade-offs, and provisioning for peak workloads.

8 Conclusion

ScaleBench_AI significantly advances the LLM inference benchmarking landscape by introducing a self-optimizing, dynamic, and production-ready benchmarking tool, purpose-built to evaluate the scalability and performance of large language models under real-world constraints. Building on the foundation of EchoSwift version 1 [3], ScaleBench_AI integrates larger dataset, dynamic traffic pattern generation, threshold-driven validation, and binary search-based backtracking to automatically determine the optimal number of concurrent users a system can support without exceeding the validation criteria for performance metrics such as **Time to First Token (TTFT) and token latency.**

ScaleBench_AI introduces a **multi-phase benchmarking workflow** that begins with progressive load testing, automatically adjusting concurrency levels based on validation criteria. The tool remains model-agnostic and compatible across LLM types, including quantized models (INT4, INT8 etc.), fine-tuned variants, and full-scale pretrained models deployed across CPUs, GPUs, and dedicated accelerators. Designed with a focus on **production realism, repeatability, and extensibility**, ScaleBench_AI enables organizations to evaluate LLM serving infrastructure not just for peak performance, but also for threshold-based load validation, cost-efficiency, and resilience at scale, sizing and capacity planning.

Acknowledgments. Authors would like to thank Sushanth Gowda, Kammara Prasad Achari who are AI engineers from InfobellIT who helped test and develop this benchmark.

Disclosure of Interests. It is now necessary to declare any competing interests or to specifically state that the authors have no competing interests. Please place the statement with a third level heading in 9-point font size beneath the (optional) acknowledgments, for example: The authors have no competing interests to declare that are relevant to the content of this article. Or: Author A has received research grants from Company W. Author B has received a speaker honorarium from Company X and owns stock in Company Y. Author C is a member of committee Z.

References

1. https://seekingalpha.com/article/4746448-amd-stock-accelerates-product-development-to-close-competitive-gap
2. https://mlcommons.org/working-groups/benchmarks/inference/
3. Krishna, K., Bandili, R.: EchoSwift: an inference benchmarking and configuration discovery tool for large language models (LLMs). In: Proceedings of the 15th ACM/SPEC International Conference on Performance Engineering (ICPE 2024), South Kensington, London, UK, 7–11 May 2024. ACM, New York (2024).https://doi.org/10.1145/3629527.3652273
4. ScaleBench_AI. https://github.com/Infobellit-Solutions-Pvt-Ltd/ScaleBench_AI
5. Dataset-20k. https://huggingface.co/datasets/epsilondelta1982/Dataset-20k
6. ShareGPT.https://huggingface.co/datasets/pvduy/sharegpt_alpaca_oa_vicuna_format/tree/main
7. Open Orca https. https://huggingface.co/datasets/Open-Orca/OpenOrca

Tectonic: Bridging Synthetic and Real-World Workloads for Key-Value Benchmarking

Alexander H. Ott(✉), Shubham Kaushik(✉), Boao Chen, and Subhadeep Sarkar

Brandeis University, Waltham, MA, USA
{alexanderott,kaushiks,boaochen,subhadeep}@brandeis.edu

Abstract. Key-value stores are the backbone of many modern SQL- and NoSQL-based data systems, serving a variety of real-world applications. Despite their widespread adoption, existing key-value benchmarks fall short across multiple dimensions when accurately replicating complex and dynamic real-world workloads. For instance, state-of-the-art key-value benchmarks, such as YCSB, KVBench, and db_bench, are unable to (i) emulate dynamic workloads where the workload composition and distribution changes arbitrarily over time; (ii) generate composite keys with different prefix distributions; and (iii) generate workloads with varied degrees of data sortedness. These limitations result in inaccurate performance evaluations and limit the ability to understand how a commercial key-value store performs under dynamically shifting workloads.

In this paper, we introduce Tectonic, a highly configurable and resource-efficient Rust-based key-value workload generator designed to model the temporal, structural, and dynamic properties of real-world workloads. Tectonic offers (i) fine-grained control over data access patterns for inserts, updates, merges, point and range queries, and point and range deletes; (ii) configurable composite key generation/selection strategies; (iii) dynamic workload generation where the workload properties change over time; and (iv) generation of workloads with user-specified data sortedness. Tectonic does so (v) at a 2× higher throughput than the state-of-the-art, (vi) while recording up to 84% lower main memory footprint. By bridging the gap between synthetic and production workloads, Tectonic enables in-depth analysis of key-value data systems under conditions that better reflect the demands of real-world applications. We benchmark Tectonic's performance against YCSB and KVBench in terms of latency, resource utilization, and ability to emulate production workloads. The code for Tectonic is available at: https://github.com/SSD-Brandeis/tectonic.

Keywords: Key-value benchmark · Dynamic workload · Scalability

A. H. Ott and S. Kaushik—Both authors contributed equally and are corresponding authors for this work.

R. Nambiar and M. Poess (Eds.): TPCTC 2025, LNCS 16261, pp. 69–88, 2026.
https://doi.org/10.1007/978-3-032-18070-4_5

1 Introduction

Key-value stores are widely used as the storage engine of a wide number of NoSQL data stores, including RocksDB [16] at Meta, Bigtable [8] and LevelDB [20] at Google, FoundationDB [4] at Apple, Cassandra [2] and HBase [3] at Apache, Azure CosmosDB [30] and FASTER [7] at Microsoft, and DynamoDB [13] at Amazon. Many relational databases also employ key-value stores underneath in the storage layer. For example, CockroachDB [11] uses Pebble as the storage engine, and TiDB [21] and MyRocks [14] both use RocksDB as the underlying storage. While the key-value paradigm allows for low-latency writes and high operational throughput in general, the performance of a key-value store can vary significantly based on the workload characteristics, such as the proportion of different operations, the distribution of keys, and the data access patterns, as well as the variability of the workload over time [6,9,24,28,41]. Thus, there is a strong need for effective benchmarking tools that can (i) generate workloads that closely resemble production workloads and (ii) evaluate the performance of key-value stores under diverse and dynamic workloads.

Limitations of the State of the Art. State-of-the-art key-value benchmarks, such as YCSB [12], KVBench [47], and db_bench [15], are widely used to evaluate the performance of key-value stores. However, these workload generators are **unable to capture the complexity of real-world workloads across multiple dimensions**, as shown in Table 1.

(1) Inability to Generate Dynamic Workloads: In practice, production workloads often exhibit temporal variations, such as diurnal shifts, seasonal trends, and gradual transitions in access patterns [6,23,47]. For instance, over a 7-day window production workloads at Meta, such as UDB, ZippyDB, and UP2X, vary across multiple dimensions, including (i) the composition of the workload, (ii) the distribution of the operations, (iii) access patterns of queries, as well as (iv) the sizes of key-value pairs [6]. UDB shows a diurnal pattern for writes to the database, which peaks each day at 17:00 PST, and then quickly reaches its nadir at 23:00 PST. Moreover, during the weekends, some column families experience a significant (by up to 10×) jump in the query frequency. One of the biggest limitations of state-of-the-art key-value benchmarks is their **inability to capture dynamic variations in the workload altogether and model shifting workloads**. In fact, the only way to emulate temporal variation in workloads is by generating segments of the dynamic workload separately and then stitching them together manually. This is a very crude emulation of dynamic workloads, as each phase operates on a disjoint keyspace, thus failing to preserve key-sharing across phases. As a result, the workloads generated lack coherence, which in turn, undermines the accuracy of performance evaluation.

(2) No Support for Composite Keys and Prefix-based Access Patterns: In production workloads, often the database name, the relation/column family name, as well as the user ID are added as a prefix to the *actual* application-generated key to constitute a **synthetic composite key**. Prefixes

Table 1. Tectonic supports a wide range of operations, distributions, and structural controls, enabling accurate modeling of real-life workloads.

		YCSB	KVBench	db_bench	Tectonic
operations	insert	✓	✓	✓	✓
	update	✓	✓	✓	✓
	read-modify-write	✓		✓	✓
	point query	✓	✓	✓	✓
	empty point query		✓	✓	✓
	range query	✓	✓	✓	✓
	point delete		✓	✓	✓
	empty point delete		✓		✓
	range delete		✓	✓	✓
distributions	uniform	✓	✓	✓	✓
	normal		✓	✓	✓
	beta		✓		✓
	zipfian	✓	✓		✓
	exponential			✓	✓
	log normal				✓
	poisson				✓
	weibull				✓
	pareto			✓	✓
properties	dynamic workload shifts		*	*	✓
	context-aware shifting				✓
	data sortedness				✓
	variable query selectivity	✓		✓	✓
	variable key-value length				✓
	temporality-based access			✓	✓
	customizable key prefix			*	✓
	composite keys				✓

* requires significant manual intervention

to this composite key are used as identifiers for a key-value pair's origin and domain, enabling efficient filtering and grouping. For instance, a composite key `cf-EMP:edge:alex` indicates the key `alex` was generated by an application `edge` and is stored in the column family `EMP` [37]. Existing key-value benchmarks are unable to model prefix-based key layouts altogether. Generating composite key in YCSB, db_bench, or KVBench would entail significant manual development, which is both complex and time-consuming. This makes it very hard to evaluate the performance of key-value stores that use prefix-based operations, such as indexing [19], membership checks [38], and data layout reorganization [26].

(3) Lack of Sortedness Benchmarks: Production workloads often exhibit a *correlation between attributes*, such that when the entries are sorted on one attribute, they are also *nearly sorted* on another [35,36]. For instance, in TPC-H [45], the `lineitem` table has three date columns, namely, `shipdate`, `commitdate`, and `receiptdate`, and sorting the data on `shipdate` would cause the data to be very close to being sorted on `commitdate` and `receiptdate` as well (but not fully-sorted) [5]. Sortedness of data affects the ingestion, indexing, and query cost significantly; thus, benchmarking the performance of a storage engine under varied data sortedness is crucial in practice. While existing key-value benchmarks can generate data following a number of key distributions [15,47], they are **unable to generate data with variable sortedness**. The only available sortedness benchmark, Benchmark on Data Sortedness (BoDS) [34], has two major limitations. First, it is not designed as a general-purpose key-value workload generator, as it does not support basic operations, such as deletes and updates, cannot generate interleaved operations, and does not support different key distributions beyond sortedness. Second, BoDS supports only numeric key generation, and the keys are always generated serially (and not randomly).

(4) Lack of a Unified Benchmarking Framework: Modern application requirements are heterogeneous, exhibiting diverse and dynamic data access patterns [6,29,33]. It is critical for a database practitioner to benchmark the performance of different key-value stores under diverse and shifting workloads to ascertain the suitability of a database for a given workload and performance target. Existing key-value benchmarks, however, **fall short in emulating the rich space of key-value workloads** along one or more dimensions. For instance, YCSB only supports a small set of distributions (i.e., uniform and Zipfian) and can not generate workloads with point or range deletes [12,47]. db_bench is tightly coupled with RocksDB and LevelDB only and, hence, has a limited applicability [15]. KVBench does not support read-modify-write operations and has a remarkably high memory footprint (we discuss this in Sect. 3).
Due to these limitations, state-of-the-art key-value benchmarks are **unable to accurately replicate real-world workloads, leading to poor benchmarking and suboptimal data system optimizations**.

Contributions. In this paper, we present Tectonic, a Rust-based, scalable, and highly configurable key-value benchmarking suite that can generate a diverse array of dynamic workloads while being faster and more resource-efficient than the state of the art. The contributions of Tectonic are as follows.

1. *Dynamic and Evolving Workloads*: Tectonic exposes a rich set of tunable knobs, providing the users fine-grained control over the workload generation process. Tectonic allows the user to model dynamically shifting workloads by specifying the workload characteristics for each phase. Each phase is independently configurable, allowing the keyspace to be either disjoint or shared according to the application requirements.
2. *Structured Key Generation*: Tectonic allows configurable composite key generation, allowing the users to have control over the size and domain of each

key segment. Each key segment may have distinct distributions, which allows modeling the "hotness" of key range, as observed in production workloads.
3. *Sortedness-Aware Ingestion*: Tectonic supports generating entries with varied degrees of sortedness. Unlike the state of the art [34], entries in Tectonic can be generated as interleaved with other database operations and following any key distribution, while following a user-specified sortedness.
4. *Fast and Resource Efficient*: We show through experiments that the Rust-based implementation of Tectonic makes it significantly faster than state-of-the-art workload generators, such as YCSB and KVBench, while recording an, on average, 7.5× lower memory footprint.

2 The Tectonic Benchmark Suite

Tectonic is a highly configurable and resource-aware key-value benchmark that supports a diverse set of operations, distributions, and properties (see Table 1) to ensure accurate emulation of real-world workloads. Tectonic's Rust-based codebase allows for orders of magnitude faster workload generation (by up to 12×) with a significantly smaller main memory footprint (by up to 84%) and comparable CPU utilization. To the best of our knowledge, **Tectonic is the first key-value benchmark that supports benchmarking storage engines under dynamically shifting workloads**.

2.1 Architecture and Overview of Tectonic

Execution Pipeline. Benchmarking in Tectonic happens over a five-step process as shown in Fig. 1.

Step ①: Tectonic takes as input a JSON file, which contains the specification of the benchmarking workload. At the top level of the specification, we have a list of one or more *Sections*. A *Section* is defined as an ensemble of *Groups* of operations. Each *Group*, in turn, is a collection of an arbitrary number of insert, update, empty and non-empty point query, range query, read-modify-write, and point and range delete operations. In the resulting workload, the operations in different *Sections* and *Groups* within a *Section* are executed serially. Operations within the same *Group* are interleaved.

Step ②: Tectonic parses the JSON input and converts it to a structure holding *Sections*, the containing *Groups*, and the distribution details necessary to generate the workload. At this stage, Tectonic identifies the different phases in the benchmarking setup by analyzing the *Sections* and *Groups*. Operations in the same *Group* are (i) to be executed as interleaved, (ii) share the same keyspace, and (iii) are affected by preceding operations within the same group. For every *Section* in the workload, the generator in Tectonic performs the following steps.

Step ③: The generator chooses the appropriate data structure to create an *ActiveKeySet* that stores the **set of "live" keys** at any point during workload generation. The *ActiveKeySet* is a critical component of the generator as it allows for (i) differentiating between unique inserts and updates, (ii) differentiating

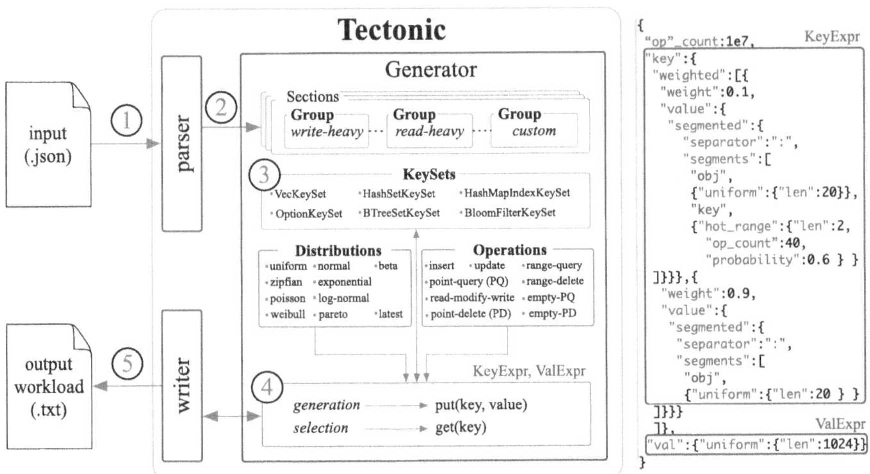

Fig. 1. The components of Tectonic and a flow for generating workloads.

between empty and non-empty operations (such as point queries and deletes), (iii) supporting a large number of access distributions, and (iv) generating data with varied degrees of sortedness. Based on the specification of the operations in a *Section*, Tectonic chooses the appropriate data structure (vector, hash set, hash-map, B$^+$-tree, etc.) to implement the *ActiveKeySet*. Each *Section* operates on an independent *ActiveKeySet*, allowing for *Sections* to be generated in parallel.

Steps ④ & ⑤: Next, Tectonic performs the generation (from unique inserts) and selection (which key to query) phases and passes the output to the writer for execution (or persistent storage). For inserts, updates, and read-modify-writes, the values associated with the keys are generated on the fly.

Key Construction. Tectonic constructs keys based on the specification in the input file. A `NumberExpr` (`NumExp`) defines a numeric expression that evaluates to a numeric key. A `StringExp` (`StrExp`), similar to `NumExp`, is an expression that evaluates to the desired string key. `StrExp` has five variants: (i) `constant`, evaluates to a constant string, (ii) `uniform`, produces a string of a specific length composed of uniform characters (defaulting to alphanumeric), (iii) `weighted`, randomly selects from an array of `StrExp` according to configured probability weights, (iv) `segmented`, evaluates different segments independently based on a configured distribution and joins them together using a delimiter to form a complete key, and (v) `hot-range`, generates certain prefixes more frequently.

The `NumExp` is used by both key generation and key selection. During key generation, it controls the parameters such as the lengths of the keys and values, as well as the selection of hot key ranges. The selection process selects keys from the existing *ActiveKeySet* for operations such as updates, read-modify-write, point queries, range queries, point deletes, and range deletes. Keys are selected by sampling by a specified distribution (defaults to uniform $[0.0, 1.0)$), clamping the value to $[0.0, 1.0)$, and multiplying the total count of keys to calculate the index, which is used to retrieve the key from the *ActiveKeySet*.

2.2 Basic Key-Value Operations

We now describe the implementation of core key-value operations in Tectonic.

Insert in Tectonic adds a key-value pair with a **unique key** to the database. Tectonic maintains the *ActiveKeySet* (KS) to store and track all "live" or active keys of a workload at any point in time. The *value* for a key is generated on the fly by the writer when a record is written to the output file. Users can configure the insert workload by defining a `"inserts"` block with `StrExp` for `"key"` and `"val"` within `"groups"` as: `{"groups":[{"inserts":{"op_count":NumExp, "key":StrExp, "val":StrExp}}]}`.

Updates and Read-Modify-Writes. Updates overwrite the value of an existing key-value pair in the database, while read-modify-writes (also known as *merge*) append a new value to the existing one or run a user-defined function to merge the values [12,16]. In both cases, the key must already exist in the database and not be logically invalidated. When generating an update or a read-modify-write, Tectonic selects a key from the *ActiveKeySet*, KS, after sampling based on the user-specified distribution (`Dist`) in `"selection"`. The default distribution is: `Uniform(0, 1)`. It then generates a value to be updated or merged while writing keys to the workload file, similarly to inserts. Users must pass an `"updates"` and `"merges"` key to generate update and merge operations, respectively, as: `{"groups":[{"updates":{"op_count":NumExp,"val":StrExp, "selection":Dist}}]}`.

Point Query. Tectonic can generate point queries (PQs) that are (i) *empty*, i.e., when the target key does not exist in the database or has been logically invalidated, or (ii) *non-empty*, i.e., when the target key is live. To differentiate between empty and non-empty PQ, Tectonic uses the metadata in KS. To generate an empty PQ, the generator first randomly generates a key k, and then checks if $k \in KS$. If it is, Tectonic re-generate a key at random; otherwise, it adds a PQ on k to the output. For non-empty PQs, Tectonic selects a key from the KS after sampling it on the distribution provided in the input file. Users must specify `"point_queries"` or `"empty_point_queries"` key to generate the corresponding operations as: `{"groups":[{"point_queries":{"op_count":NumExp,"selection":Dist}` and `{"empty_point_queries":{"op_count":NumExp,"key":StrExp}]}`.

Range Query. To generate range queries (RQs), Tectonic first probes KS and selects a start key by sampling based on a specified distribution. Then, the end key is determined based on the query selectivity. The RQ selectivity in Tectonic can be specified as constant or to follow a user-specified distribution. To generate RQs, the input JSON should have `"range_queries"` as: `{"groups":[{"range_queries":{"op_count":NumExp,"selectivity": NumExp,"selection":Dist}]}`.

Point Delete. Tectonic can distinguish between *empty* and *non-empty* point deletes [39,40]. Similarly to PQs, to distinguish between empty and non-empty PDs, Tectonic probes KS for membership checks. For non-empty PDs, Tectonic selects a key from KS, and once the delete is generated, the key is removed from KS. Users can generate `"point_deletes"` or `"empty_point_deletes"`, by specifying: `{"groups":[{"point_deletes":{"amoun"t:NumExp},{"empty_point_deletes": {"op_count":NumExp,"key":StrExp}]}`.

Range Delete. Similar to RQs, Tectonic can generate range deletes with a given selectivity. After generating the RQ, Tectonic removes all keys within the deleted range from KS. User can generate `"range_deletes"`, as follows: `{"groups":[{"range_deletes":{"op_count":NumExp,"selectivity":NumExp}}]}`.

2.3 Modeling Workload Skews

Tectonic supports nine distributions for key generation and selection: (1) uniform, (2) normal, (3) beta, (4) Zipfian, (5) exponential, (6) log-normal, (7) Poisson, (8) Weibull, and (9) Pareto. It leverages the `rand_distr` Rust library, which readily provides the implementations of the distributions, enabling fast sampling. Tectonic uses these distributions to sample keys from the `ActiveKeySet` and clamp them to the interval $[0.0, 1.0)$, to ensure validity.

Each operation in Tectonic, such as inserts, updates, point queries, or range deletes, can have its own independent key distribution. This allows modeling diverse access patterns across operations, such as *uniformly* distributed inserts followed by a workload of *skewed* updates, or range queries with a *uniform* selectivity interleaved with non-empty point queries on the *recently inserted* entries.

2.4 What Sets Tectonic Apart

Ability of Generating Dynamic Workloads. Production workloads are often non-uniform and evolve over time due to changes in user behavior, application requirements, or specific periodic events. Tectonic is designed to support the generation of dynamically shifting workloads as it allows the user to separately specify the composition of multiple workload phases (through *Groups* and *Sections* in the JSON file). Each phase has its own access distribution, operation mix, and key selection policy. Below, we present two real-world workloads that state-of-the-art key-value benchmarks are unable to produce, and we discuss how Tectonic is able to emulate them.

Example 1: Production workloads at Meta and X experience a *burst of inserts and updates* during peak hours (i.e., during sports matches, political debates,

```
1 {
2  "groups":[{
3   "inserts":{
4    "op_count":1e6,
5     "key":{"uniform":{"len":32}},
6     "val":{"uniform":{"len":1024}}
7   },
8   "updates":{
9    "op_count":1e4,
10   "val":{"uniform":{"len":1024}}
11  }
12 },
13 {
14  "point_queries":{
15   "op_count":1e3,
16   "selection":{"uniform":{"len":32}}
17  },
18  "range_queries":{
19   "op_count":50,
20   "selectivity":{
21    "uniform":{"min":0.01,"max":0.1}},
22   "selection":{"uniform":{"len":32}}
23  }
24 }]}
```

Fig. 2. Dynamic workload specification in Tectonic: Phase 1: (Lines 1–12) for a write-heavy workload; Phase 2: (Lines 13–24) for a read-heavy workload.

etc.) [10], when user activity soars high [6]. The workload pattern during these hours is distinctively different from other times of a day, when users are primarily browsing content, leading to a *high volume of point and range queries* on popular or recently updated content. Note that the point and range queries in the later phase must share the keyspace with the preceding inserts and updates. To simulate this workload scenario, Tectonic requires two groups in a section, one which can simulate bursty inserts and updates (Fig. 2 (Lines 1–12)) where key size is $32B$ and value is of $1024B$, two which can simulate high volume of point and range queries (Fig. 2 (Lines 13-24)) where both point queries and range queries follows a uniform distribution.

Example 2: E-commerce platforms, such as Amazon, often process workloads where different phases focus on separate segments of the keyspace. For instance, during off-peak hours, a bulk of the operations target the product catalog, such as *filtering products by vendors*. This leads to skewed accesses to data with a specific key-prefix, such as `product:<vendor_id>:<sku>`. On the other hand, during peak hours when customers are active, operations such as *checking a user's order history* lead to frequent accesses that use a completely different set of keys with a prefix, like `order_history:<user_id>:<timestamp>`. Since the keys across these phases are from disjoint parts of the keyspace, Tectonic models this workload by implementing each phase in a separate *Section*, thereby enabling distinct prefix layouts, key distributions, and operation interleaving for each phase.

Tunable Sortedness for Keys. Tectonic can generate workloads with varied degrees of sortedness. In several production workloads, data arrives in nearly sorted order [36,45], but not as fully sorted. Tectonic, like BoDS, uses the K, L-sortedness metric to generate a collection of data that is arbitrarily sorted. K denotes the fraction of entries that are out of place in the workload, and L denotes the maximum displacement of such an out-of-place entry. However, unlike BoDS, Tectonic (i) can support string keys as well as composite keys, (ii) generates the data following a specific distribution, and (iii) allows other database operations to be interleaved with the inserts.

Emulating "Hot" Key-Ranges. Similarly to UDB, ZippyDB, and UP2X, many production workloads exhibit strong skew in access patterns, where a small subset of "hot" keys are accessed far more frequently [6,22]. These hot regions may shift over time depending on application behavior. For instance, during flash sales on e-commerce platforms, only a few products receive the majority of user queries and orders. These product IDs form hot key ranges that dominate the workload for a short window. Tectonic supports fine-grained control over key selection by allowing users to define hot key ranges and assign access probabilities to them. The range for hot key ranges is defined using non-uniformly generated prefixes. The length of the prefix, the number of hot prefixes, and the probability of selecting a hot prefix over a non-hot one during string generation are specified.

Support for Prefix-Based and Composite Key. Key-value stores often rely on structured keys to encode metadata, such as relation names or user types, for more efficient data partitioning and access. Thus, commercial key-value stores frequently use prefix-based or composite keys, e.g., `user:12345:profile` or `org:abc:project:xyz:log`, to colocate related records and enable fast prefix scans. Tectonic support prefix-based and composite key generation, allowing users to configure multiple segments with different distributions, or hot ranges. When describing the composition of a key, users can specify (i) the key length, (ii) how to construct each key segment, and (ii) the distribution of each segment.

3 Benchmark Workloads

Tectonic uses a JSON specification file as input to generate synthetic workloads that closely resemble real-life production workload characteristics. This input file is human-readable and is easy to configure. In this section, we show Tectonic can not only efficiently generate the benchmark workloads of YCSB and KVBench, but also generate a large set of workloads that the state of the art is unable to generate. We then compare Tectonic's performance against the state of the art in terms of end-to-end latency, throughput, and memory footprint.

Defining Workloads. Workloads in Tectonic are described by a JSON file. The top-level structure contains *Sections*, a list of isolated phases in the workload, where operations in different sections do not share keyspace. The second level contains *Groups*, a list of sequential phases, where operations are aware of the previous phase (e.g., preloading followed by querying phase on the same keyspace). Each group specifies one or more operations that are interleaved. The most common one is *op_count*, which refers to the number of operations to generate for a specific operation type. The *key/val* specifies the process for generating keys and values, e.g., uniformly random, segmented with a hot prefix, or composite keys. A workload can have multiple sections, with each section comprising various groups, and each group can have multiple types of operations.

Experimental Setup. We use a machine with an Intel(R) Xeon(R) Gold 6240R CPU, 2.40 GHz cores, 192 GB of RAM, 240 GB SSD, and running

Ubuntu 20.04 LTS. We use the GNU time utility (version 1.7) [17] to collect all system-level performance metrics such as user time, system time, and maximum resident set size. We simulate YCSB and KVBench workloads through Tectonic and compare the total execution time, CPU usage, and memory footprint.

3.1 Emulating YCSB Workloads

The YCSB key-value benchmark is widely used to evaluate the performance of key-value and NoSQL systems. It has six benchmark workloads (YCSB-A - YCSB-F), each representing a specific access pattern and read-write ratio. Tectonic can natively simulate all YCSB workloads using a simple JSON specification. To run a specific YCSB workload using Tectonic, the user provides a corresponding specification file (e.g., a.spec.json for YCSB-A) and executes: `tectonic-cli generate -w ycsb-specs/a.spec.json`. Each specification file encodes the YCSB workload logic using sections, groups, and operations, while maintaining consistency with the original YCSB design in terms of data model and access patterns. We include full specifications for all six YCSB workloads as part of the Tectonic repository under ycsb-specs/, making it easy to modify, extend, or compose them with additional workload phases.

3.2 Emulating KVBench Workloads

KVBench is a recent key-value benchmarking suite designed to capture a range of data access patterns observed in production systems [47]. It defines five distinct workload profiles (KVBench-I – KVBench-V), each representing a unique combination of operations, key distributions, and data sizes. Tectonic can reproduce these workloads using declarative JSON specifications, enabling users to experiment with the same access behaviors under a unified and extensible framework. To run a specific workload using Tectonic, users can provide the corresponding configuration file, e.g., 1.spec.json for KVBench-I: `tectonic-cli generate -w kvbench-specs/i.spec.json`

3.3 The Tectonic Benchmark

We define seven benchmark workloads to show Tectonic's flexibility in simulating complex key-value access patterns, as shown in Table 2.

Tec-1 *(Multi-phased dynamic)* models three sequential workload phases, transitioning from a write-heavy phase to a read-heavy one and ending with a balanced mix of operations, including range queries and updates, each following a different access distribution.

Tec-2 *(Interleaved multi-distributional)* generates a workload with interleaved operations, including insert, point, and range queries, point and range deletes, and empty point queries. Each operation uses its distinct statistical distribution, ideas for stress-testing systems under mixed and concurrent loads.

Tec-3 *(Near-sorted ingestion)* simulates scenarios where data arrives mostly in order, such as time-series databases, but includes controlled disorder in key insertion order to evaluate tolerance to near-sortedness.

Tec-4 *(Soft phase transitioning)* captures a gradual transition of the workload characteristic over time, such as reducing insert rates and increasing both point and range query volume across phases.

Tec-5 *(Discrete phase transitioning)* represents a sharp transition from write-heavy to read-heavy behavior across two phases, helpful in evaluating system responsiveness under sudden access pattern changes.

Tec-6 *(Variable key-value size)* explores workloads with varying key and value sizes—ranging from 32B to 256B to simulate document stores or blob systems where entry size variability influences I/O and memory usage.

Tec-7 *(Skewed access)* focuses on skewed data access, where a small portion of keys dominate both inserts and point queries, a typical pattern in caching workloads and real-time analytics.

Together, these workloads highlight Tectonic's ability to capture complex temporal, structural, and statistical variations in realistic system benchmarks.

4 Experimental Evaluation

In this section, we first evaluate the performance of Tectonic against YCSB and KVBench across the six YCSB workloads (YCSB-A - YCSB-F). We use three system-level metrics: (i) end-to-end workload generation latency, (ii) operational throughput, and (iii) the peak main memory footprint, measured by the maximum resident set size. Next, we evaluate Tectonic's against KVBench using the five KVBench benchmark workloads. We show that Tectonic scales efficiently with increasing workload sizes. We then compare the similarity of workload between YCSB and Tectonic by comparing the database performance using a workload generated by YCSB and Tectonic from the same specification.

Tectonic Dominates the State of the Art when Generating YCSB Workloads. To run these experiments, we set up all the benchmarks to generate an equal number of operations with the exact proportions and wrote them to an output file. The YCSB benchmark generates operations on the fly to improve memory utilization. To ensure an apples-to-apples comparison, we adapted YCSB to write all operations in an output file (using Java's `BufferedWriter`), and set the same buffer size (1 MB). Other benchmarks, such as KVBench and Tectonic, follow the same pattern and construct a workload file beforehand. We do not compare against RocksDB's db_bench benchmark, as it is closely tied to RocksDB internals, and collecting all operations in an output file was not straightforward. The Tectonic generates all different YCSB workloads 12× and 10× faster than KVBench and YCSB itself, respectively (Fig. 3(A). It shows an improved throughput of $\approx 90\%$, Fig. 3(B), as it performs random key generation efficiently (using the `rand_xoshiro` Rust library) while optimizing the operation generation process using `ActiveKeySet` containers and custom data structures.

Table 2. Benchmark workloads supported by Tectonic

workload composition	distribution of operations
Tec-1: Multi-phased dynamic	
p1: 95% insert, 5% non-empty point deletes; p2: 100% empty point query; p3: 50% insert, 50% range query (sel: 0.01)	p1: Zipfian (both ops.); p2: uniform; p3: uniform (both ops.)
Tec-2: Interleaved multi-distributional	
50% insert, 20% non-empty point query, 10% empty point query, 10% non-empty point delete, 10% range delete (sel=0.0001)	Zipfian, latest normal, uniform Pareto
Tec-3: Near-sorted ingestion	
100% insert with $K = 1\%$ and $L = 10\%$	uniform
Tec-4: Slow phase transitioning	
p1: 70% insert, 20% non-empty point query, 10% range query; p2: 50% insert, 30% non-empty point query, 20% range query; p3: 30% insert, 40% non-empty point query, 30% range query	range query selectivity varies uniformly between 0.1 and 0.2 in p1, p2 & p3
Tec-5: Discrete phase transitioning	
p1: 90% insert, 5% empty point query, 5% range query; p2: 10% insert, 70% non-empty point query, 20% range query	transition from p1 to p2 write-heavy to read-heavy
Tec-6: Variable entry size	
50% insert, 50% non-empty point query	key varies from 32B–256B value varies from 32B–256B
Tec-7: Skewed access	
50% insert (10% hot keys with a given prefix), 50% non-empty point query (90% queries with a given prefix)	10% hot keys in inserts 90% point query on hot keys

Tectonic does an excellent job in optimizing the total memory usage, showing an improvement of 84%, Fig. 3(C), making it capable of generating larger workloads. KVBench is unable to simulate YCSB-F, as it does not support read-modify-write, and hence, is omitted in Fig. 3. For YCSB-E, which involves short-range queries that read up to 100 records, KVBench shows higher end-to-end latency. This is because the vector is sorted every time a new range query is generated; as an insert operation appends a new key to the vector, it becomes unsorted. On the other hand, Tectonic is capable of generating range queries in two formats: (i) the YCSB format, which features an open range query with a specified *scan length*, and (ii) the KVBench format, which generates both start and end keys.

For Fig. 3, Tectonic follows the YCSB way of generating range queries, which does not require sorting.

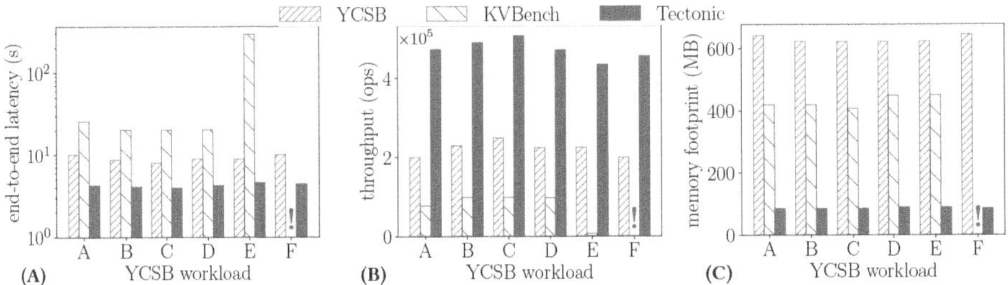

Fig. 3. Tectonic is faster than all state-of-the-art key-value generators (A) and provides better throughput (B) while using less memory (C) for all YCSB types of workloads. Note that KVBench can not simulate YCSB-F workload.

Tectonic Outperforms KVBench Across the Board. We again configure both benchmarks to produce the same number of operations with the same key and value sizes, as well as the same distribution or selectivity, if applicable. To run KVBench workloads I, III, and IV, we required preloading of inserts. In the first phase, we generate 1M insert operations, and then use this count to compute other operation compositions. In Fig. 4, we show the performance of Tectonic when generating KVBench workloads. The observations are as follows: (i) Tectonic simulated all five different KVBench workloads with 1.5 order of magnitude faster than KVBench, Fig. 4(A); (ii) it provided more than 1.5 order of magnitude better throughput, Fig. 4(B); and (iii) it only utilized 70% less memory than KVBench Fig. 4(C). The workload IV in KVBench generates 50% range deletes with selectivity 0.0001% and exhibits poor throughput comparatively. Tectonic can emulate KVBench workloads more efficiently than KVBench itself. Tectonic outperforms KVBench because it uses efficient data structures to store the `ActiveKeySet`, such as Bloom filters, which enables it to achieve higher throughput with a lower memory footprint.

Tectonic Scales Better than the State of the Art. In this experiment, we vary the total number of operations (from 1M to 100M) while proportionately scaling the constituent operations. The benchmark first generates 50% inserts for preloading, followed by 40% inserts, 5% point queries, and 5% updates in an interleaved fashion. Figure 5(A) shows that Tectonic offers 1.6× and 6.4× higher throughput than YCSB and KVBench, respectively. As we increase the size of the workload, we observe that Tectonic's advantages over the state of the art hold in terms of throughput. This is because the process is CPU-bound on generating random strings (as shown in Fig. 5(A)), and Tectonic's String generation implementation is faster and more efficient compared to both YCSB and KVBench. In Fig. 5(B), however, we observe that as the workload size increases, Tectonic has a

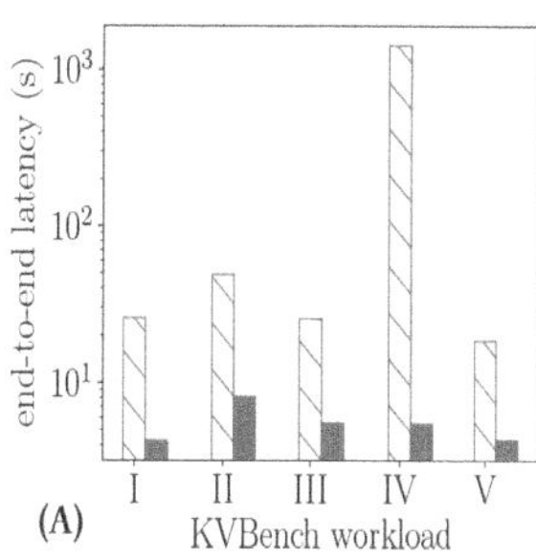

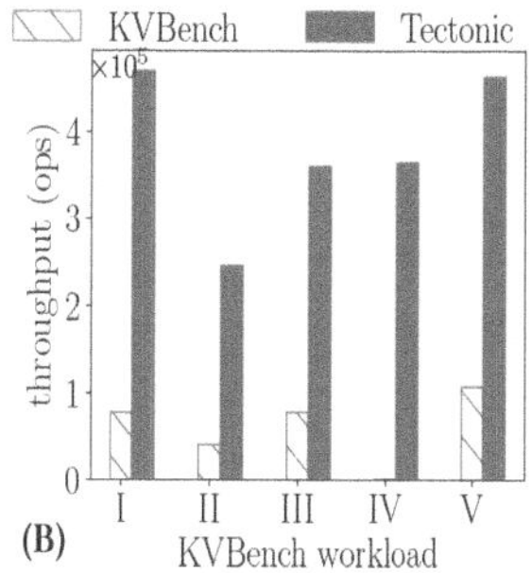

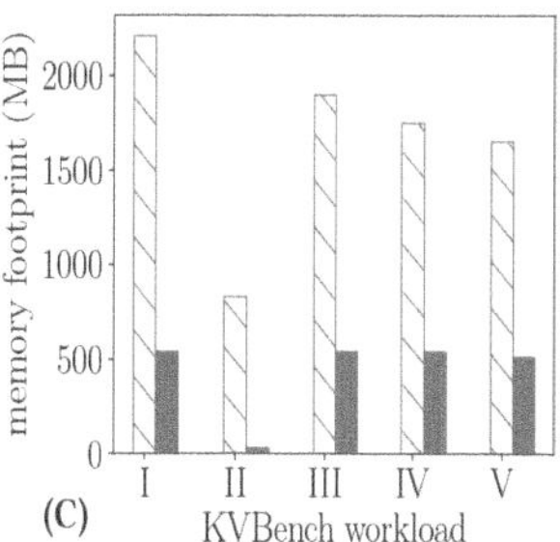

Fig. 4. Tectonic emulates all KVBench generic workloads more efficiently, showing (A) more than 1.5× improvement in end-to-end execution latency, (B) enhanced throughput, and (C) a reduced memory footprint.

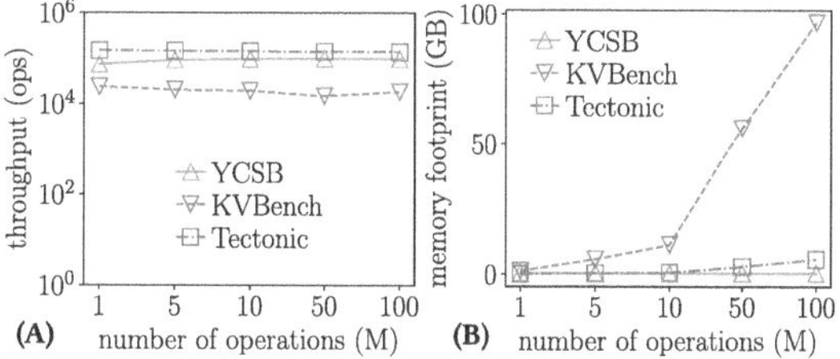

Fig. 5. Tectonic scales better than the state of the art in terms of performance at the cost of a slight increase in the memory footprint.

slightly higher memory footprint than YCSB. This is because workload generation in YCSB is *memoryless*, and hence, YCSB does not support operations such as empty point queries and empty point deletes. For 1M operation Tectonic still shows less memory footprint than YCSB, see Fig. 3(C). While KVBench supports all core key-value operations, it requires significantly more metadata to enable them, requiring up to 2 orders of magnitude more memory than Tectonic.

Workload Similarity with State of the Art. In Fig. 6, we compare two workloads with the same specifications (YCSB-A with 20 million operations, 1123 bytes per entry) – one is generated by Tectonic and the other by YCSB – by analyzing the database performance. We use RocksDB with default configurations for this. The rate of bytes read and written into the database when running the same specification workloads yields similar results, as shown in Fig. 6(A). Inserts and updates show a similar latency pattern. Point queries too exhibit comparable $P0, P25, P75$ values, as shown in Fig. 6(B). The total number of bytes read and written during the execution of the workload shows less than 1% difference (Fig. 6(C)). This indicates that RocksDB experienced a comparable amount of data movement due to compactions and flushes. The cache reflects the locality of data access in the database, and Fig. 6(D) shows exactly the same cache hits and misses for both workload runs on RocksDB. Tectonic offers broader distribution and operation support with high accuracy, while effectively mimicking state-of-the-art workloads to produce similar database behaviors.

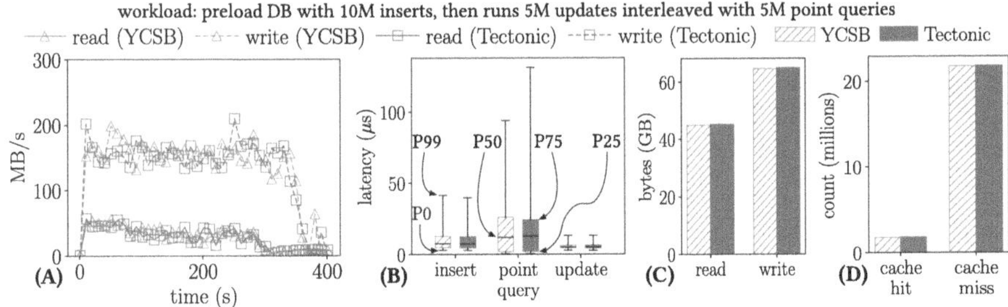

Fig. 6. Workloads generated by Tectonic and YCSB perform similarly when run on a production database offering (A) comparable performance for both reads and writes, (B) latencies for inserts, point queries, and updates, (C) total data movement, and (D) cache behavior (hit and miss counts).

5 Related Work

YCSB. The Yahoo! Cloud Serving Benchmark (YCSB) [12] is a widely used key-value benchmark for evaluating the performance of cloud-native NoSQL databases. It provides a flexible architecture with support for various database backends and is easily extensible. YCSB's primary workload module, `CoreWorkload`, includes support for inserts, updates, read-modify-writes, point queries, and range queries (scans). Point queries and updates can be configured to follow distributions such as uniform, exponential, sequential, Zipfian, latest, and hotspot. However, YCSB lacks support for point and range deletes, and is unable to distinguish between empty and non-empty point queries. Additionally, it requires point queries and updates to share the same distribution.

db_bench. db_bench [15] is a benchmarking utility tightly integrated with RocksDB [16] and LevelDB [20], offering detailed insights into internal behaviors and metrics. db_bench supports inserts, updates, read-modify-writes, point queries, range queries, point deletes, and range deletes. It can simulate empty point queries by generating keys that are guaranteed not to exist. However, modifying db_bench to serve as a general-purpose key-value benchmark requires a significant amount of development, which has led to its limited adoption.

KVBench. KVBench [47] supports a comprehensive set of operations, including inserts, updates, range queries, range deletes, as well as both empty and non-empty point queries and deletes. Each operation can be assigned its own access distribution, such as uniform, normal, beta, or Zipfian. KVBench allows limited control over operation sequencing (e.g., interleaved vs. sequential), but it does not support dynamic or time-varying workloads. Additionally, it lacks support for read-modify-writes, variable-length keys and values, and complex key formats.

BoDS. Benchmark on Data Sortedness (BoDS) [34] is designed to evaluate key-value and relational systems under varying degrees of data sortedness. It only supports five workload types: bulk loading, individual inserts, and mixed read/write workloads with or without preloading. BoDS allows control over data ordering using sortedness parameters K, L, and the beta distribution $B(a, b)$. However, BoDS does not support several basic key-value operations, such as read-modify-writes, deletes, and empty point lookups, lacks support for dynamically shifting workloads, and can not emulate complex multi-distributional workloads.

Emulating Production Workload Traces. Cao *et al.* presented a detailed characterization of the real-world workload for use cases at Facebook [6]. They presented three main workloads: UDB, a MySQL-compatible storage layer for social graphs; ZippyDB, a distributed KV store for metadata; and UP2X, a distributed KV store for AI/ML services with frequent updates. They emulated the real-world workloads with YCSB and db_bench, and while db_bench was able to more accurately emulate the workloads, there is still room for improvement.

Relational Data Generators. Relational database benchmarking has a long history, leading to the development of both industry standards and research-focused data generators. Benchmarking suites such as TPC-C [46], TPC-DS [43], and TPC-E [44] define schema structures and workloads for evaluating transaction processing and decision-support systems. Complementing these standards, research prototypes such as MUDD [42], Myriad [1], PDGF [32], and more recent tools [18,27,31] have been proposed to generate large-scale multi-table datasets that satisfy relational constraints. Each system targets specific challenges in SQL-based models. For instance, MUDD separates data distribution from data generation and supports snowflake schemas for decision-support benchmarks. Myriad and PDGF provide mechanisms to ensure referential integrity by regenerating valid keys, while others explore efficient updates, adaptability testing, and workload shifts. These approaches primarily focus on static relational schemas and maintaining inter-table consistency. However, they lack the fine-grained control needed for non-relational storage engines. In particular, existing tools do not adequately emulate multi-phase dynamic workloads with mixed operations and shifting access patterns, nor do they expose mechanisms for controlling the granularity of key distribution or entry size.

6 Conclusion

In this paper, we present Tectonic, a highly configurable and resource-efficient key-value benchmark that can accurately model complex real-world key-value workloads as well as generate dynamic workloads that change over time. Tectonic outperforms state-of-the-art key-value benchmarks, namely, YCSB and KVBench, in terms of performance and resource utilization, while scaling similarly to the state of the art. Tectonic also offers a fine-grained control over data access patterns, sophisticated key and value generation strategies, dynamic workload parameters, and support for shifting, sorted, and near-sorted workloads.

Acknowledgements. The experiments presented in this paper were conducted using the Chameleon Cloud platform [25]. We thank the Chameleon team for providing this valuable testbed to the research community.

References

1. Alexandrov, A., Schiefer, B., Poelman, J., Ewen, S., Bodner, T.O., Markl, V.: Myriad: parallel data generation on shared-nothing architectures. In: Proceedings of the 1st Workshop on Architectures and Systems for Big Data (ASBD 2011), pp. 30–33 (2011). https://doi.org/10.1145/2377978.2377983. https://dl.acm.org/doi/10.1145/2377978.2377983
2. Apache: Cassandra (2023). http://cassandra.apache.org
3. Apache: HBase (2023). http://hbase.apache.org/
4. Apple: FoundationDB (2018). https://github.com/apple/foundationdb
5. Athanassoulis, M., Ailamaki, A.: BF-tree: approximate tree indexing. Proc. VLDB Endow. **7**(14), 1881–1892 (2014). http://www.vldb.org/pvldb/vol7/p1881-athanassoulis.pdf
6. Cao, Z., Dong, S., Vemuri, S., Du, D.H.C.: Characterizing, modeling, and benchmarking RocksDB key-value workloads at Facebook. In: Proceedings of the USENIX Conference on File and Storage Technologies (FAST), pp. 209–223 (2020)
7. Chandramouli, B., Prasaad, G., Kossmann, D., Levandoski, J.J., Hunter, J., Barnett, M.: FASTER: a concurrent key-value store with in-place updates. In: Proceedings of the ACM SIGMOD International Conference on Management of Data, pp. 275–290 (2018). https://doi.org/10.1145/3183713.3196898. http://doi.acm.org/10.1145/3183713.3196898
8. Chang, F., et al.: Bigtable: a distributed storage system for structured data. ACM Trans. Comput. Syst. (TOCS) **26**(2), 4:1–4:26 (2008). https://doi.org/10.1145/1365815.1365816
9. Chatterjee, S., Jagadeesan, M., Qin, W., Idreos, S.: Cosine: a cloud-cost optimized self-designing key-value storage engine. Proc. VLDB Endow. **15**(1), 112–126 (2021). https://doi.org/10.14778/3485450.3485461
10. Cheng, A., et al.: TAOBench: an end-to-end benchmark for social networking workloads. Proc. VLDB Endow. **15**(9), 1965–1977 (2022). https://doi.org/10.14778/3538598.3538616. https://www.vldb.org/pvldb/vol15/p1965-cheng.pdf
11. CockroachDB: CockroachDB (2021). https://github.com/cockroachdb/cockroach
12. Cooper, B.F., Silberstein, A., Tam, E., Ramakrishnan, R., Sears, R.: Benchmarking cloud serving systems with YCSB. In: Proceedings of the ACM Symposium on Cloud Computing (SoCC), pp. 143–154 (2010). https://doi.org/10.1145/1807128.1807152. http://doi.acm.org/10.1145/1807128.1807152
13. DeCandia, G., et al.: Dynamo: Amazon's highly available key-value store. ACM SIGOPS Oper. Syst. Rev. **41**(6), 205–220 (2007). https://doi.org/10.1145/1323293.1294281
14. Facebook: MyRocks (2023). http://myrocks.io/
15. Facebook: db_bench (2024). https://github.com/facebook/rocksdb/wiki/Benchmarking-tools
16. Facebook: RocksDB (2024). https://github.com/facebook/rocksdb
17. Foundation, F.S.: Gnu operating system. https://www.gnu.org/software/time/
18. Frank, M., Poess, M., Rabl, T.: Efficient update data generation for DBMS benchmarks. In: Third Joint WOSP/SIPEW International Conference on Performance Engineering, ICPE 2012, Boston, MA, USA - April 22–25, 2012, pp. 169–180 (2012). https://doi.org/10.1145/2188286.2188315
19. Geffner, S., Agrawal, D., El Abbadi, A., Smith, T.R.: Relative prefix sums: an efficient approach for querying dynamic OLAP data cubes. In: Proceedings of the IEEE International Conference on Data Engineering (ICDE), pp. 328–335 (1999). https://doi.org/10.1109/ICDE.1999.754948

20. Google: LevelDB (2021). https://github.com/google/leveldb/
21. Huang, D., et al.: TiDB: a raft-based HTAP database. Proc. VLDB Endow. **13**(12), 3072–3084 (2020). https://doi.org/10.14778/3415478.3415535. http://www.vldb.org/pvldb/vol13/p3072-huang.pdf
22. Huang, G., et al.: X-engine: an optimized storage engine for large-scale E-commerce transaction processing. In: Proceedings of the ACM SIGMOD International Conference on Management of Data, pp. 651–665 (2019). https://doi.org/10.1145/3299869.3314041
23. Huynh, A., Chaudhari, H.A., Terzi, E., Athanassoulis, M.: Endure: A Robust Tuning Paradigm for LSM Trees Under Workload Uncertainty. CoRR 2110.13801 (2021). https://arxiv.org/abs/2110.13801
24. Huynh, A., Chaudhari, H.A., Terzi, E., Athanassoulis, M.: Endure: a robust tuning paradigm for LSM trees under workload uncertainty. Proc. VLDB Endow. **15**(8), 1605–1618 (2022). https://doi.org/10.14778/3529337.3529345
25. Keahey, K.: Chameleon: Experimental Platform for Cloud Computing Research (2018). https://www.chameleoncloud.org/media/cms_page_media/17/GENI-lex.pdf
26. Kryczka, A.: Compaction Styles (2020). https://github.com/facebook/rocksdb/blob/gh-pages-old/talks/2020-07-17-Brownbag-Compactions.pdf
27. Li, Y., Zhang, R., Li, Y., Ke, S., Zhang, S., Zhou, A.: Lauca: Generating Application-Oriented Synthetic Workloads. CoRR abs/1912.0 (2019). http://arxiv.org/abs/1912.07172
28. Mo, D., Chen, F., Luo, S., Shan, C.: Learning to Optimize LSM-trees: Towards A Reinforcement Learning based Key-Value Store for Dynamic Workloads. CoRR abs/2308.0 (2023). https://doi.org/10.48550/ARXIV.2308.07013
29. Nuessle, C., Kennedy, O., Ziarek, L.: Benchmarking pocket-scale databases. In: Nambiar, R., Poess, M. (eds.) TPCTC 2019. LNCS, vol. 12257, pp. 99–115. Springer, Cham (2020). https://doi.org/10.1007/978-3-030-55024-0_7
30. Power, C., et al.: The cosmos big data platform at microsoft: over a decade of progress and a decade to look forward. Proc. VLDB Endow. **14**(12), 3148–3161 (2021). https://doi.org/10.14778/3476311.3476390. http://www.vldb.org/pvldb/vol14/p3148-jindal.pdf
31. Rabl, T., Lang, A., Hackl, T., Sick, B., Kosch, H.: Generating shifting workloads to benchmark adaptability in relational database systems. In: Nambiar, R., Poess, M. (eds.) TPCTC 2009. LNCS, vol. 5895, pp. 116–131. Springer, Heidelberg (2009). https://doi.org/10.1007/978-3-642-10424-4_9
32. Rabl, T., Poess, M.: Parallel data generation for performance analysis of large, complex RDBMS. In: Proceedings of the International Workshop on Testing Database Systems (DBTest), p. 5 (2011). https://doi.org/10.1145/1988842.1988847
33. Raman, A., Huynh, A., Lu, J., Athanassoulis, M.: Benchmarking learned and LSM indexes for data sortedness. In: Proceedings of the International Workshop on Testing Database Systems (DBTest), DBTest 2024, pp. 16–22 (2024). https://doi.org/10.1145/3662165.3662764
34. Raman, A., Karatsenidis, K., Sarkar, S., Olma, M., Athanassoulis, M.: BoDS: a benchmark on data sortedness. In: Performance Evaluation and Benchmarking - TPC Technology Conference (TPCTC), pp. 17–32 (2022)
35. Raman, A., Karatsenidis, K., Xie, S., Olma, M., Sarkar, S., Athanassoulis, M.: QuIT your B+-tree for the quick insertion tree. In: Proceedings of the International Conference on Extending Database Technology (EDBT), pp. 451–463 (2025). https://doi.org/10.48786/EDBT.2025.36

36. Raman, A., Sarkar, S., Olma, M., Athanassoulis, M.: Indexing for near-sorted data. In: Proceedings of the IEEE International Conference on Data Engineering (ICDE), pp. 1475–1488 (2023)
37. RocksDB: Prefix seek. https://github.com/facebook/rocksdb/wiki/Prefix-Seek
38. RocksDB: Prefix Bloom Filter (2020). https://github.com/facebook/rocksdb/wiki/Prefix-Seek#configure-prefix-bloom-filter
39. Sarkar, S., Papon, T.I., Staratzis, D., Athanassoulis, M.: Lethe: a tunable delete-aware LSM engine. In: Proceedings of the ACM SIGMOD International Conference on Management of Data, pp. 893–908 (2020). https://doi.org/10.1145/3318464.3389757
40. Sarkar, S., Papon, T.I., Staratzis, D., Zhu, Z., Athanassoulis, M.: Enabling timely and persistent deletion in LSM-engines. ACM Trans. Database Syst. (TODS) **48**(3), 8:1–8:40 (2023). https://doi.org/10.1145/3599724
41. Sarkar, S., Staratzis, D., Zhu, Z., Athanassoulis, M.: Constructing and analyzing the LSM compaction design space. Proc. VLDB Endow. **14**(11), 2216–2229 (2021). https://doi.org/10.14778/3476249.3476274. http://vldb.org/pvldb/vol14/p2216-sarkar.pdf
42. Stephens, J.M., Poess, M.: MUDD: a multi-dimensional data generator. In: Proceedings of the Fourth International Workshop on Software and Performance, WOSP 2004, Redwood Shores, California, USA, 14–16 January 2004, pp. 104–109 (2004). https://doi.org/10.1145/974044.974060
43. TPC: Specification of the TPC-DS benchmark. http://www.tpc.org/tpcds/
44. TPC: Specification of TPC-E benchmark. http://www.tpc.org/tpce/
45. TPC: TPC-H benchmark (2021). http://www.tpc.org/tpch/
46. TPC: Specification of TPC-C benchmark (2022). http://www.tpc.org/tpcc/
47. Zhu, Z., Saha, A., Athanassoulis, M., Sarkar, S.: KVBench: a key-value benchmarking suite. In: International Workshop on Testing Database Systems (DBTest), pp. 9–15 (2024). https://doi.org/10.1145/3662165.3662765

Benchmarking Considerations for Agentic AI Systems

Ajay Dholakia[1], Sachin Gopal Wani[1(✉)], David Ellison[1], Miro Hodak[2], Debojyoti Dutta[3], Shishir Nagaraja[4], and Raj Ranjan[4]

[1] Lenovo, Infrastructure Solutions Group, Morrisville, NC, USA
{adholakia,swani1,dellison}@lenovo.com
[2] AMD, San Jose, CA, USA
Miro.Hodak@amd.com
[3] Nutanix, San Jose, CA, USA
debo.dutta@nutanix.com
[4] Newcastle University, Newcastle, UK
{Shishir.Nagaraja,Raj.Ranjan}@newcastle.ac.uk

Abstract. This panel discussion will address the top-of-mind subject of Agentic AI Systems. With the rise of Generative AI and associated Large Language Models (LLMs) and Foundation Models (FMs), the focus of research and practice is shifting to building AI Agents for targeted tasks. Furthermore, a collection of AI Agents are being stitched together to design and deploy Agentic AI systems for enterprise-level workflows and use cases. While the excitement around building such systems that employ LLMs and FMs as building blocks grows, the need to assess the performance of multi-agent systems is growing in importance as well. Metrics such as latency, throughput, accuracy and power consumption are, of course, necessary, but also not sufficient. Additional consideration must be given to the type of workflow, the criticality and resiliency of the use-case, and the target infrastructure for deployment. The panelists will bring their perspectives about building distributed autonomous Agentic AI systems, leveraging their experience spanning industry as well as academia. Factors crucial to developing a comprehensive framework for useful benchmarks will be discussed, with the goal of highlighting best practices for as well as limitations in current state of the art in AI system benchmarking.

Keywords: Agentic AI · AI Agents · Benchmarking · Generative AI

1 Introduction

Agentic AI has been identified as a top technology trend for 2025, marking a pivotal shift in the artificial intelligence landscape. The challenge for all AI practitioners is to design and implement effective and usable Agentic AI systems. However, considerable confusion persists regarding the definition and terminology related to this technology.

Unlike generative AI, which acts as a sophisticated tool for content creation, an agentic system is defined by its ability to interact with an environment to achieve a goal

R. Nambiar and M. Poess (Eds.): TPCTC 2025, LNCS 16261, pp. 89–98, 2026.
https://doi.org/10.1007/978-3-032-18070-4_6

with a degree of autonomy. An action taken by a separate entity in the surrounding environment, triggered by the output of an augmented LLM in response to a query, is what qualifies the AI software as an AI agent [1]. Such agents enable a dynamic flow of actions and offer the advantage of making decisions based on the data and outcomes encountered in real-time. A system composed of multiple, interconnected AI agents then becomes an Agentic AI system [2].

This methodical view of building blocks, workflows, and agents lays the foundation for benchmarking purposes. The transition from generative tools to autonomous actors creates an urgent need for new evaluation paradigms focused on process, safety, and reliability. Developing benchmarks that assess the capabilities of such Agentic AI systems is a difficult but necessary requirement for driving broader adoption and building trust.

The rest of the paper is as follows. Section 2 describes related work on early benchmarks. Section 3 outlines the benchmark creation and adoption by organizations such as MLPerf. Section 4 delves into broader considerations about Agentic AI systems ranging from governance, standardization and compliance. Section 5 positions Agentic AI in the edge deployment scenario and focuses on security related requirements from a benchmarking perspective. Section 6 pulls together the key discussion points from the prior section. Finally, Sect. 7 provides a summary and outlines key next steps needed to make progress towards a comprehensive benchmark for Agentic AI systems.

2 Related Work

The evaluation of agentic AI systems necessitates a fundamental departure from the benchmarks traditionally used for large language models (LLMs). While metrics for generative models have focused on the quality of a static output—such as accuracy on multiple-choice questions or fluency in text generation—agentic evaluation must assess a dynamic, interactive process [3, 4]. An agent's performance is defined not just by its final answer, but by the entire trajectory of actions it takes: its ability to reason through multi-step problems, use external tools, interact with a changing environment, and adapt to unforeseen circumstances [2]. This paradigm shift has spurred the development of a new generation of benchmarks designed specifically to measure these agentic capabilities.

Early efforts to standardize agent evaluation led to the creation of broad, multi-dimensional benchmarks designed to assess the core competencies of LLMs acting as agents. A prime example is AgentBench [5], a comprehensive framework that evaluates an LLM's general reasoning and decision-making abilities across eight distinct and relatively self-contained environments. These environments test a wide array of skills in isolation, from operating system and database manipulation to web browsing and solving lateral thinking puzzles. By assessing performance across this diverse task set, AgentBench provides a crucial baseline for comparing the raw agentic potential of different foundational models, revealing significant performance gaps between proprietary and open-source LLMs.

While general capability benchmarks are essential for evaluating the underlying models, the practical application of agentic AI in enterprise settings demands evaluation grounded in the complex realities of specific professional domains. This has led to the emergence of highly specialized, task-oriented benchmarks. In the software engineering domain, SWE-bench [6] has become a prominent example. It moves beyond simple code generation tasks by presenting agents with real-world problems sourced directly from GitHub issues in popular Python repositories. An agent is given an entire codebase and an issue description and is tasked with generating a code patch to resolve the problem. Success is not determined by semantic similarity but by a rigorous, execution-based "fail-to-pass" criterion, where the agent's patch must cause a predefined set of failing unit tests to pass without breaking existing functionality.

Complementing SWE-bench's focus on codebase modification, ITBench [7, 8] addresses the distinct challenge of live system operations. It is designed to evaluate an agent's ability to perform the job of a Site Reliability Engineer (SRE), Compliance Officer, or FinOps analyst. The benchmark's scenarios are derived from real-world production incidents and industry security standards, requiring agents to diagnose failures, assess compliance, or optimize costs within a simulated but realistic IT environment. Its evaluation framework incorporates business-relevant metrics such as Mean Time to Repair (MTTR) and the novel Normalized Topology-Aware Match (NTAM), which assesses the accuracy of a diagnosis within the system's dependency graph. Other domain-specific benchmarks like WebArena [9] for GUI-based web navigation and the DO Challenge [10] for drug discovery further illustrate this trend toward high-fidelity, job-specific evaluation.

Recognizing that a binary success metric is insufficient for complex, multi-step tasks, recent work has shifted focus toward evaluating the agentic process itself. This philosophy acknowledges that in a long chain of actions, the overall probability of success is the product of the success of each step, making it critical to understand where and why failures occur [11]. Benchmarks like TRAIL [12] are explicitly designed to evaluate an LLM's ability to debug and localize errors within long-context agent traces. Similarly, the AgentQuest [13] framework introduces novel metrics like "progress rate" and "repetition rate" to provide deeper insight into an agent's behavior and identify failure modes like looping or stagnation. This move toward process-based evaluation is coupled with a growing call to incorporate measures of economic and operational viability, such as API costs, token usage, and latency, into the evaluation framework to assess if an agent's solution is practical for real-world deployment.

Finally, as agents are poised for deployment in high-stakes environments, evaluating their safety, trustworthiness, and ability to collaborate has become a critical research frontier. Dedicated safety benchmarks like Agent-SafetyBench [14] and AgentHarm [15] have been developed to probe for common failure modes and test an agent's adherence to safety guardrails. Looking toward the future of more complex, distributed systems, frameworks like MultiAgentBench [16] are pioneering the evaluation of multi-agent collaboration and competition, assessing the effectiveness of different coordination protocols and communication strategies. Together, these diverse threads of research illustrate a field rapidly maturing to meet the multifaceted challenge of building and validating agentic AI systems that are not only capable but also efficient, reliable, and safe.

3 Benchmarking Methodology

Benchmarking Agentic AI is not an easy task. Established AI benchmarking suites consider a single model giving a prediction for a given input. In contrast, agentic AI systems consist of multiple components that interact with each other, making the flow non-linear and stateful. Figure 1 illustrates the comparison between these two paradigms.

Agentic AI has an input and output, but instead of a single AI model, it has multiple components. In a simplified scheme, an AI model does the planning step, deciding on the action to recommend. Next, a task is executed using a tool, such as creating computer code or searching the internet. After this, another AI model evaluates the result. If the result is deemed sufficient, an output is generated. If not, the initial AI model is asked to generate a different action. This iterative, state-dependent flow makes benchmarking difficult because it is not clear what should be measured. One approach is to treat the part between input and output as a black box effectively achieving the traditional AI benchmarking case. However, this is insufficient because it ignores the fact that internal flow is non-linear due to the conditional at the evaluation step.

Proper benchmarking needs to consider all the following components:

- AI model executing the planning step
- Tools that execute actions
- AI model evaluating the result

In addition, the non-linear flow needs to be accounted for as well. This means that the benchmark needs to consider both accuracy (as defined by the AI model evaluation) and performance of the system at the same time.

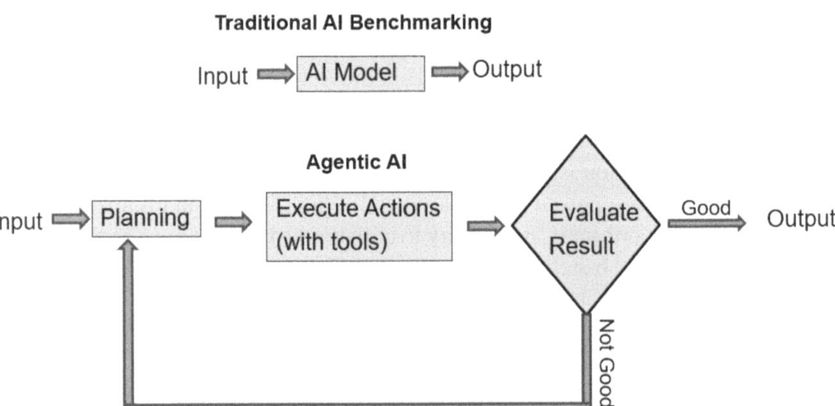

Fig. 1. Comparison between traditional benchmarking (top) and Agentic AI (bottom).

4 Governance Considerations

The autonomy and complexity that make agentic AI powerful also make it difficult to govern. Traditional governance frameworks are often insufficient for systems that can make independent decisions, adapt to changing conditions, and exhibit emergent behaviors

[17]. A robust governance strategy is therefore a prerequisite for the responsible deployment of agentic AI. This involves integrating established risk management frameworks, adhering to international standards, and ensuring comprehensive auditability.

A foundational tool for this is the NIST AI Risk Management Framework (AI RMF), a voluntary framework designed to help organizations manage the risks associated with AI. Its core functions—Govern, Map, Measure, and Manage—provide a structured approach that can be adapted for agentic systems. Organizations can use the AI RMF to assess the risks of an agent, define the scope of its authority, determine requirements for human oversight, and establish protocols for monitoring and feedback [18, 19].

On the international stage, standardization bodies are creating frameworks to ensure global compatibility and trust. The joint committee ISO/IEC JTC 1/SC 42 [20] is dedicated to AI standardization, developing standards that cover the entire AI lifecycle. A key output is ISO/IEC 42001 [21, 22], the first international standard for AI Management Systems. It provides a certifiable framework for organizations to develop, provide, or use AI systems responsibly, addressing quality, security, transparency, and reliability. Similarly, regulations like the EU AI Act, while not specifically naming agentic AI, establish a risk-based framework that applies to all AI applications, ensuring they are deployed ethically and transparently [23].

A central challenge in governing agentic AI is the "accountability gap" created by its often-opaque decision-making processes [24]. Without clear traceability, it is difficult to assess compliance, detect bias, or assign responsibility when an agent fails. This necessitates building systems with auditability and traceability as core features. Best practices include implementing immutable audit trails that log every agent action, decision, and interaction. These logs must capture not only the final output but also the agent's reasoning path, including the data inputs, tools used, and intermediate steps taken [25–28]. Emerging automated auditing tools, such as Anthropic's Petri [29], further assist researchers in systematically exploring model behaviors to identify misalignments before deployment.

5 Case Study: Agentic AI Security

5.1 Safety, Liability, and Economics of Agentic AI

Security will be the new safety in Agentic AI – where agents autonomously take decisions, security failures will manifest as safety failures. Agentic AI transforms the web experience from a data-and-content centric one to an experiential-and-execution centric world. Instead of supplying false or misleading data leading to execution failures, the agent will take charge of execution itself.

This means big changes for liability; taking charge of execution puts a higher legal onus on companies. The responsibility for decision quality and execution of decisions lies with the decision maker i.e. the AI agent, rather than the data supplier, or the system deployer. Due to this, software companies may no longer be able to escape legislative scrutiny as security failures manifest as safety failures. This is particularly evident when Agentic AI interacts with the physical world where medical devices are covered by significant legislation.

AI agents themselves fall under the broad definition of an "AI System"; So, what happens to shared liability when multiple automated systems interact unpredictably? Perhaps that is not as complex as the next question: who will patch the system when it fails?

Execution-time security failures are safety failures and will be dealt with as breaches of safety – e.g. misdiagnosis of cancer where the healthcare agent is in charge. This is due to a fundamental shift in the nature of the safety frameworks when considering security issues. Safety-as-security is different from conventional safety which deals with stochastic failure as against adversarial failure [30]. Current safety frameworks work on the basis of a design that is reviewed and assessed on the basis of an upfront safety capital. However, security issues will be discovered over the lifetime of the Agentic-Physical infrastructure and require continuous patching with an unpredictable maintenance cycle. The safety capital thus changes from an upfront and predictable one to a continuous and unpredictable one. This means companies will have to start thinking differently as well, and profit margins may be hard to pin down.

5.2 Safety-As-Security Challenges in Agentic AI

Agentic AI don't just generate data, they manage entire workflows and act on our behalf. To trust them, we must consider how Agentic AI changes power and control. The confidentiality of data flows and the integrity of decision fusion are key security properties. Agentic decision-integrity can be affected in several ways.

- **Goal-integrity:** Mimicry attacks can incrementally corrupt decision boundaries, which enables the gradual shift of agentic objectives from purposeful to influenced and undeclared ones – goal hijacking. An Agentic AI workflow can be nudged. For instance, an agent takes decisions in favor of a pharma equipment manufacturer rather than the patient.
- **Pattern integrity:** Over repeated interactions with adversarial agents, honest agents can end up learning harmful patterns. For instance, agentic anti-malware technologies may be persuaded by ransomware agent behavior to allow active encryption, thus crippling privacy-enhancing tools.
- **Input integrity:** Like their conventional ML counterparts, Agentic AI can also suffer from poisoned-well attacks where a lack of input integrity controls can permit poisoning of its knowledge base. For instance, adversarial content e.g. via fake tumor imagery poisons the agent's accumulated knowledge and beliefs.

The promise of Agentic AI is to enhance the gains in efficiency from content-generation to a whole host of new sectors via automated-execution. However, changing technology often leads to an erosion in security controls. In an authority-misuse attack an agent executes high-stakes decisions without oversight. The problems with Agentic AI will start once we start trusting the agent. But what security controls do we need to ensure transactional integrity? A trusted AI agent is the one that can damage, but trust is emergent rather than static.

6 Discussion

6.1 From Single Agent to Multi Agent Complexity

A central challenge in benchmarking agentic AI is the shift from evaluating an isolated model to evaluating a system of interacting agents [3]. Traditional language model evaluations emphasized static outputs, but agentic systems unfold through sequences of actions in changing environments. An agent is judged by its entire trajectory of planning, tool use, interaction, and adaptation. As agents are combined into larger workflows, evaluation must capture emergent behavior that arises from coordination and information exchange.

As systems graduate from a single agent to teams of agents, complexity grows because small errors can compound. If two competent agents each succeed most of the time, the probability of joint success across multiple steps can still fall sharply when errors propagate. Multi-agent benchmarks therefore focus not only on final task completion but also on the quality of coordination. MultiAgentBench [16] evaluates teams of language model agents on collaborative and competitive tasks and tracks indicators of coordination quality in addition to completion rates.

6.2 Beyond Accuracy and Latency

Although accuracy, throughput, and latency remain necessary, agentic AI demands additional metrics that better reflect real-world viability. Process-oriented metrics have emerged to diagnose failure modes within long traces. AgentQuest [13] introduces progress rate and repetition rate to detect whether an agent advances through a plan or falls into loops. The TRAIL [12] benchmark evaluates an agent's ability to locate and repair its own errors in long execution traces, which is critical for sustained autonomy.

Resiliency under failure is equally important. Effective systems should recognize when subtasks fail, recover, and continue safely. IT-focused evaluations now borrow reliability measures such as mean time to repair to quantify how quickly agents diagnose and remediate faults. Safety-focused benchmarks such as Agent-SafetyBench [14] and AgentHarm [15] probe adherence to guardrails under pressure and illuminate failure modes that accuracy alone would miss.

6.3 Cost Per Task

Practical deployment depends on whether an agent can deliver value at acceptable cost. Benchmarks increasingly report tokens, external tool calls, compute time, and energy as part of a normalized cost per task. Survey work recommends that evaluations include resource consumption to level the playing field between elaborate agent stacks and simpler baselines. Reporting cost alongside success and resiliency guides engineering toward solutions that are both accurate and efficient.

6.4 Choosing the Right Infrastructure

Infrastructure decisions shape agent behavior and therefore should be part of benchmarking. Edge deployment can reduce latency and preserve privacy, while cloud deployment provides elasticity for heavy reasoning. Many organizations adopt hybrid patterns. Evaluations should therefore measure the same task under edge, cloud, and hybrid configurations to capture context-dependent performance. Hardware also matters. GPUs, TPUs, and NPUs offer different advantages [31]. Benchmarks should capture how agents scale across these tiers and how gracefully they degrade when a tier is unavailable.

6.5 Responsible Agentic AI

As agent autonomy increases, responsible design principles become part of what it means to perform well. Robustness under partial failure is a first requirement. The question is whether the system detects an anomaly, chooses a safe fallback, and documents what happened. Process-centric evaluation that inspects traces is essential for this goal. Practical tracing frameworks already record intermediate actions, tool inputs and outputs, and state transitions so that reviewers can see exactly where a plan went wrong. Such traceability is foundational for both debugging and trust.

Auditability and explainability extend this idea across teams of agents. Evaluations should check for clear provenance of inputs, rationales that can be tied to evidence, and complete action logs that attribute changes to specific agents. Definitions of agentic AI for enterprise use stress the need for transparency and accountability so that operations teams can validate behavior and satisfy governance reviews [32].

6.6 Human in the Loop

Even strong agents should defer to humans for high-risk or irreversible actions. Responsible evaluation therefore asks whether an agent knows when to escalate and whether it respects policy boundaries. Safety-oriented benchmarks that simulate adversarial or ambiguous instructions are useful for testing whether an agent refuses unsafe actions and seeks human confirmation when appropriate. In enterprise workflows, the ability to pause, ask for approval, and present a concise summary with evidence is a capability to be measured.

6.7 Discussion Conclusion

Benchmarks for agentic AI must evolve from single-model accuracy toward system-level assessment. The move to multi-agent systems requires evaluation of interaction dynamics and coordination quality. Metrics should include end-to-end task completion, resiliency under failure, and cost per task. Infrastructure choices change the performance envelope and should be reflected in benchmark design. Responsible operation requires robustness, auditability with trace-based inspection, and clear human-in-the-loop safeguards. By integrating these elements, researchers can guide the field toward systems that are effective, efficient, and trustworthy.

7 Summary and Next Steps

Benchmarks are necessary for the broader adoption of Agentic AI systems. As discussed in this paper, the challenge of developing benchmarks for general Agentic AI systems is monumental. These benchmarks must go beyond individual building blocks like LLMs and evaluate the holistic performance of complex, multi-agent workflows.

The next phase in this journey needs to address both functional and non-functional requirements. Functional requirements focus on performance, efficiency, and correctness, while non-functional requirements encompass the critical domains of governance, security, and cost-effectiveness. The call to action for practitioners in industry and academia is to collaborate on a combined harness for evaluating general Agentic AI systems. This involves developing dynamic benchmarks that can evolve to prevent data contamination, creating standardized environments to ensure reproducibility, and integrating multi-objective evaluation frameworks that measure not just if a task was completed, but if it was completed safely, efficiently, and responsibly.

References

1. Anthropic: Building Effective Agents. https://www.anthropic.com/research/building-effective-agents. Accessed 16 Sept 2025
2. IBM: What is agentic AI?. https://www.ibm.com/think/topics/agentic-ai. Accessed 10 Oct 2025
3. IBM Research: The next frontier in AI evaluation: a survey of agent benchmarks. https://research.ibm.com/blog/AI-agent-benchmarks. Accessed 16 Sept 2025
4. Wang, L., et al.: A Survey on Evaluating Large Language Model based Agents. arXiv preprint arXiv:2308.11432v7 (2025)
5. Liu, X., et al.: AgentBench: evaluating LLMs as agents. arXiv preprint arXiv:2308.03688 (2023)
6. Jimenez, C.E., et al.: SWE-bench: can language models resolve real-world github issues?. In: Proceedings of the Twelfth International Conference on Learning Representations (2024)
7. Jha, S., et al.: ITBench: evaluating AI agents across diverse real-world IT Automation Tasks. arXiv preprint arXiv:2502.05352 (2025)
8. IBM Research: ITBench: a new yardstick to measure AI agents for IT automation. https://research.ibm.com/blog/it-agent-benchmark. Accessed 16 Sept 2025
9. Zhou, S., et al.: WebArena: a realistic web environment for building autonomous agents. arXiv preprint arXiv:2307.13854 (2023)
10. Smbatyan, K., et al.: Can AI agents design and implement drug discovery pipelines?. arXiv preprint arXiv:2504.19912 (2025)
11. Bloor Research: The Domino Effect - benchmarking agentic AI. https://www.bloorresearch.com/the-domino-effect-benchmarking-agentic-ai/. Accessed 16 Sept 2025
12. Patronus AI: Introducing TRAIL: A Benchmark for Agentic Evaluation. https://www.patronus.ai/blog/introducing-trail-a-benchmark-for-agentic-evaluation. Accessed 16 Sept 2025
13. Gioacchini, L., et al.: AgentQuest: A modular benchmark framework to measure progress and improve LLM agents. arXiv preprint arXiv:2406.06411 (2024)
14. Zhang, Z., et al.: Agent-SafetyBench: evaluating the safety of LLM agents. arXiv preprint arXiv:2412.14470 (2024)
15. Andriushchenko, M., et al.: AgentHarm: a benchmark for measuring harmfulness of LLM agents. arXiv preprint arXiv:2410.09024 (2024)

16. Zhu, K., et al.: MultiAgentBench: evaluating the collaboration and competition of LLM agents. arXiv preprint arXiv:2503.01935 (2025)
17. IBM: AI agent governance: Big challenges, big opportunities. https://www.ibm.com/think/insights/ai-agent-governance. Accessed 09 Oct 2025
18. NIST: AI Risk Management Framework. https://www.nist.gov/itl/ai-risk-management-framework. Accessed 09 Oct 2025
19. Tabassi, E.: Artificial Intelligence Risk Management Framework (AI RMF 1.0). NIST AI 100–1, National Institute of Standards and Technology, Gaithersburg, MD (2023). https://doi.org/10.6028/NIST.AI.100-1
20. Nemko: ISO/IEC JTC 1/SC 42. https://digital.nemko.com/standards/iso-iec-jtc-1sc-42. Accessed 09 Oct 2025
21. UNESCO: How ISO and IEC are developing international standards for the responsible adoption of AI. https://www.unesco.org/ethics-ai/en/articles/how-iso-and-iec-are-developing-international-standards-responsible-adoption-ai. Accessed 09 Oct 2025
22. ANSI: Using AI Responsibly: U.S. Leads Efforts to Develop ISO/IEC 42001. https://www.ansi.org/standards-news/all-news/12-27-23-using-ai-responsibly-us-leads-efforts-to-develop-iso-iec-42001. Accessed 09 Oct 2025
23. CX Network: How to use agentic AI in line with the EU AI Act. https://www.cxnetwork.com/artificial-intelligence/articles/how-to-use-agentic-ai-in-line-with-the-eu-ai-act. Accessed 09 Oct 2025
24. ISACA: The Growing Challenge of Auditing Agentic AI. https://www.isaca.org/resources/news-and-trends/industry-news/2025/the-growing-challenge-of-auditing-agentic-ai. Accessed 09 Oct 2025
25. KPMG: A foundation for agentic AI. https://kpmg.com/kpmg-us/content/dam/kpmg/pdf/2025/ai-governance-for-agentic-ai-era.pdf. Accessed 09 Oct 2025
26. Phelps: Agentic AI: Opportunities and Compliance Considerations for Community Banks. https://www.phelps.com/insights/agentic-ai-opportunities-and-compliance-considerations-for-community-banks.html. Accessed 09 Oct 2025
27. Rubrik: Take Control with Rubrik Agent Rewind. https://www.rubrik.com/insights/ai-issues-take-control-with-rubrik-agent-rewind. Accessed 09 Oct 2025
28. NexaStack: Ensure Trust with Traceability for Agentic AI. https://www.nexastack.ai/blueprints/agentic-ai-traceability/. Accessed 09 Oct 2025
29. Anthropic: Petri: Open-source auditing for AI systems. https://www.anthropic.com/research/petri-open-source-auditing. Accessed 09 Oct 2025
30. Gardiner, J., Cova, M., Nagaraja, S.: Command & control: understanding, denying and detecting - a review of malware C2 techniques, detection and defences. arXiv preprint arXiv:1408.1136 (2015)
31. Bigelow, S. J.: TechTarget WhatIs? GPUs vs. TPUs vs. NPUs: comparing AI hardware options. https://www.techtarget.com/whatis/feature/GPUs-vs-TPUs-vs-NPUs-Comparing-AI-hardware-options. Accessed 09 Oct 2025
32. Raveesh-Babu, S.: Advanced tracing and evaluation of generative AI agents using LangChain and Amazon SageMaker AI MLFlow. https://aws.amazon.com/blogs/machine-learning/advanced-tracing-and-evaluation-of-generative-ai-agents-using-langchain-and-amazon-sagemaker-ai-mlflow/. Accessed 09 Oct 2025

DataGenX: Generating Synthetic Relational Data from Annotated SQL Schemas

Ahmad Ghazal[1(✉)], Kenny Chan[1], Sunny Bains[1], and Hanumath Maduri[2]

[1] PingCAP, Inc., 440 N Wolfe Rd, Sunnyvale, CA 94085, USA
{ahmad.ghazal,chenqingjing,sunny.bains}@pingcap.com
[2] Workday, Pleasanton, USA
hanumath.maduri@workday.com

Abstract. Synthetic data generation is essential for database development, allowing for the simulation, benchmarking and testing of the customer workload in scenarios where real data is unavailable due to privacy, scale or accessibility constraints. In practice, developers often have only the database schema and a handful of statistics, such as table cardinalities, value distributions, number of distinct values, TOP-N values, and range-based histograms. Despite this common setting, existing tools fall short: benchmark-specific generators (e.g., TPC-H, TPC-C) are rigid and tied to fixed schemas; UI-based tools like Mockaroo ignore relational semantics; and model-based approaches such as SDV require access to real data to learn patterns.

We present DataGenX (part of the TiDB toolchain), a lightweight and flexible synthetic data generator designed for this under-served but common scenario. DataGenX operates directly on annotated SQL DDL, where comments are used to specify column-level statistics and inter-table relationships (e.g., foreign key join cardinalities). Then it generates synthetic data that conforms to these annotations, producing realistic and consistent datasets without requiring access to real data. DataGenX also supports multi-threaded row generation, where each thread produces a disjoint set of rows and writes to a separate file, enabling scalable and efficient data generation on multi-core systems.

To validate the fidelity of DataGenX, we reimplemented the TPC-C and TPC-H schemas using annotated DDL and generated data using DataGenX. We compared the resulting datasets to those produced by the official TPC data generators and DataGenX that achieved fidelity 99%, accurately reproducing distributions, key relationships and table sizes. This demonstrates DataGenX's capability to simulate realistic workloads purely from schema-level specifications and a small set of statistical annotations.

Keywords: Synthetic Data Generation · Declarative Data Generation · Query Optimizer Statistics · SQL Annotations

K. Chan—Main developer of DataGenX.

R. Nambiar and M. Poess (Eds.): TPCTC 2025, LNCS 16261, pp. 99–114, 2026.
https://doi.org/10.1007/978-3-032-18070-4_7

1 Introduction

Modern database systems are increasingly reliant on robust testing, simulation, and benchmarking to ensure correctness, performance, and scalability. A fundamental requirement in these processes is access to representative datasets that reflect realistic schema structures, data distributions, and inter-table relationships. However, acquiring such datasets is often challenging due to privacy restrictions, business sensitivity, or the simple unavailability of production data—especially in early-stage development environments.

Existing solutions for synthetic data generation fall short in key ways.

Benchmark-specific tools such as those from TPC-C [9] offer high-fidelity datasets (closely mimicking real data distributions and relationships), but they are tightly bound to fixed schemas and hardcoded generation logic, limiting their applicability to customized or evolving workloads. On the other end of the spectrum, user-interface–driven tools like Mockaroo [10] allow basic data generation from schema definitions but lack support for referential integrity and cross-table dependencies. Finally, model-based approaches such as SDV [7] require real data to learn from, making them unusable in greenfield development or privacy-sensitive contexts.

To bridge this gap, TiDB [8] introduced **DataGenX**, a schema-driven and annotation-based synthetic data generator. DataGenX allows developers to embed data generation logic directly into standard SQL DDL via structured comments. These annotations express a wide variety of statistical and relational properties, including:

- **Column-level distributions**: Developers can specify numerical distributions using expressions like `/*{{ rand.uniform(0, 10000) }}*/` to simulate continuous values or use value histograms and top-N lists for skewed distributions.
- **Boolean logic and conditionals**: Using `CASE` expressions, one can inject conditional variation—e.g., setting a discount to 0.0 for the first 2,100 rows, and a random value thereafter: `/*{{ case when rownum <= 2100 then 0.0 else rand.range(1,1000000)/100 end }}*/`.
- **Regular expression–based generation**: Text fields can be populated using patterns, such as `/*{{ rand.regex('[A-Z]{2}') }}*/` for U.S. state codes or `/*{{ rand.regex('[0-9a-zA-Z]{10,20}') }}*/` for alphanumeric strings.
- **Referential constraints and parent-child relationships**: DataGenX supports generating dependent tables using shared variables and derived table loops. For example, in modeling orders and order lines, an order row can define the number of associated line items via `@ol_cnt := rand.range_inclusive (5, 15)`, followed by a loop that generates exactly `@ol_cnt` rows in the child `order_line` table with consistent foreign key values.

By treating each row as an independent unit unless explicitly linked through shared variables or derived table rules, DataGenX can scale generation across threads or machines. While it does not take a single scale factor as input, its architecture supports generating large volumes of data efficiently—similar in spirit to the scale-out capabilities of TPC benchmarks—making it well-suited for both local testing and large-scale system evaluation.

We validate DataGenX by re-implementing the TPC-C [19] benchmark schema with annotations and show that the tool can accurately reproduce the dataset's structural and statistical properties. This includes key metrics such as table cardinalities, distribution shapes, and inter-table consistency, demonstrating that DataGenX can achieve high-fidelity simulation from schema-level specifications alone.

DataGenX provides a flexible, lightweight, and expressive solution for generating synthetic datasets, tailored to meet the needs of database developers, engine researchers, and system testers. By requiring nothing more than an annotated schema and high level statistics both of which are commonly available in practice—DataGenX fills an important gap in the ecosystem of data generation tools.

In addition to flexibility and fidelity, DataGenX is designed for performance at scale. It uses a multi-threaded runtime to parallelize row generation across available logical CPU cores. Each thread independently generates a subset of rows and writes its output to a separate file, achieving efficient utilization of hardware resources for large-scale data generation.

The rest of the paper is organized as follows. Section 2 reviews related work in synthetic data generation, highlighting the limitations of existing tools. Section 3 details the design and implementation of DataGenX, including the annotation syntax, data generation engine, and support for inter-table relationships. Section 4 presents an empirical evaluation of DataGenX using the TPC-C benchmark, demonstrating its ability to generate high-fidelity, large-scale synthetic datasets. We conclude with directions for future work in Sect. 5.

2 Prior Work

Synthetic data generation plays a central role in database system development, testing, and benchmarking. A wide range of techniques have been proposed, from benchmark-specific generators to declarative and machine-learning–based tools, but they vary considerably in scalability, realism, constraint fidelity, and usability. A recent comprehensive survey by Davila et al. [20] offers an in-depth examination of Tabular Data Synthesis (TDS), identifying key challenges such as handling missing values, imbalanced datasets, diverse column types, and preserving statistical correlations, temporal dependencies, and integrity constraints. The paper evaluates 37 tools against functional and non-functional requirements, providing guidance for tool selection and highlighting gaps in the data management capabilities of existing solutions.

Benchmark-specific generators like **TPC-H**, **TPC-DS**, and **TPC-C** produce large-scale datasets with known schemas but offer limited flexibility: they are tied to static schemas and distributions and lack support for constraint and statistical customization. **Star Schema Benchmark (SSB)** [13] (e.g., spatial [14] and NoSQL [15]) also remain tightly coupled to fixed schema designs.

While these tools are widely used in benchmarking, their lack of adaptability limits their usefulness for diverse application scenarios. Efforts such as [1,2] analyze how schema characteristics impact query performance, while proposals like [17] offer abstract, non-executable conceptual models. StarBench [17] introduces a schema-driven generator specific to SSB, but is narrowly focused.

UI-driven tools like **Mockaroo** [10] allow for schema-aware generation but provide minimal support for inter-table relationships or statistical accuracy. ML-driven systems like **SDV** [7] and commercial platforms like **Tonic.ai** [11] learn from real datasets to produce statistically faithful synthetic data, though they depend on access to sensitive real-world data—often unavailable in early-stage development or privacy-sensitive settings.

Declarative, academic tools such as **DataSynth** [4], **XData** [5], and **QAGen** [6] prioritize constraint satisfaction and query validity but often lack the scalability, usability, and schema generality needed for practical adoption. For example, **XData** supports SQL reasoning but scales poorly and has limited customization. **QAGen** is query-aware but specialized and non-open source. **DataSynth** supports constraint-based generation but may encounter scalability bottlenecks and constraint conflicts.

Several systems have explored schema- and workload-driven data synthesis. **PiGen**, proposed by Sanghi et al. [18], addresses a key limitation in prior data generators: the inability to honor projection cardinality constraints. **PiGen** employs linear programming and subspace partitioning strategies to enforce such constraints, along with symmetric refinement and workload decomposition techniques. This makes it well-suited for detecting optimizer bugs and evaluating performance in Big Data systems, though it does not target general-purpose schema flexibility.

Dscaler, introduced by Zhang and Tay [22] as part of the ASPECT framework, focuses on scaling empirical datasets while preserving statistical similarity. Users can apply a sequence of "tweaking" operations to enforce specific dataset properties. While effective for scaling real-world datasets for benchmarking, it requires an original dataset and is not schema-independent like **DataGenX**.

Rabl et al. [21] propose a high-throughput big data synthesis engine aimed at stress-testing large-scale systems. Their work emphasizes performance and volume, especially at the bit-level, but does not support schema-level constraints or flexible, user-defined generation interfaces.

These efforts highlight a tradeoff landscape: tools offering high statistical fidelity often require real data and lack schema generality, while declarative tools support constraints but struggle with scalability or usability. A persistent gap exists in delivering a scalable, schema-independent, declarative tool that does not rely on sample data but still supports realistic and constraint-aware dataset generation.

To address this, we introduce **DataGenX**, a system built upon the open-source dbgen engine (distinct from the **TPC-H** version). **DataGenX** supports fully annotated DDLs, large-scale generation, inter-table constraints (e.g., primary and foreign keys), and optimizer-relevant statistics. It features a SQL-like declarative interface, requires no access to real datasets, generalizes across schemas, and is fully open source—positioning it as a scalable and practical solution for modern benchmarking and testing workflows.

To provide a more scalable and user-friendly solution, this paper introduces **DataGenX**, a system built upon the open-source generator formerly known as `dbgen` (see https://github.com/kennytm/dbgen). The new name, `DataGenX`, is used to distinguish it from the unrelated `dbgen` tool in the TPC-H benchmark kit. `DataGenX` enables large-scale data generation, supports inter-table constraints (including primary and foreign keys), and captures optimizer-relevant statistics. It features a declarative, SQL-like interface, requires no access to sample data, is schema-independent, and remains fully open source.

In Table 1 defines key features of data generation tools. "Scale" refers to their ability to produce small to very large data sets. "Constraints" supports integrity rules like primary and foreign keys. "Sample" shows whether real or training data is needed. "Statistics" describes the ability to control column-level distributions such as top-N values or histograms. "Schema" specifies whether tools support arbitrary schemas or rely on fixed or partial ones. "Programmatic" denotes the use of scripted or compiled code, as seen in TPC benchmarks. The terms "Limited" and "Weak" signal partial or minimal feature support.

Table 1. Comparison of Synthetic Data Generation Tools by Functionality and Accessibility

Tool	Functionality				Flexibility & Access		
	Scale	Constraints	Sample	Stats	Schema	API	Open Source
DataGenX	✓	✓	✗	✓	Any	Declarative	✓
TPC Benchmarks	✓	✗	✗	✗	Fixed	Programmatic	✓
DataSynth	~	~	✗	~	Fixed	Declarative	✓
XData	✗	✓	✓	~	Partial	Scripted	✗
QAGen	✗	✓	✓	✗	Partial	Query-Aware	✗
SDV	~	~	✓	✓	Any	Python SDK	✓
Mockaroo	✗	✗	✗	~	Any	GUI + API	~
Tonic.ai	✓	✓	✓	✓	Any	GUI + SDK	✗

Legend:, ✓= Supported, ✗= Not Supported, ~= Limited;

As shown in Table 1, DataGenX fills an important gap by combining declarative control, support for schema-level statistics and constraints, and performance-scalable generation—all while avoiding the need for real datasets. This makes it uniquely positioned for realistic workload simulation, testing, and optimizer behavior reproduction.

3 DataGenX

3.1 Specification

DataGenX generates synthetic relational data by interpreting annotated SQL `CREATE TABLE` statements, referred to as *templates*. Each template defines the schema of a single table and embeds data generation logic within structured comments. These annotations, written in either `/*{{ ... }}*/` or `{{ ... }}` blocks, provide row-wise generation expressions evaluated dynamically for every row.

Annotation Syntax. Annotations specify how values should be produced for associated columns. For example:

```
CREATE TABLE "table" (
    "id"    INTEGER,              /*{{ rownum }}*/
    "name"  CHAR(40),             /*{{ rand.regex('[a-zA-Z ]{40}') }}*/
    UNIQUE KEY ("id")
);
```

In this example:

- `rownum` yields the row number (starting from 1).
- `rand.regex(...)` generates a random string matching the specified regular expression.

During generation, DataGenX evaluates these expressions to produce `INSERT` statements or data files, such as:

```
INSERT INTO "table" VALUES
(1, 'ExampleStringOne'),
(2, 'ExampleStringTwo'),
...
```

Expression Semantics. The annotation language supports a rich SQL-inspired expression syntax, including:

- **Literals**: Integers, floats, booleans, and strings.
- **Operators**: Arithmetic (`+`, `-`, `*`, `/`), logical (`AND`, `OR`, `NOT`), comparison (`=`, `<>`, `<`, `>`, `<=`, `>=`), and bitwise (`&`, `|`, `^`, `~`).
- **Control Flow**: `CASE WHEN` expressions for conditional logic.
- **Functions**: A variety of built-in functions for random data generation, string manipulation, date/time operations, and more.

Variable Binding. Variables can be declared and reused across columns or rows using the `@var := ...` assignment syntax. This allows the expression of complex generation patterns, such as correlated columns or derived table semantics. For instance:

```
CREATE TABLE correlated (
    "a" BOOLEAN NOT NULL,        /*{{ @flag := rand.bool(0.3) }}*/
    "b" BOOLEAN NOT NULL,        /*{{ @flag }}*/
);
```

In this example, both columns `a` and `b` will have the same randomly generated boolean value for each row.

Supported Functions and Features. DataGenX provides a comprehensive set of functions and features for data generation:

- **Random Generators**:
  - `rand.range(min, max)`: Uniform integer in [min, max).
  - `rand.uniform(min, max)`: Uniform float in [min, max).
  - `rand.bool(p)`: Boolean with probability `p` of being `TRUE`.
  - `rand.zipf(n, s)`: Zipfian distribution over `n` elements with exponent `s`.
  - `rand.log_normal(mu, sigma)`: Log-normal distribution with parameters `mu` and `sigma`.
  - `rand.regex(pattern)`: Random string matching the given regular expression.
  - `rand.uuid()`: Random UUID generation.
  - `rand.weighted(ARRAY[w_1, ..., w_n])`: Returns a random integer `i` ($1 \leq$ `i` $\leq$ `n`) with probability proportional to `w_i`. Useful for simulating categorical skew.
- **String Functions**:
  - `substring(str, from, len)`: Extract substring.
  - `char_length(str)`: Character length of a string.
  - `overlay(str placing replacement from pos for len)`: Replace substring.
- **Date and Time Functions**:
  - `current_timestamp`: Current timestamp.
  - `INTERVAL n UNIT`: Time interval.
  - `rand.u31_timestamp()`: Random timestamp between 1970-01-01 and 2038-01-19.
- **Array Functions**:
  - `ARRAY[...]`: Array construction.
  - `generate_series(start, end, step)`: Generate a series of numbers.
  - `rand.shuffle(array)`: Shuffle an array.
- **Miscellaneous**:
  - `coalesce(v1, v2, ...)`: First non-NULL value.
  - `debug.panic(...)`: Trigger a runtime error with a message.

Supported Data Types. DataGenX supports a rich set of SQL-compatible data types essential for modeling realistic relational datasets. Supported types include: *NULL* values, with explicit support for nullable columns; *numerics*, including booleans, 64-bit integers (`i64`), and 64-bit floating-point values (`f64`); *strings*, which are treated as binary data but interpreted as UTF-8 when possible; *date/time values*, limited to UTC timestamps; *time intervals*, with resolution ranging up to calendar weeks; and *arrays*, including heterogeneous arrays of the above types. This comprehensive type system enables the simulation of a wide range of production-grade schemas, including transactional (e.g., TPC-C) and analytical (e.g., TPC-H) workloads.

3.2 Optimizer Statistics

A central insight in DataGenX is that database optimizer statistics offer a compact and meaningful representation of a dataset. Modern query optimizers rely on these statistics to make planning decisions such as join orderings, index selections, and access paths. By reproducing these statistics synthetically, we can simulate the optimizer's behavior and regenerate execution plans that closely resemble those observed in real systems.

Our approach leverages the annotation constructs described in the previous section to encode key statistics about tables and columns directly into the schema template. These annotations then guide synthetic data generation in a way that aligns with the statistical expectations of the optimizer.

We assume a generic model for optimizer statistics that includes:

- **Table-level statistics:** The number of rows in each table.
- **Column and index statistics:**
  - **Top-N values:** A list of the most frequent values in a column, along with their frequencies.
  - **Histograms:** A set of non-overlapping value ranges with associated row counts.
  - **Number of distinct values (NDV):** The number of unique values within each histogram bucket.

The following annotated template demonstrates how Top-N values and histogram buckets with NDV constraints can be encoded:

```
create table t (
    pk bigint unsigned primary key {{ rownum }},
    val bigint unsigned not null {{
        case rand.weighted(array[10, 12, 14, 14, 14])
            when 1 then 0
            when 2 then 1
            when 3 then div(rand.range(0, 3) * (10 - 4), 3 - 1) + 4
            when 4 then div(rand.range(0, 4) * (21 - 11), 4 - 1) + 11
            when 5 then div(rand.range(0, 3) * (36 - 22), 3 - 1) + 22
        end
    }}
);
```

This expression models the following statistical profile:

Low Bound	High Bound	Count	NDV
0	0	10	1
1	1	12	1
4	10	14	3
11	21	14	4
22	36	14	3

Description:

- The `CASE WHEN` block uses standard SQL semantics to assign different generation logic based on weighted selection.
- `rand.weighted(array)` takes a list of non-negative weights and returns an integer $k \in [1, N]$, with probability proportional to the weight at position k.
- For Top-N values (e.g., 0 and 1), the corresponding branches return fixed constants.
- For histogram buckets, where a value must be drawn uniformly from M distinct values in a numeric range $[L, U]$, the expression:

  ```
  div(rand.range(0, M) * (U - L), M - 1) + L
  ```

  maps M (NDV) discrete values to evenly spread integers within $[L, U]$. For example:
  - Bucket [4–10] with NDV=3 yields {4, 7, 10}
  - Bucket [11–21] with NDV=4 yields {11, 14, 17, 21}
  - Bucket [22–36] with NDV=3 yields {22, 29, 36}
- This construction ensures the correct number of distinct values per bucket and aligns generated frequencies with the intended distribution. When the number of rows increases or decreases, each bucket's contribution remains proportional to its relative row count, i.e., `count[i] / total-count`, where `count[i]` is the number of rows in the ith bucket.

Running this template with 64 rows will yield a synthetic column distribution that closely matches the optimizer's statistical model—supporting high-fidelity testing, cost-based query planning, and execution plan verification.

3.3 Implementation

Each annotation is applied row-by-row and can be done independently. This enables DataGenX to parallelize generation across threads or machines. By default, the number of threads is bounded by the number of logical CPU cores. Each thread is assigned a distinct range of rows to generate using an independent random seed and writes its output to a separate file. This design ensures scalable and reproducible data generation with minimal synchronization overhead.

Figure 1 illustrates the overall architecture of DataGenX. It highlights the annotation parser, the parallel data generation engine, and the configuration layer, showing how input DDL files are processed and transformed into scalable synthetic datasets. The architecture is designed for modularity and performance, enabling seamless integration into test pipelines.

Configuration. DataGenX provides several configuration parameters that control the generation process. These include the number of rows to generate, a random seed (with a default value if unspecified), and the output format—either CSV or SQL DML. When the DML option is used, users can also specify how

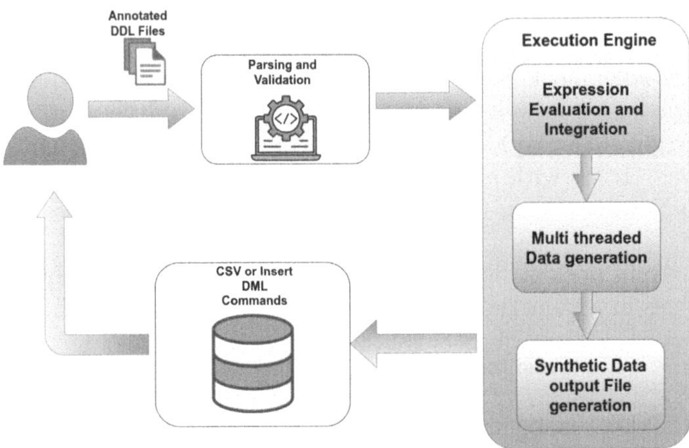

Fig. 1. DataGenX Architecture.

many rows to group per INSERT statement. While DML is useful for immediate loading into databases, the CSV format is a more scalable choice for large datasets and is recommended for performance benchmarking scenarios. All configuration options can be specified either through a configuration file or directly via command-line arguments, enabling flexible integration into test workflows and CI pipelines.

Parsing and Validation. Input SQL DDL files are parsed using a custom parser built with the PEG-based PEST [3] framework. This parser processes annotated column definitions and performs validation checks, including syntax correctness and annotation completeness. For each column, if no annotation is explicitly provided, DataGenX falls back to a default behavior of generating random values matching the column's data type. Errors in annotation syntax or unsupported constructs are reported clearly to aid rapid correction and iteration.

Execution Engine. Each annotated table template is processed row-by-row, with expressions dynamically evaluated to generate synthetic data. By default, generation is parallelized across multiple threads—bounded by the number of logical CPUs on the host machine. Each thread is seeded independently and assigned a disjoint row range. Threads operate in isolation and write their output to separate files to minimize synchronization overhead and I/O contention. This design allows DataGenX to scale with available hardware and produce large datasets efficiently.

Expression Evaluation and Integration. At runtime, each annotation expression is compiled into an executable form using TiDB's native expression evaluation engine. This ensures consistency between the semantics of synthetic data generation and the execution logic within TiDB itself. Built-in functions include numeric, string, date/time, and array operations, as well as probabilistic and histogram-based generators. Users can define variable bindings, use CASE logic, or include regex-based constraints to generate highly customized data profiles.

Generation Flow. The full generation workflow begins by parsing the schema and resolving annotations. Next, metadata is initialized based on user configuration, and the workload is distributed across threads. Each thread executes the data generation loop, evaluates expressions, and streams output in the configured format. The system ensures both consistency and performance through stateless execution, isolated file writes, and deterministic random seeds. The final result is a set of realistic, annotated, and scalable synthetic datasets

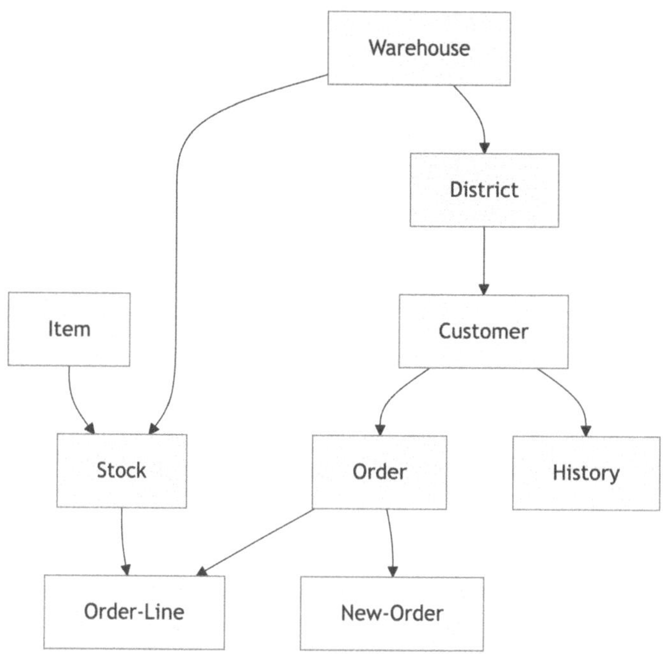

Fig. 2. TPC-C Schema.

4 Evaluations

4.1 Overview of TPC-TC

TPC-C is a standard OLTP benchmark from the Transaction Processing Council that simulates a wholesale supplier with multiple warehouses. The overall schema is shown in Fig. 2. It models a transactional workload across nine tables—Warehouse, District, Customer, Order, Order-Line, New-Order, History, Stock, and Item—connected by ten foreign key relationships.

The schema scales with the number of warehouses (W), with most tables growing linearly except Item, which is fixed at 100,000 rows. For each warehouse, there are 10 districts, 30,000 customers and orders, over 300,000 order lines, around 9,000 new orders at any time, and 100,000 stock items. History is insert-only and grows with transaction volume.

In addition to its structural complexity, the TPC-C schema includes a rich variety of SQL data types. It uses integers for identifiers, quantities, and scaling parameters; fixed-length and variable-length strings (e.g., CHAR and VARCHAR) for names, addresses, and status fields; and DATE/TIMESTAMP columns to track transaction times and delivery dates. This mix reflects common patterns in production OLTP databases and challenges data generators to produce syntactically valid and semantically coherent values. For example, realistic name fields, timestamps within valid business ranges, and numeric relationships (e.g., totals and quantities) must all be preserved.

TPC-C defines five transactions—New-Order, Payment, Order-Status, Delivery, and Stock-Level—that stress the system with varied access patterns: read-only (Item), read-write (Warehouse, District, Customer, Stock), queue-like (New-Order), delayed updates (Order, Order-Line), and insert-only (History).

This combination of schema scaling, transactional diversity, and varied data types makes TPC-C a comprehensive and realistic benchmark for evaluating DatagenX's ability to generate complex, high-fidelity transactional datasets.

4.2 Test Setup

We ran the benchmark on a TiDB cluster running version 8.5. The cluster consists of three TiDB servers, which are stateless nodes responsible for receiving client requests, parsing SQL, performing optimization, and generating execution plans. Each TiDB server is provisioned with 16 CPU cores and 128 GB of RAM. The cluster also includes three TiKV (row-store) nodes, each equipped with 16 CPU cores, 64 GB of RAM, and 1 TB of local disk storage.

To evaluate the fidelity and performance of synthetic data generation, we used two tools to generate TPC-C datasets at a scale of 80 warehouses. This corresponds to approximately 5 GB of raw data, which is sufficiently large to demonstrate relational integrity and statistical consistency, while remaining small enough to enable repeatable experimentation and result verification.

The first dataset was generated using **DataGenX**, configured to run with 8 parallel threads. DataGenX produced the synthetic TPC-C dataset in CSV format, which was then ingested into the TiDB cluster using its native bulk import utilities. The second dataset was produced using the **BenchmarkSQL** tool [12]. We chose BenchmarkSQL because it is a widely used, open-source TPC-C implementation that adheres to the official TPC-C benchmark specification. It serves as a practical wrapper around the standard logic and is compatible with modern database systems, making it a reproducible and accessible baseline for comparison. BenchmarkSQL was configured to generate the same 80-warehouse dataset, which was also loaded into the same TiDB cluster for comparison.

To illustrate DataGenX's annotation model, consider a simplified example involving the `order` and `order_line` tables. In the DDL snippet below, each field in the table is annotated using structured comments that specify how its values should be generated. Local variables (denoted by `@`) are assigned values during row generation and reused to ensure referential consistency across tables. For instance, the warehouse ID `o_w_id` is computed and saved as `@w_id`, which is then reused in the `order_line` table as `ol_w_id`. The variable `@o_entry_d` stores the order timestamp and is later reused as the delivery timestamp for fulfilled orders.

```
create table order (
  o_w_id      integer not null,   /*{{ @w_id := div(rownum-1, 30000)+1
    }}*/
  o_d_id      integer not null,   /*{{ @d_id := mod(div(rownum-1, 3000),
     10)+1 }}*/
  o_id        integer not null,   /*{{ @o_id := mod(rownum-1, 3000)+1
    }}*/
  o_c_id      integer,            /*{{ @c_ids[@o_id] }}*/
  o_carrier_id integer,           /*{{ case when @o_id <= 2100 then rand
    .range_inclusive(1, 10) end }}*/
  o_ol_cnt    integer,            /*{{ @ol_cnt := rand.range_inclusive
    (5, 15) }}*/
  o_entry_d   timestamp           /*{{ @o_entry_d := current_timestamp
    }}*/
);

/*{{ for each row of order generate @ol_cnt rows of order_line }}*/

create table order_line (
  ol_w_id      integer not null,  /*{{ @w_id }}*/
  ol_d_id      integer not null,  /*{{ @d_id }}*/
  ol_o_id      integer not null,  /*{{ @o_id }}*/
  ol_number    integer not null,  /*{{ subrownum }}*/
  ol_delivery_d timestamp,        /*{{ case when @o_id <= 2100 then
    @o_entry_d end }}*/
  ol_amount    decimal(6,2),      /*{{ if @o_id > 2100 then rand.range
    (1,1000000)/100 else 0.0 }}*/
  ol_supply_w_id integer,         /*{{ @w_id }}*/
  ol_quantity integer,            /*{{ 5 }}*/
  ol_dist_info char(24)           /*{{ rand.regex('[0-9a-zA-Z]{24}')
    }}*/
);
```

The `for each row` construct specifies a parent-child relationship between `order` and `order_line`, where each `order` row generates multiple `order_line` rows. The variable `subrownum` automatically tracks the line number (from 1 to `@ol_cnt`) within each group, enabling realistic multi-line order structures.

This example demonstrates how DataGenX combines row-indexed variables, reuse of local context, and hierarchical generation to model relational structures faithfully.

4.3 Results

To assess the fidelity of the synthetic data produced by DataGenX, we conducted a series of validation checks comparing its output against the reference dataset generated by BenchmarkSQL [12]. These validations focused on structural consistency and relational integrity. Specifically, we verified (i) row counts per table to ensure correct table sizes, and (ii) distinct value counts for selected key columns to validate distribution and uniqueness constraints. DataGenX's generated data matched the BenchmarkSQL dataset on all these metrics, confirming that annotated DDL specifications in DataGenX can reproduce relational structures and cardinalates with high fidelity.

We evaluated the output of DataGenX against a reference dataset generated using BenchmarkSQL [12] to assess both the fidelity of the generated data and its suitability for performance benchmarking.

Data Validation. We conducted a series of structural and integrity checks on the DataGenX-generated dataset. These included (i) row count comparisons across all tables, (ii) distinct value counts to verify key cardinalities, and (iii) primary-foreign key join validations. The results were consistent with those obtained from the BenchmarkSQL dataset, confirming that DataGenX accurately reproduces the relational structure, cardinalities, and data distributions defined by the TPC-C schema.

Benchmark Execution. To assess runtime suitability, we ran the official TPC-C workload on datasets generated by both DataGenX and BenchmarkSQL, each scaled to 30 warehouses. The benchmark was configured to run for 30 s after a warm-up period, simulating concurrent transaction execution across active terminals.

Transaction throughput was measured in TPM-C (Transactions Per Minute for New-Order table), the standard TPC-C performance metric that counts successfully completed `New-Order` transactions under load. As shown in Fig. 3, both datasets yielded comparable throughput. DataGenX achieved an average of 19,749 TPM-C across four runs, while BenchmarkSQL averaged 19,762 TPM-C. This validates that DataGenX-generated data can support realistic OLTP performance evaluation.

Performance Comparison. In addition to data fidelity, we evaluated the runtime performance of DataGenX relative to BenchmarkSQL for generating the TPC-C dataset at a scale of 80 warehouses. Both tools were configured to use 8 parallel threads on the same hardware environment. DataGenX completed the data generation in approximately 30 s, whereas BenchmarkSQL required around 50 s for the same dataset. This 40% reduction in generation time is likely attributable to differences in implementation languages—DataGenX is written

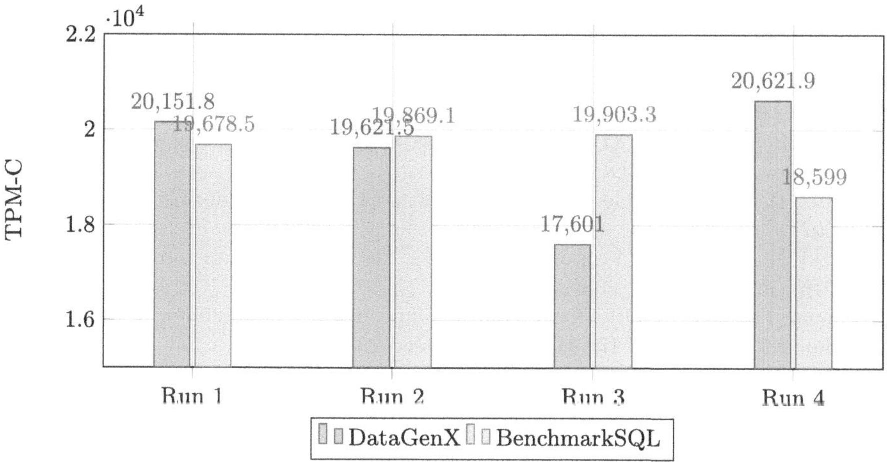

Fig. 3. TPM-C Results for TPC-C at 30 Warehouses

in Rust and benefits from low-level memory safety and compilation to native code, while BenchmarkSQL is implemented in Java and incurs additional runtime overhead. These results demonstrate that DataGenX not only achieves high-fidelity dataset generation but also provides significant performance advantages for large-scale workloads.

5 Future Work

Looking ahead, several directions may enhance the capabilities of DataGenX. One potential extension is the automation of annotations, where schema definitions and collected statistics can be analyzed to infer appropriate generation rules. This would streamline the setup process and reduce the manual effort required to simulate realistic datasets. Another promising area is benchmark verification—particularly for complex suites like TPC-DS—where integrated mechanisms could ensure the synthetically generated data satisfies both structural and statistical expectations. Finally, as datasets continue to grow in size, column-level parallelism may be introduced to complement row-level threading, allowing high-volume columns to be generated concurrently for even faster throughput.

References

1. Rabl, T., Poess, M., Jacobsen, H.A., O'Neil, P., O'Neil, E.: Variations of the star schema benchmark to test the effects of data skew on query performance (2013). https://doi.org/10.1145/2479871.2479927
2. Sanchez, J.: A review of star schema benchmark, arXiv preprint arXiv:1606.00295 (2016)

3. Tiselice, D.: "pest: The Elegant Parser," pest.rs. https://pest.rs/. Accessed 19 May 2025
4. Gillenwater, J., et al.: DataSynth: generating realistic synthetic graph data. In: VLDB (2020)
5. Joglekar, M., et al.: XData: testing data-intensive applications with generated query-aware data. VLDB J. (2015)
6. Arab, B., et al.: QAGen: generating query-aware test databases. In: SIGMOD (2007)
7. Patki, N., Wedge, R., Veeramachaneni, K.: The synthetic data vault. In: NeurIPS (2016). https://github.com/sdv-dev/SDV
8. Huang, D., et al.: TiDB. Proc. VLDB Endow. **13**(12), 3072–3084 (2020). https://doi.org/10.14778/3415478.3415535. Accessed 25 Feb 2022
9. TPC Current Specs/Source. www.tpc.org/tpc_documents_current_versions/current_specifications5.asp
10. Mockaroo. https://mockaroo.com
11. Tonic.ai. https://www.tonic.ai
12. BenchmarkSQL: A TPC-C like benchmark for relational databases. https://github.com/benchmarksql/benchmarksql. Accessed 29 May 2025
13. Star Schema Benchmark (2009). https://www.cs.umb.edu/~poneil/StarSchemaB.PDF
14. The Spatial Star Schema Benchmark (2011). https://api.semanticscholar.org/CorpusID:53418785
15. Dehdouh, K., Boussaid, O., Bentayeb, F.: Columnar NoSQL Star Schema Benchmark (2014). https://api.semanticscholar.org/CorpusID:28006623
16. Conceptual Model for Star Schema Data Warehouse (2023). https://api.semanticscholar.org/CorpusID:259626460
17. Hanumath Rao. StarBench: A Schema-Driven Data Generator for the Star Schema Benchmark. Proceedings of TPC Technology Conference (TPC-TC) (2024). https://github.com/HanumathRao/StarBench
18. Sanghi, A., Salihoglu, S., Jorge, T., Miller, R.J.: Projection-compliant database generation. Proc. VLDB Endow. **15**(12), 3562–3574 (2022)
19. TPC-C Homepage. Tpc.org (2025). www.tpc.org/tpcc/
20. Davila R, M.F., Groen, S., Panse, F., Wingerath, W.: Navigating tabular data synthesis research understanding user needs and tool capabilities. ACM SIGMOD Rec. **53**(4), 18–35 (2025). https://doi.org/10.1145/3712311.3712315
21. Rabl, T., Danisch, M., Frank, M., Schindler, S., Jacobsen, H.-A.: Just can't get enough: synthesizing big data. In: Proceedings of the 2015 ACM SIGMOD International Conference on Management of Data (SIGMOD 2015), pp. 1457–1462. Association for Computing Machinery, New York (2015). https://doi.org/10.1145/2723372.2735378
22. Zhang, J.W., Tay, Y.C.: Dscaler: synthetically scaling a given relational database. Proc. VLDB Endow. **9**(14), 1671–1682 (2016). https://doi.org/10.14778/3007328.3007333

DiStash: A Disaggregated Multi-stash Transactional Key-Value Store

Yiming Gao[1], Hieu Nguyen[2], Jun Li[2], and Shahram Ghandeharizadeh[1(✉)]

[1] University of Southern California, Los Angeles, CA 90089, USA
{gaoyiming,shahram}@usc.edu

[2] eBay Inc., 2025 Hamilton Avenue, San Jose, CA 95125, USA
{hieunguyen,junli5}@ebay.com

Abstract. A stash is a storage medium such as Dynamic Random Access Memory (DRAM), Solid State Disk (SSD), Hard Disk Drive (HDD), or Non-Volatile Memory (NVM). This paper presents a disaggregated transactional key-value (KV) store, DiStash, that governs KVs cross pools of stash types. It enables an application to use a single transaction to read and write different copies of one or more key-value pairs across the different pools of stashes. It simplifies the application logic by (a) preventing undesirable race conditions that may cause copies of data across different stash pools to become inconsistent and/or (b) failures that may result in loss of key-value pairs. A configuration of DiStash may use a pool of stashes as either ephemeral or durable storage. The application dictates whether the content of its participating stashes are inclusive (replicated) or exclusive (tiered). We implement a DiStash by extending FoundationDB. We quantify the tradeoffs with its design decisions using microbenchmarks and eBay's production workload. We open source our implementation at https://github.com/ebay-USC/DiStash.

Keywords: Disaggregated Storage · Transaction · Consistency

1 Introduction

Advances in computing, networking, and mass storage devices have introduced disaggregation of storage. Dynamic Random Access Memory (DRAM) [3,24], Solid State Disk (SSD) [4,7], Hard Disk Drive (HDD) [12,18,31], and alternative forms of Non-Volatile Memory (NVM) [30,33] including NVDIMM [5,22,23] are a type of stash that offer different speed, storage capacity, failure characteristics, and price points [13,14]. To provide online access to a large data set, an application may construct pools of stash types. It may either duplicate or migrate data across the different pools with the objective to maximize the number of references to the pool with the fastest stash. This principle is the cornerstone of cache-augmented database management systems [1,15,26–28], load balancing techniques using a front-end cache [9,20], and hierarchical storage structures [6,10,35]. A challenge of such systems is how to maintain copies of

R. Nambiar and M. Poess (Eds.): TPCTC 2025, LNCS 16261, pp. 115–133, 2026.
https://doi.org/10.1007/978-3-032-18070-4_8

data consistent across different stash pools. The current practice of using different transactional storage managers with different pools may result in undesirable race conditions that cause copies of the data to become inconsistent. This means the value of a data item may reflect different values produced by the execution of different transactions [17,32].

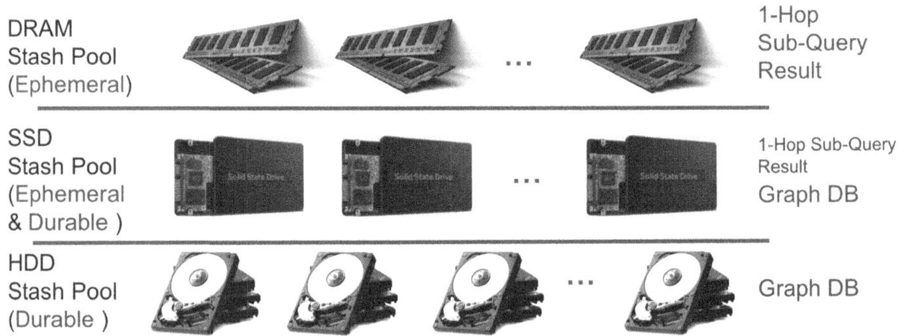

Fig. 1. DiStash with three pools of stashes: DRAM, SSD, and HDD. The pool of DRAM stashes is for ephemeral storage of 1-hop sub-query results [27]. The pool of HDD stashes is for durable storage of graph data. The pool of SSD stashes is ephemeral storage for graph data and durable storage for 1-hop sub-query results. A graph query processor may lookup sub-query results in either DRAM or SSD, and process queries using either SSD or HDD.

DiStash[1] is a disaggregated software architecture that builds upon the FoundationDB [36,37]. It enables its application to manage data across different stash pools using one transaction. The stash pools may be scattered across different data centers. A configuration of DiStash may specify a different degree of replication for data in a stash pool. This is to tolerate failures of stashes in that pool. An application may maintain a copy of the data on different stash types as illustrated in Fig. 1.

A stash type may be volatile or non-volatile, see the x-axis of Fig. 2. While a volatile stash such as DRAM loses its data after a power recycle, a non-volatile stash preserves its data. A DiStash deployment supports the designation of a stash type's operational mode as ephemeral or durable, see the y-axis of Fig. 2. Ephemeral may provide the illusion of an infinite amount of storage space by maintaining a subset of data and evicting others. Examples include a cache manager such as memcached [25], Kosar [11], or Redis [2]. Durable maintains data permanently and has a fixed storage capacity. Once it acknowledges storage of a key-value pair, the key-value pair persists. Examples include POSIX-compliant file systems such as EXT2 and database management systems, DBMSs, such as SQLite.

[1] DiStash is a play on the word "destash" which means to declutter or switch locations.

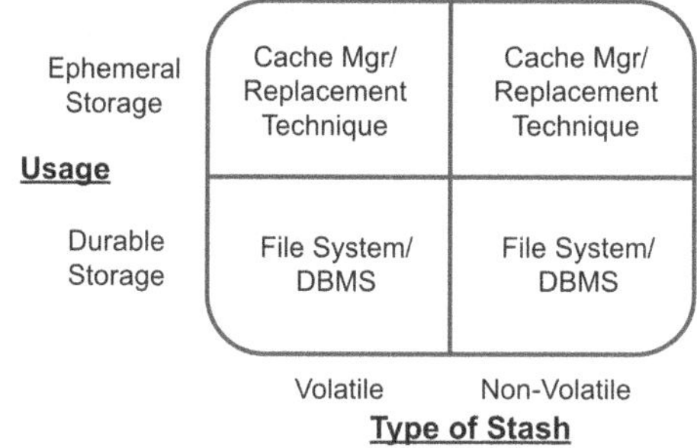

Fig. 2. A taxonomy of stash types and their usage.

Ephemeral and durable behave differently once their storage capacity is exhausted. Should the application attempt to insert additional data, ephemeral may delete perviously inserted key-value pairs to free space for the new key-value pair. Durable returns an error, e.g., ENOSPC (Error No SPaCe) with EXT2 and SQLITE_FULL with SQLite.

Contributions of this paper include:

1. DiStash, a transactional storage manager that supports pools of stashes each with a different number of instances and degree of replication. The stashes may be spread across multiple data centers. Section 3.
2. A DiStash transaction may read and write data from different pools of stashes. Section 3.2.
3. An implementation of DiStash using FoundationDB [36,37]. It may be deployed across multiple data centers. Section 4.
4. An evaluation of two DiStash deployments across 3 data centers using eBay production workload. Section 5.
5. We open source our software at https://www.github.com/ebay-USC/DiStash.

The rest of this paper is organized as follows. Section 2 motivates DiStash by presenting several use cases of it. Subsequently, we describe each of the above contributions in turn. Section 6 presents related work. Brief conclusions and future research directions are presented in Sect. 7.

2 Motivation: Applications of DiStash

DiStash has wide applicability described by the following use cases.

2.1 Cache-Augmented Data Stores

DiStash may be used to implement cache augmented data stores [27,28] in support of read dominated workloads such as social networking [28] or fraud detection [26]. It may consist of 2 stash pools. SSD for durable storage of data used for query processing. DRAM for ephemeral storage of query results for their fast lookup with repeat queries. Conceptually, the data on the different stashes is inclusive (replicated). However, the physical representation of data is exclusive (tiered) because the result of queries is different than the data used to process those queries. With eBay's production workload, a cache-augmented graph database lowers 95th and 99th percentile of query response times by at least 2x and 1.63x, respectively [27].

Section 3.1 presents cache-augmented data stores in greater detail. Briefly, an update may be required to modify data on SSD and the impacted query results in DRAM. DiStash enables the application to perform both in one transaction. Section 3.2 highlights the significance of using one transaction. It shows with multiple transactions to manage data across different pools of stashes, undesirable race conditions may cause copies of data across these stash pools to reflect different values produced by different transactions. DiStash frees the developer to focus on the application requirement instead of identifying the different race conditions and writing software to prevent them. Writing software is expensive because it must be designed, developed, tested, and maintained. DiStash eliminates this expense.

2.2 Load Balancing

A challenge of using a pool of n SSD stashes is uneven distribution of load across individual stashes [9,20]. While data placement schemes help balance an aggregate load, they do not balance the dynamic load. Hotspots may occur with a transient skewed access pattern. One way to balance load is to use a small front-end stash (a cache) for frequently accessed data items [9]. An implementation of this solution has been shown to improve throughput by 3–10x [20]. The front-end stash must be fast enough to keep the n slow SSD stashes busy. While a skewed access pattern negatively impacts the load balancing of the (n) slow stashes, it simultaneously enhances the effectiveness of the fast frontend stash in two key ways. Firstly, it achieves a higher hit rate. Secondly, it results in a more balanced distribution of uncached data across the (n) slow stashes. It has been shown that the cache is required to only store $O(n \ log \ n)$ data items where n is the total number of slow stashes, i.e., SSDs [9].

The resulting two-tier deployment must cope with unpredictable shifts in the query workload, e.g., flash crowds [9]. A miss for a data item in the front-end stash may populate the cache with a fixed probability. A concurrent write for the same data item may implement one of the write policies such as write-around (Fig. 3), write-through (Fig. 4), and write-back [1,15]. This write may race with the population of cache by the miss, causing the miss to populate the front-end stash with stale data. See discussion of Fig. 7 in Sect. 3.2.

DiStash prevents the undesirable race condition by enabling the load balancing solution to use one transaction to update copies of the data in the fast front-end stash and one or more of the slow stashes.

2.3 Hierarchical Data Storage

A storage hierarchy [10,35] may consist of h pools of stashes, S_0 to S_{h-1}. These stash pools may be ordered with S_0 as the fastest and S_{h-1} as the slowest[2]. Typically S_0 is the most expensive and provides the least amount of storage compared with the other layers of the hierarchy. The KV pairs migrate across the stashes based on their popularity and the working set of an application. Ideally, the application working set should reside in the fastest stash, S_0 [6].

Given a read request for a key, if it is not found in Stash S_0 then the system must look for it in the next stash S_1. If it is not found in S_1 then it must search for it in S_2. This process repeats until either the referenced key is found or all the h stashes have been searched. Bloom filters may be used to expedite identifying a missing key in a stash [8,19]. A key found in stash S_i, $i \geq 1$, might be moved to Stash S_0 based on the anticipation that it will be referenced again. The application may delete its copy from Stash S_i to ensure data across different stashes is exclusive.

A write to a key-value pair may be written to S_0. As S_0 becomes full, the application may migrate the infrequently referenced data to S_1. This process may repeat for the other intermediate stashes with S_{h-1} providing the highest density[3] [6].

Flashstore [6] is an example key-value store, consisting of three stash pools: DRAM, SSD, and HDD. It has been shown to outperform BerkeleyDB with two stash pools by providing 85x cost efficiency (ops/sec/dollar) [6]. Using our terminology, its durable storage is the HDD where the key-values reside. It has two ephemeral storage. One for SSD to materialize the working set of an application. A second for the DRAM to maintain the least recently referenced key-value pairs, a write buffer, and a hash index that points to the physical location of the keys in the SSD. The potential race conditions that may result in data inconsistency are well documented, see Sect. 4.6 of [6]. In addition, this study identifies consistency with multiple stash as non-trivial, differing it to future work, see Sect. 4.7 of [6].

DiStash may be used to implement a system similar to Flashstore [6]. This implementation preserves consistency of data while allowing for multiple instances of a stash type. A stash pool in the hierarchy may scale independently and have a different degree of replication. See Sect. 3.

2.4 Hybrids

It is possible to have a hybrid of the above possibilities. This is shown in Fig. 1. The DRAM, SSD, and HDD is a hierarchy similar to Flashstore [6]. The DRAM and SSD is a cache augmented solution similar to [27]. This figure shows the SSD pool as both ephemeral and durable storage. It is ephemeral for graph

[2] It is possible for two or more adjacent stash pools to provide approximately the same performance [35].

[3] Typically S_{h-1} provides the lowest cost per byte and slowest service time.

data and durable for 1-hop sub-query results. The configuration of DiStash that implements the hybrid maintains 4 stash pools: one DRAM, one HDD, and two SSD. The two SSD stash pools are independent: One for durable storage of 1-hop sub-query results and a second for ephemeral storage of graph data.

A graph query consisting of one or more 1-hop sub-queries may be processed as follows. The query processor looks up the result of each 1-hop sub-query in DRAM. If it is not found there, the query processor looks it up in the SSD durable storage. If it is not found there then the query processor executes the query using the instance of the graph database on the SSD ephemeral storage. If the referenced vertices and edges by the query are missing from SSD then they are staged from HDD to SSD. The query processor may compute the result of the missing 1-hop sub-query results to populate the DRAM stash. As the DRAM stash becomes full, it writes its entries to SSD.

3 DiStash in the Context of Cache Augmented Data Stores

A DiStash is a disaggregated storage manager for migrating and replicating copies of data across pools of stashes in a transactional manner. An application may use it to implement a cache augmented solution. Below, we describe how the concept of a transaction prevents undesirable race conditions that result in loss of data or inconsistencies across different replicas of a data item.

Without loss of generality, for the rest of this paper, the term stash and stash pool is used synonymously.

3.1 Cache Augmented Data Store

An application may configure DiStash with SSD as durable storage for use by a query processing engine and DRAM as ephemeral storage for the result of queries. When a query is issued, the application looks up the result of the query in the cache. If found then the application has observed a cache hit, returning the cache entry as the result of the query. Otherwise, a cache miss, the application executes the query, computes its results, generates a cache entry, and inserts it in the cache for future lookup [28].

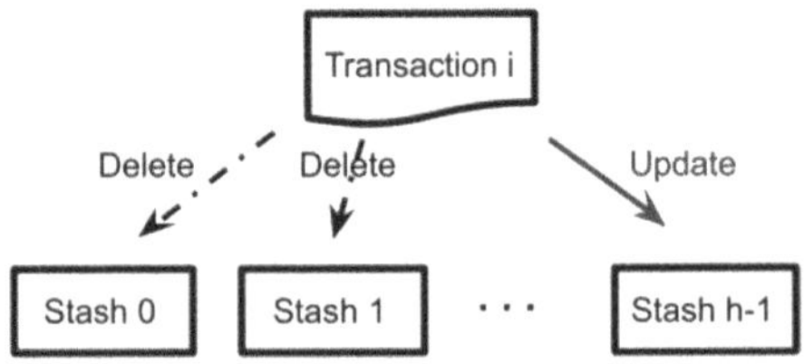

Fig. 3. Write-Around.

In the presence of writes to the data in the durable storage, the application must maintain the cache entries in the ephemeral storage consistent. It may use different write policies [15,21]. Figure 3 shows the *write-around* policy with a hierarchy of h stash pools. It requires the application to issue a transaction that deletes all copies of a cache entry and updates the original data. Copies of the cache entries typically reside on the fastest stashes with the original data residing on the slowest stash. With two stash pools, h=2, the copy of query results in DRAM, i.e., the fast stash, is deleted while the original data on the SSD, i.e., the slowest stash, is updated.

Figure 4 shows the *write-through* policy. It requires the application to issue a transaction to update all copies of a cache entry and the original data across all h stash pools. The update to a stash pool might be in the form of an SQL update command, a memcached append command, or Read-Modify-Write (RMW). With the latter, the transaction may read the impacted data from a stash, modify its value, and write it back. Figure 4 shows the RMW against one stash pool. However, it may be performed across 2 or more and possibly all stash pools.

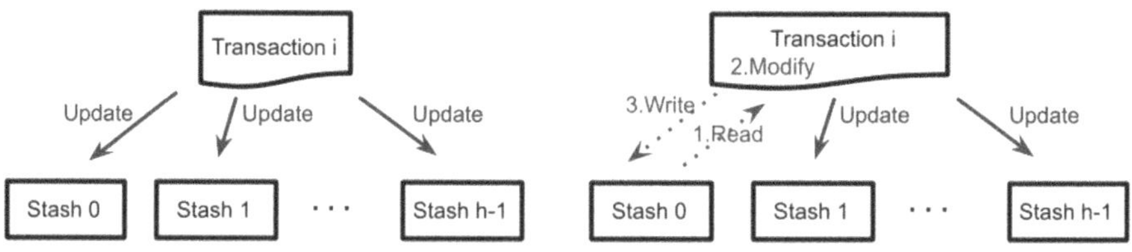

Fig. 4. Write-Through.

DiStash enables an application to use the write-around and write-through policies in different transactions concurrently.

Figure 5 shows an implementation of a read and a write with DiStash for two stashes: DRAM and SSD. The transaction that reads data from DRAM becomes a read-write when it does not find its data in DRAM, see Fig. 5a. The write implements the write-through policy by updating both the SSD and DRAM stashes in one transaction. Both assume each stash represents its data as key-value pairs. A key concept is one transaction that either reads or writes data from both stashes.

3.2 Why One Transaction?

Without the concept of one transaction that implements ACID semantics across the same copy of data (either logical or physical) across all stashes, an implementation may suffer from race conditions that result in the loss of latest write. We illustrate this with a deployment that consists of two different transactional storage managers: one manages the DRAM stash while the other manages the

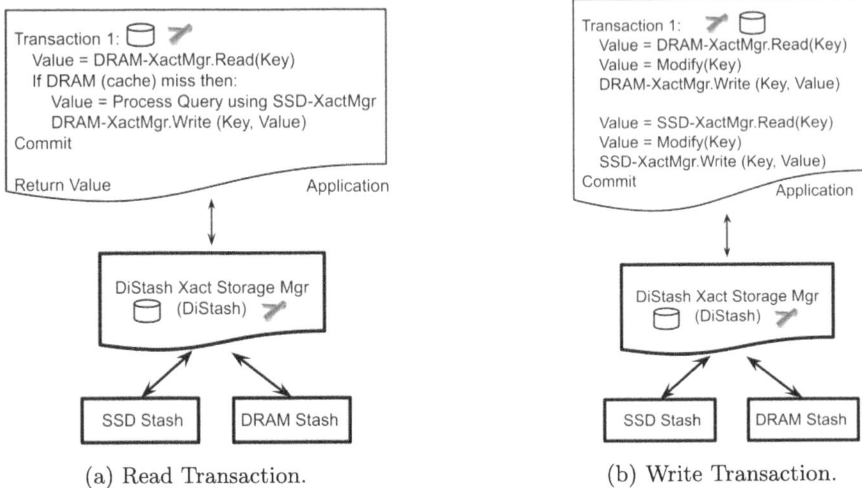

(a) Read Transaction.

(b) Write Transaction.

Fig. 5. Read and write transactions with DiStash.

SSD stash. This causes the application to implement the alternative policies by issuing different transactions to each stash.

Figure 6a shows the potential transactions issued by a read to the DRAM stash. When the referenced key is found, it consists of one transaction. However, with a miss, it consists of three transactions. The second transaction references the SSD storage manager to compute the result of the query. The third transaction populates the DRAM with the result of the query.

Figure 6b shows the write with two storage managers. It consists of two independent transactions. One per storage manager (that manages a different stash) to implement the write-through policy.

The two storage manager solution suffers from undesirable race conditions that may cause the different stashes to reflect inconsistent values. One such race condition is shown in Fig. 7. Client 1 issues a write that updates the SSD and DRAM stashes in turn per Fig. 6b. Client 2 issues a read that observes a cache miss. Hence, it issues a second transaction that reads data from the SSD stash. This transaction overlaps with the SSD write of Client 1. The underlying storage manager may use multi-version concurrency control (MVCC), enabling Client 2 to read an obsolete value of data. If Transaction 3 of Client 2 executes after Transaction 2 of Client 1, the value written to DRAM does not reflect the value produced by the latest transaction that wrote SSD[4]. A subsequent read using DRAM does not observe the value produced by the latest transaction. This violates the isolation and durability properties of transactions.

Figure 7 highlights the fact that while the transactions issued to each storage manager are serializable, transactions across the two storage managers are not serializable. This causes copies of the same data item on two or more stashes to

[4] Unless V1=V2.

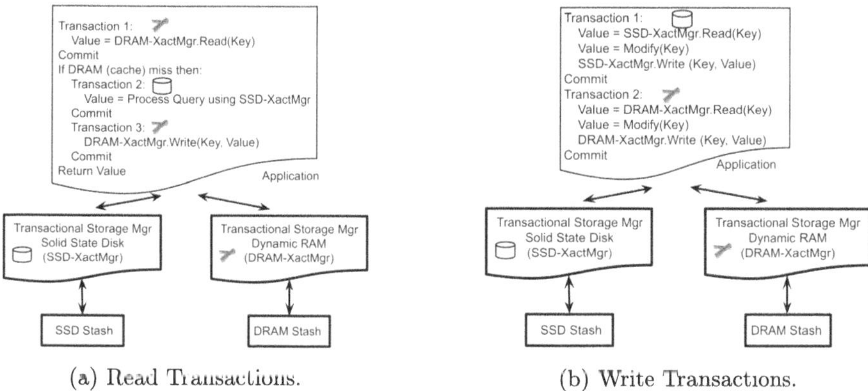

(a) Read Transactions. (b) Write Transactions.

Fig. 6. Read and write transactions with different stashes being managed by different storage managers.

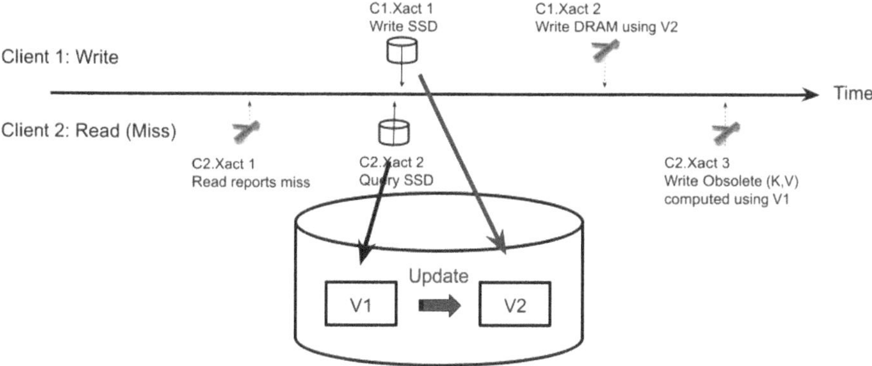

Fig. 7. An undesirable race condition results in inconsistent data across DRAM and SSD.

reflect inconsistent values. DiStash addresses this by using one storage manager and one transaction to read and write from different stashes, see Fig. 5. This forces the transactions by Client 1 and 2 to be serialized: Client 1's transaction followed by 2's transaction, or Client 2's transaction followed by 1's transaction. Should the operations overlap as shown in Fig. 7, DiStash will abort one of the two transactions, forcing its client to retry its transaction. This ensures copies of a data item across different stashes to have consistent values. This preserves the isolation and durability properties of transactions.

4 An Implementation

We extended FoundationDB to implement DiStash, see Fig. 8:

- Support h pools of stashes.

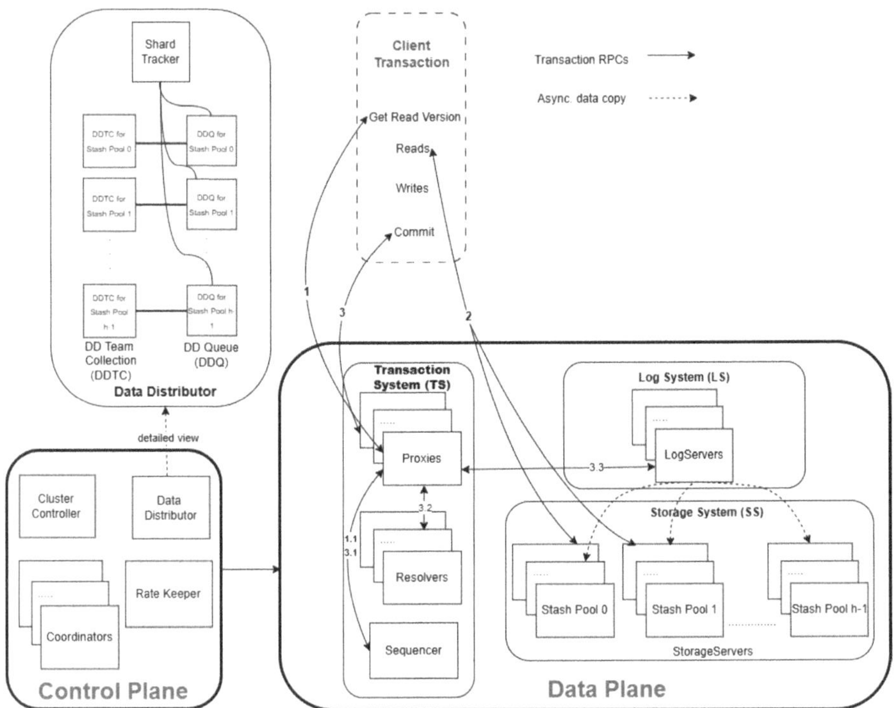

Fig. 8. An implementation of DiStash. See [37] for definition of arrows.

- Each stash pool may have a different degree of replication.
- One log server for all h stash pools.
- A transaction may reference key-value pairs that reside across all h stash pools.
- Balancing of load across the individual stashes that constitute a pool.
- Support for both ephemeral and durable storage using volatile and non-volatile stash pools. See Fig. 2.
- Recovery of a non-volatile stash is different than a volatile stash. With the latter, the recovery process uses a replica to maintain hit rate.
- One may extend a volatile stash with non-volatile storage for local logging, enabling the volatile stash to recover its data from short lived failures faster than 60 s. The threshold 60 s is adjustable.

Key changes to FoundationDB include:

- A Data Distributor (DD) team collection and queue for each stash pool. The queue facilitates re-location of shards for load balancing across the stashes in a pool.
- A new Storage Server (fdbserver/KeyValueStoreCache.actor.cpp) that extends FDB's existing in-memory implementation with the LRU replacement technique in support of DRAM ephemeral storage.

- Extensions of the configuration file to specify the h stash pools in the system and whether each is ephemeral or durable.
- Initialization of the FDB to read from the configuration files. This serves two purposes. First, initialize DD for each stash pool. Second, initialize the storage servers for each stash pool with the pre-specified degree of replication.
- A different prefix is used for each stash pool. This prefix is specified in the configuration files. The DD is aware of this prefix and this information is fetched by the client.
- We changed the Data Distributor Team Collection (DDTC) to maintain a different degree of replication for each stash pool. We also changed the initialization of the DD to verify the specified degree of replication for a stash satisfies the current deployment. If this is not satisfied then DD constructs replicas to meet the requirements of the deployments.

One may use an existing implementation of SQLite or RocksDB with a durable stash. A future research activity is to implement an SSD optimized ephemeral storage similar to Flashstore.

DiStash partitions data across the stashes by assigning a unique prefix to a stash pool. These prefixes are specified in a configuration file. The Data Distributor (DD) directs keys with a prefix to its unique stash pool. It consists of $2h+1$ processes: one shard tracker process (DDST), h Team Collection (DDTC) processes, and h Queue (DDQ) processes[5]. The DD Shard Tracker ensures the data is partitioned across the stashes consistent with the prefix boundaries defined for each stash pool. A DDTC is responsible for grouping the machines and servers within its corresponding stash pool to construct replica groups. A DDQ is responsible for migrating logical partitions, i.e., ranges, of data across the nodes of each stash pool by migrating ranges across its stashes. The DDST may construct new ranges by splitting existing ranges and merging existing ranges into larger ones.

5 Performance Evaluation

We evaluate DiStash using both microbenchmarks and eBay's production knowledge graph. This evaluation considers normal and failure modes of DiStah. The failure mode consists of epochs. Each epoch starts with the failure of x stashes and ends with the insertion of x new stashes.

The microbenchmark quantifies the performance of DiStash with different stash types. It focuses on data ingest by writing a fixed amount of data to either a DRAM stash or a SSD stash. It shows how DiStash's use of MVCC [36] results in a lower rate of data ingest with the SSD stashes. Due to strict page limits, we do not present the microbenchmark results.

eBay's knowledge graph facilitates search using a graph representation of data. It is a read dominated workload with the database refreshed periodically,

[5] The DD of the original FDB consisted of 3 (2+1) processes, one of each of shard tracker, DDTC, and DDQ. In our implementation, there is one extra process that is not shown. It is called the Shard forwarder. It is introduced to simplify the implementation.

approximately every 2 weeks. It generates a persistent database consisting of final query result for a subset of query templates that require a low latency. We use a trace driven evaluation of the production workload to compare (a) 1Stash, a durable store using 40 SSDs for both graph data and query result in each of two data centers, with (b) 2Stash, that separates durable store for graph data using 40 SSDs from ephemeral store for query results using 5 DRAMs in each of two data centers. The size of the production graph database is approximately 2.1 Terabytes. It is replicated 3 times across the 40 SSDs. The size of the query result is approximately 12.6 Gigabytes. It is replicated 3 times across 40 SSDs with 1Stash and 5 DRAMs with 2Stash. A third data center maintains the log records using SSD.

The eBay workload consists of 5 query templates [27]. Three of these query templates are cached and constitute approximately 45% of the workload. We considered two workloads: *Light* and *Moderate*. Light uses 100 pods each with 10 threads to generate the workload. Moderate uses 200 pods each with 10 threads to generate the workload. In failure mode, an epoch starts with the failure of $x = 2$ stashes and ends with the insertion of $x = 2$ stashes. With 2Stash, the failure epochs apply to the DRAM stash pool only.

5.1 Normal Mode of Operation

Summary of Results: With the eBay workload, we consider the latency of the overall workload and the fraction that benefits from the query results, i.e., cache hits. 2Stash improves the 95th and 99th overall latencies by 10% when compared with 1Stash. With a low system load, the latency of the cache hits with 1Stash is superior to 2Stash. This observation disappears with a moderate system load.

Table 1. Latency with 1Stash and 2Stash, moderate workload.

	50th	95th	99th
1Stash	2.23	23.36	80.36
2Stash	2.18	20.93	72.33
% Improvement	2%	10.4%	10%

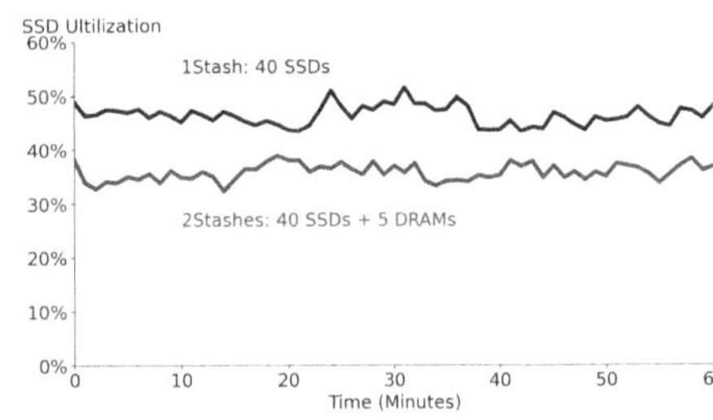

Fig. 9. SSD Utilization, moderate workload.

Detailed Results. In these experiments, all references to the three cached query templates that constitute 45% of the workload observe a cache hit. Hence, approximately 45% of the workload is processed using the query results. This fraction uses 40 SSDs with 1Stash and 5 DRAMs with 2Stash. With the light workload, 1Stash and 2Stash provide comparable performance. With the moderate workload, Table 1 shows the average of 50th, 95th, and 99th latencies based on one hour of execution time. While the 50th latency is comparable, 2Stash improves the 95th and 99th latencies by approximately 10%. The DRAM stashes reduce the SSD utilization with 2Stash, see Fig. 9. These freed SSD resources are used to expedite processing of the queries that do not observe a cache hit, i.e., 55% of the workload.

With a moderate workload, the 50th, 95th and 99th latencies of queries that observe a cache hit is comparable with both 1Stash (40 way parallelism using SSD) and 2Stash (5 way parallelism using DRAM). The buffer pool manager of SQLite maintains the cache entries in its memory (DRAM), serving them as fast as the DRAM of the 2Stash. This is at the expense of 55% of the workload that reference disk pages for query processing. This expense is shown with a higher SSD utilization in Fig. 9.

Cache Hit Latency. During normal mode of operation and with a light system load, the 50th latency of 1Stash and 2Stash are comparable. However, 1Stash reduces the 95th and 99th latencies, compare the start (x-axis = 0) of Figs. 10a and 10b. This is because, with 2Stash, the load is not uniformly distributed across the 5 DRAMs. Figure 12 (origin until 23:28) shows two of the stashes have a lower utilization than the other three. Balancing the load across a few stashes with a light system load is non trivial. The observed performance gap disappears with a moderate system load. With this load, while the 50th latency remains unchanged, the 95th latency of both configurations increases to 5.3 ms, and their 99th latency increases to 15 ms.

5.2 Failure Mode of Operation

Summary of Results: DiStash is able to tolerate failure of $R-1$ stash failures where R is the degree of data replication with the stash pool. Its DD re-constructs replicas of those shards with fewer than R replicas aggressively. DiStash uses these same replicas for query processing. This causes the load on the servers hosting these replicas to increase. Depending on the system load, there may be a noticeable increase in the 50th, 95th, 99th latencies.

Insertion of one or two stashes (at the end of an epoch) causes DiStash, i.e., its DD, to reorganize data across stashes. With a few stashes (5 DRAMs of 2Stash), this increases the 95th and 99th latencies temporarily with a light system load. With a large number of stashes (40 SSDs of either 1Stash or 2Stash), there is no noticeable change in latency with a light system load.

Detailed Results. We evaluated the impact of stash failures on 1Stash and 2Stash cluster configurations. This analysis specifically reports on queries that observe a cache hit. Throughout these experiments, a light workload was simulated using 100 pods. The cache is warm, providing an approximate hit rate of 100%, i.e., $\geq$99.98%.

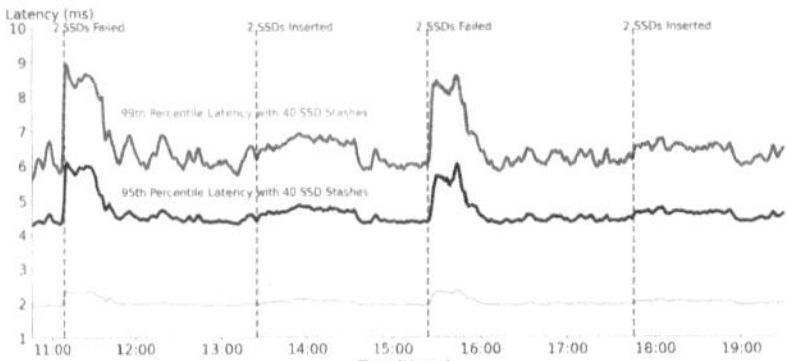

(a) 1Stash, 40 SSDs with light workload. There are two epochs. The first epoch starts at 11:09 and ends at 13:24. The second starts at 15:24 and ends at 17:45.

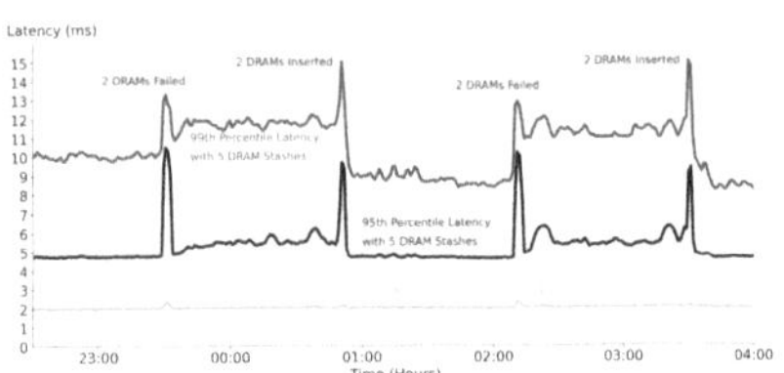

(b) 2Stash, 40 SSD + 5 DRAM with light workload. There are two epochs. The first starts at 23:28 and ends at 00:40. The second starts at 2:09 and ends at 3:29.

Fig. 10. Query result lookup (cache hit) latency of 1Stash and 2Stash. Each epoch starts with the failure of 2 stashes and ends with insertion of 2 stashes. With 1Stash, 40 SSDs process requests. With 2Stash, 5 DRAM stashes process requests.

We repeat an epoch to verify the observed trends are reproducible. Figure 10a shows the 50th, 95th and 99th latencies with 1Stash. The failure of 2 SSDs causes the DD to replicate the shards with missing replicas, i.e., those with either 1 or 2 surviving replicas. These shards correspond to both the graph data and the query result data. Their duplication across the remaining 38 SSDs causes the disk to become 100% utilized[6], see Fig. 11.

Once we insert 2 SSDs back into the 1Stash configuration, the DD starts to migrate shards to them in order to utilize their available bandwidth. This causes the utilization of some SSDs to spike to 100%. The migration is not aggressive and has minimal impact on the 95th and 99th latencies. This re-balancing requires a long time because it involves shards of both the graph data and the query result data.

Figure 10b shows the 50th, 95th and 99th latencies with 2Stash. Failure of 2 DRAM stashes results in aggressive replication of those shards with 1 or 2 missing replicas. These are depicted as spikes at time 23:28 and 2:09. Replication increases the CPU utilization of the remaining 3 DRAMs, see Fig. 12. The impacted shards correspond only to the query results[7]. They are compact in size. Hence, the duration of aggressive replication is shorter when compared with 1Stash. This is highlighted by the shorter duration of the spikes in Fig. 10b compared to those in Fig. 10a.

With 2Stash, after aggressive replication, the 95th and 99th latencies remain elevated because only 3 stashes are processing requests. This results in a higher CPU utilization during each epoch, see Fig. 12.

Once we insert the 2 DRAM stashes, the latency and CPU utilization spike as DiStash starts to migrate data to them. This re-balancing decreases the 95th and 99th latencies quickly as 5 DRAM stashes start to process requests (instead of 3).

[6] DD strives to ensure the same each stash performs its fair share of work.

[7] The graph data is separate and stored across 40 SSDs.

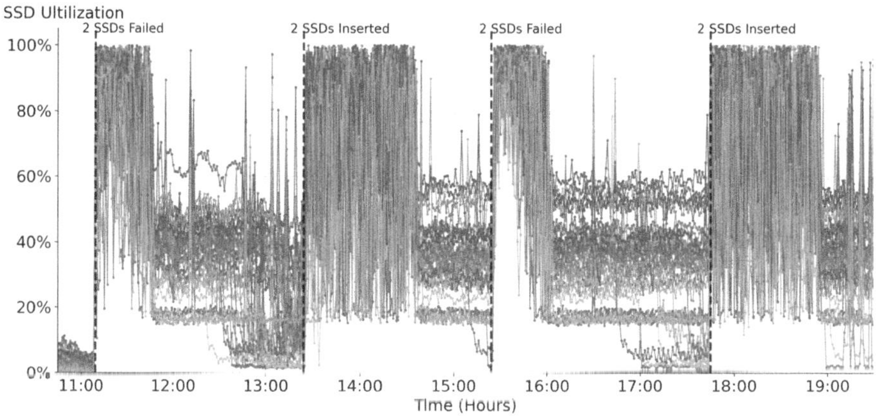

Fig. 11. Utilization of 40 SSDs with epochs of Fig. 10a.

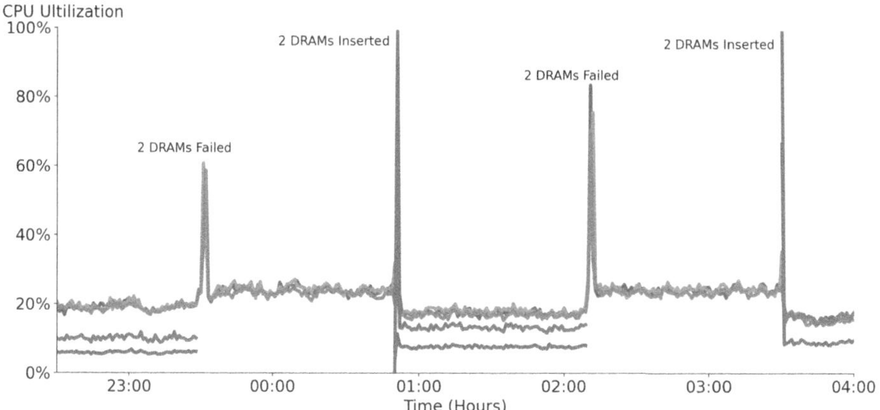

Fig. 12. CPU utilization of 5 DRAMs with epochs of Fig. 10b.

Cache Hit Latency. With 2 stash failures in the caching layer, the duration of time to replicate shards with 1 or 2 replicas is longer with 1Stash. By co-locating graph data with query results on the SSDs, 1Stash must reconstruct a larger amount of data when compared with 2Stash. 1Stash continues to provide a lower 95th and 99th latency because, after the two failures, it uses 38 SSDs in parallel instead of 3 DRAMs with 2Stash.

6 Related Work

To the best of our knowledge, DiStash is the first transactional storage manager to support h pools of stashes across multiple data centers with a different degree of data replication for each pool. It enables its application to use a transaction to migrate or copy one or more key-value pairs across one or more stashes in a pool or different stash pools.

As detailed in Sect. 2, DiStash may be used to implement cache-augmented database management systems [1,15,26–28], load balancing techniques using a front-end cache [9,20], and hierarchical storage structures [6,10,35]. However, these systems and techniques cannot be used to implement DiStash. For example, with a cache augmented solution, one may use the IQ framework [16,17] to maintain consistency of data with a query result cache. However, this framework is specific to the write-around policy. It does not support multiple stash pools or the write-through policy. Fundamentally, DiStash provides consistency using one transaction to manage data across multiple stash pools. This concept is absent from other systems.

In [13,14], we present a simple algorithm to evaluate design tradeoffs in the context of a memory hierarchy for a key-value store. This algorithm answers questions such as, given a fixed budget and a workload, which storage media should constitute a memory hierarchy? And, whether the data should be replicated or tiered. This offline algorithm may be used to size the different stash pools of DiStash for different workloads and applications.

7 Conclusions and Future Work

DiStash is a transactional storage manager for h pools of stashes. It enables an application to use a single transaction to read and write copies of key-value pairs in a stash pool and across different stash pools. A stash pool might be either ephemeral or durable. DiStash may be used to implement cache-augmented database management systems, novel load-balancing techniques, hierarchical storage structures, and a hybrid of these. We presented performance numbers from DiStash using eBay's production workload. This evaluation highlighted the flexibility of DiStash to use durable store for both graph data and query results (cache entries), and use of durable store for graph data and ephemeral store for cache entries. We showed DiStash is able to tolerate failure of stashes in either durable or ephemeral storage. Many configurations of DiStash are possible, including those based on DRAM alone, e.g., RAMCloud [29].

This workshop paper identifies many interesting future research directions. One is how to balance load with a few stashes and a light system load, see discussions of Fig. 12. This requires a global analysis of how FoundationDB (FDB) balances load with a light, moderate, and heavy system loads. At the time of this writing, FDB balances load effectively with a moderate and a heavy system load. In addition, we plan to integrate the configuration planner of [13,14] with the alternative workloads to size DiStash. This will include a comprehensive analysis of workloads with write transactions and the hybrid architecture of Fig. 1. Moreover, we plan to extend DiStash with an ephemeral storage finetuned for NVM [30,33] including NVDIMM [5,22,23].

Acknowledgments. This research was a collaborative effort between eBay and the University of Southern California, made possible through support from eBay's eRUPT program. We gratefully acknowledge CloudLab [34] for the use of their resources to enable some of the experimental results presented in this article. In addition to eRUPT, Shahram Ghandeharizadeh was supported in part by the NSF grant CMMI-2425754.

References

1. Byan, S., et al.: Mercury: host-side flash caching for the data center. In: 2012 IEEE 28th Symposium on Mass Storage Systems and Technologies (MSST), pp. 1–12. IEEE (2012)
2. Carlson, J.: Redis in Action. Simon and Schuster (2013)
3. Cenker, R.P., Clemons, D.G., Huber, W.R., Petrizzi, J.B., Procyk, F.J., Trout, G.M.: A fault-tolerant 64K dynamic random-access memory. IEEE Trans. Electron Devices **26**(6), 853–860 (1979)
4. Chen, F., Hou, B., Lee, R.: Internal parallelism of flash memory-based solid-state drives. ACM Trans. Storage (TOS) **12**(3), 1–39 (2016)
5. Clouzet, P., et al.: H2M: heuristics for heterogeneous memory. In: HMEM 2024–5th Workshop on Heterogeneity and Memory Systems (2024)
6. Debnath, B., Sengupta, S., Li, J.: FlashStore: high throughput persistent key-value store. Proc. VLDB Endow. **3**(1–2), 1414–1425 (2010). https://doi.org/10.14778/1920841.1921015
7. Dirik, C., Jacob, B.: The performance of PC solid-state disks (SSDs) as a function of bandwidth, concurrency, device architecture, and system organization. ACM SIGARCH Comput. Archit. News **37**(3), 279–289 (2009)
8. Dong, S., Callaghan, M., Galanis, L., Borthakur, D., Savor, T., Strum, M.: Optimizing space amplification in RocksDB. In: CIDR, vol. 3, p. 3 (2017)
9. Fan, B., Lim, H., Andersen, D.G., Kaminsky, M.: Small cache, big effect: provable load balancing for randomly partitioned cluster services. In: Proceedings of the 2nd ACM Symposium on Cloud Computing, SOCC 2011. Association for Computing Machinery, New York (2011). https://doi.org/10.1145/2038916.2038939
10. Ghandeharizadeh, S., Dashti, A.E., Shahabi, C.: Pipelining mechanism to minimize the latency time in hierarchical multimedia storage managers. Comput. Commun. **18**(3), 170–184 (1995)
11. Ghandeharizadeh, S., et al.: A demonstration of KOSAR: an elastic, scalable, highly available SQL middleware. In: Rouvoy, R. (ed.) Proceedings of the Middleware 2014 Posters & Demos Session, Bordeaux, France, 8–12 December 2014, pp. 23–24. ACM (2014). https://doi.org/10.1145/2678508.2678520
12. Ghandeharizadeh, S., Ierardi, D., Kim, D., Zimmermann, R.: Placement of data in multi-zone disk drives. In: Second International Baltic Workshop on DB and IS. Citeseer (1996)
13. Ghandeharizadeh, S., Irani, S., Lam, J.: On configuring a hierarchy of storage media in the age of NVM. In: 34th IEEE International Conference on Data Engineering, ICDE 2018, Paris, France, 16–19 April 2018, pp. 1380–1383. IEEE Computer Society (2018). https://doi.org/10.1109/ICDE.2018.00155
14. Ghandeharizadeh, S., Irani, S., Lam, J.: Memory hierarchy design for caching middleware in the age of NVM (2025). https://arxiv.org/abs/2506.05071
15. Ghandeharizadeh, S., Nguyen, H.: Design, implementation, and evaluation of write-back policy with cache augmented data stores. Proc. VLDB Endow. **12**(8), 836–849 (2019)

16. Ghandeharizadeh, S., Yap, J.: SQL query to trigger translation: a novel transparent consistency technique for cache augmented SQL systems. In: 28th International Workshop on Database and Expert Systems Applications, DEXA 2017 Workshops, Lyon, France, 28–31 August 2017, pp. 37–41. IEEE Computer Society (2017). https://doi.org/10.1109/DEXA.2017.24
17. Ghandeharizadeh, S., Yap, J., Nguyen, H.: Strong consistency in cache augmented SQL systems. In: Réveillère, L., Cherkasova, L., Taïani, F. (eds.) Proceedings of the 15th International Middleware Conference, Bordeaux, France, 8–12 December 2014, pp. 181–192. ACM (2014). https://doi.org/10.1145/2663165.2663318
18. Gray, J., Putzolu, F.: The 5 minute rule for trading memory for disc accesses and the 10 byte rule for trading memory for CPU time. In: Proceedings of the 1987 ACM SIGMOD International Conference on Management of Data, pp. 395–398 (1987)
19. Huang, H., Ghandeharizadeh, S.: Nova-LSM: a distributed, component-based LSM-tree Key-value store. In: Li, G., Li, Z., Idreos, S., Srivastava, D. (eds.) SIGMOD 2021: International Conference on Management of Data, Virtual Event, China, 20–25 June 2021, pp. 749–763. ACM (2021). https://doi.org/10.1145/3448016.3457297
20. Jin, X., et al.: NetCache: balancing key-value stores with fast in-network caching. In: Proceedings of the 26th Symposium on Operating Systems Principles, SOSP 2017, pp. 121–136. Association for Computing Machinery, New York (2017). https://doi.org/10.1145/3132747.3132764
21. Jouppi, N.P.: Cache write policies and performance. ACM SIGARCH Comput. Archit. News **21**(2), 191–201 (1993)
22. Lee, B., Moon, S., Park, J., Lee, S.W.: Boosting OLTP performance with per-page logging on NVDIMM. Proc. ACM Manage. Data **3**(1), 1–28 (2025)
23. Lee, C., et al.: NVDIMM-C: a byte-addressable non-volatile memory module for compatibility with standard DDR memory interfaces. In: 2020 IEEE International Symposium on High Performance Computer Architecture (HPCA), pp. 502–514. IEEE (2020)
24. Lenfant, J.: Fast random and sequential access to dynamic memories of any size. IEEE Trans. Comput. **100**(9), 847–855 (1977)
25. Memcached: Memcached. http://www.memcached.org/http://www.memcached.org/
26. Nguyen, H., Li, J., Ghandeharizadeh, S.: Graph stores with application-level query result caches. In: Nambiar, R., Poess, M. (eds.) TPCTC 2023. LNCS, vol. 14247, pp. 44–58. Springer (2023). https://doi.org/10.1007/978-3-031-68031-1_4
27. Nguyen, H., Li, J., Ghandeharizadeh, S.: One-hop sub-query result caches for graph database systems (2024). https://arxiv.org/abs/2412.04698
28. Nishtala, R., et al.: Scaling memcache at facebook. In: Proceedings of the 10th USENIX Conference on Networked Systems Design and Implementation, NSDI 2013, pp. 385–398. USENIX Association, USA (2013)
29. Ousterhout, J., et al.: The RAMCloud Storage System. ACM Trans. Comput. Syst. **33**(3) (2015). https://doi.org/10.1145/2806887
30. Patil, O., Ionkov, L., Lee, J., Mueller, F., Lang, M.: NVM-based energy and cost efficient HPC clusters. In: Proceedings of the International Symposium on Memory Systems, pp. 1–14 (2025)
31. Patterson, D.A., Gibson, G., Katz, R.H.: A case for redundant arrays of inexpensive disks (RAID). In: Proceedings of the 1988 ACM SIGMOD International Conference on Management of Data, pp. 109–116 (1988)

32. Ports, D.R.K., Clements, A.T., Zhang, I., Madden, S., Liskov, B.: Transactional consistency and automatic management in an application data cache. In: Arpaci-Dusseau, R.H., Chen, B. (eds.) 9th USENIX Symposium on Operating Systems Design and Implementation, OSDI 2010, 4–6 October 2010, Vancouver, BC, Canada, pp. 279–292. USENIX Association (2010). http://www.usenix.org/events/osdi10/tech/full_papers/Ports.pdf
33. Wang, G., Che, X., Wei, H., Chen, S., He, P., Hu, J.: Boosting file systems elegantly: a transparent {NVM} write-ahead log for disk file systems. In: 23rd USENIX Conference on File and Storage Technologies (FAST 2025), pp. 19–34 (2025)
34. White, B., et al.: An integrated experimental environment for distributed systems and networks, vol. 36, pp. 255–270. ACM, New York (2002). https://doi.org/10.1145/844128.844152
35. Wu, K., et al.: The storage hierarchy is not a hierarchy: optimizing caching on modern storage devices with Orthus. In: 19th USENIX Conference on File and Storage Technologies (FAST 2021), pp. 307–323. USENIX Association (2021). https://www.usenix.org/conference/fast21/presentation/wu-kan
36. Zhou, J., et al.: FoundationDB: a distributed unbundled transactional key value store. In: Proceedings of the 2021 International Conference on Management of Data, pp. 2653–2666 (2021)
37. Zhou, J., et al.: FoundationDB: a distributed key-value store. Commun. ACM **66**(6), 97–105 (2023)

HammerDB: From Personal Project to Open Benchmarking Standard

Steve Shaw[1(✉)] and Andy Bond[2]

[1] HammerDB Ltd., 3Rd Floor, 86-90 Paul Street, London EC2A 4NE, England
steve.shaw@hammerdb.com
[2] Red Hat Inc., 100 East Davie Street, Raleigh, NC 27601, USA
abond@redhat.com

Abstract. HammerDB is a leading open-source tool for database benchmarking, widely adopted across enterprise, cloud, and academic environments to evaluate transactional and analytic database performance. Originally developed as a personal open source project for testing the Oracle database on Linux, HammerDB has grown through a mission of accessibility, cross-platform support, and real-world relevance to become a trusted solution across the industry.

This paper presents the story of HammerDB's development, its architectural choices, major milestones, and evolution into a mature benchmarking suite with support for the most popular commercial and open source database systems. A key recent advancement is the release of HammerDB v5.0 in spring 2025, introducing a simplified installation with native packages for Linux and Windows, enhancing both performance and usability, furthering HammerDB's goal of providing modern, portable and easy to use benchmarking tools.

With its integration into the TPC-OSS subcommittee, HammerDB continues to bridge the gap between open source innovation and formal benchmarking standards. We also highlight ongoing performance collaborations with the database industry and outline future directions, including expanded workloads, cloud-native capabilities, and opportunities for community-driven contributions. This paper invites discussion on how open tools like HammerDB can shape the next era of collaborative database performance benchmarking.

Keywords: HammerDB · TPC · Benchmarking

1 Introduction

In 1994 the database industry generated about $7 billion in revenue [1], this grew to an estimated $150.38 billion by 2025 [2], representing a compound annual growth rate (CAGR) of 11.11% over 30 years. If this trend continues, the global database market could reach approximately $292 billion by 2030, accounting for a substantial share of the projected $517 billion enterprise software market by the same year [3]. Choosing the right database platform therefore, or deciding to change it, is a business decision with long-term cost and risk implications. Databases once installed are not easily replaced, requiring highly specialized and trained staff, whilst applications may depend on specific

R. Nambiar and M. Poess (Eds.): TPCTC 2025, LNCS 16261, pp. 134–154, 2026.
https://doi.org/10.1007/978-3-032-18070-4_9

functionality. This makes databases one of the most immovable components of enterprise IT. As a result, many of the database systems first deployed in the 1980s & 1990s remain in production today. At that time, relational databases dominated the market, led by Oracle, IBM DB2, Sybase, Informix, and Microsoft SQL Server. While some vendors have merged or consolidated, Oracle, Microsoft SQL Server, and IBM Db2 remain the most widely used commercial databases in 2025, underscoring the enduring importance of relational systems—which still account for 58% of the total database market today [2].

Given the competitive nature of the database landscape, vendors have always been keen to differentiate their products with performance consistently being one of the most emotive and marketable aspects. The catalyst for this was the 1985 specification of the debit/credit benchmark in the paper "A Measure of Transaction Processing Power." [4] This paper provided for the first time a standardized process for comparing databases and triggered a focus in database vendors on improving performance [5,6]. In turn this led to the foundation of the Transaction Processing Performance Council (TPC) in 1988 by a consortium of database as well as hardware vendors to define the industry-standard benchmarks for transaction processing. [7] The database industry now had an expert body to define standards and specifications and made the crucial decision to disseminate these specifications freely to the public at no charge.

The collaboration between database software and hardware vendors reflected the rise of client-server architecture and the dominance of the Unix operating system such as Sun Microsystems' Solaris, Hewlett-Packard's HP-UX and IBM's AIX, each delivering proprietary RISC platforms tailored for database workloads.

These companies sponsored and participated in the refinement of the official TPC benchmarks. As a result, hardware and database vendors aligned closely, employing highly specialized experts to further standardize workloads and develop benchmark kits beyond debit/credit such as the TPC-A, TPC-B, and later TPC-C transactional benchmarks and the TPC-H analytic benchmarks. Although the barrier to entry and the cost of developing and executing an official TPC benchmark were high, the benefits of publishing a leading result were widely considered to outweigh these costs, delivering substantial returns through increased sales of the systems used to run the benchmarked databases [8].

The 1990s and 2000s however proved to be a high-point for the publication of TPC benchmarks and over time the number of official publications declined as illustrated in Fig. 1 updated from data originally compiled by the TPC. The primary driver behind the decline of proprietary architectures for database systems was the encroachment of x86-based processors from AMD and Intel—once confined largely to desktop computing—into the enterprise domain. With the introduction of the x86–64 extension, AMD's Opteron and Intel's Xeon product lines rapidly gained dominance in both server and desktop markets, supported by major vendors such as Dell and HP, and running operating systems including Microsoft Windows and the open-source, Unix-derived Linux.

In September 2001 when Sun Microsystems withdrew from participating in TPC benchmarks, the move was widely interpreted as stemming from the Sun Fire server's underwhelming performance relative to competing systems [9]. In contrast a combination of Red Hat Enterprise Linux and the IBM DB2 database exceeded one million transactions per minute (tpmC) on an x86-based system for the first time in 2009 [10].

Increased competition from x86-based systems drove a dramatic reduction in costs, while differentiation between platforms using the same x86 architecture became increasingly difficult. At the same time, the absence of official TPC publications created a gap in the available knowledge for comparing database performance.

Software tools such as Mercury LoadRunner and Quest Benchmark Factory emerged during this period to execute benchmark-style workloads against databases. However, their use was constrained by commercial application licensing, and typically only being available for Windows-based x86 systems. This created a growing need for cost-effective database performance benchmarking solutions capable of running on x86 platforms across both Windows and Linux environments.

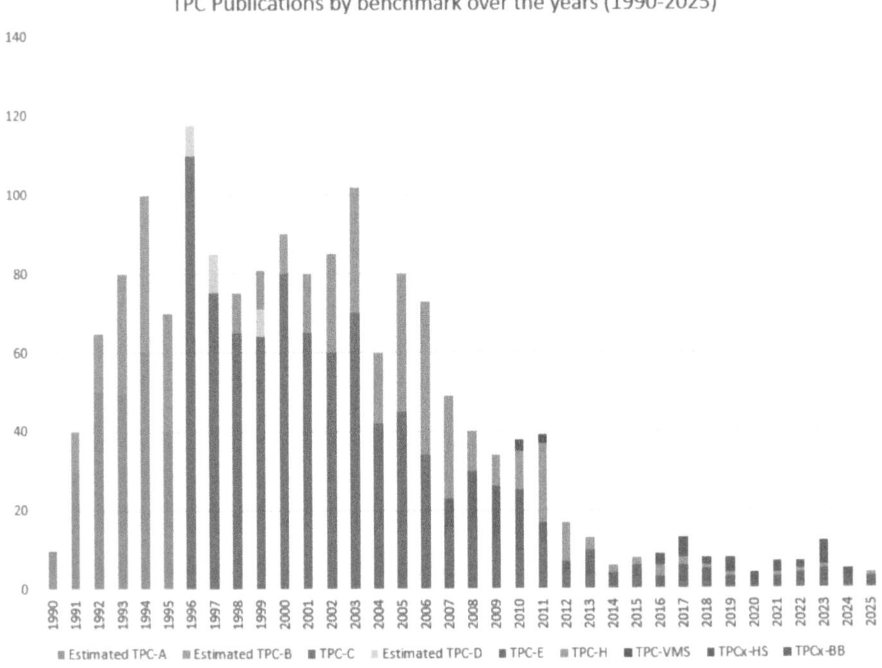

Fig. 1. TPC publications by benchmarks over the years

2 Hammerora v1.0 & v2.0

Intel had a direct interest in accelerating the decline of RISC and the rise of enterprise x86 systems and at the time, Steve Shaw one of the authors of this paper was employed a consultant to customers comparing RISC Unix to x86 Linux systems running Oracle. In particular the Oracle Real Application Clusters (RAC) extension brought x86 into competition with even the most powerful proprietary RISC based systems because it allowed single database systems to outscale proprietary RISC based sys-tem by using massive scale-out [11]. The TPC workloads were as relevant as ever, however the requirements had changed and dissatisfied with the availability of database benchmarking software, Steve Shaw decided to write an application to run database benchmarks to compare Oracle RAC on Linux systems.

2.1 OSDL

At that time Steve Shaw had a strong interest in open source and had already served as the technical reviewer for the O'Reilly publication Oracle and Open Source [12] and therefore an open source solution was the preferred solution. A proposal was put to Intel to develop a tool for their use, but this was declined. Nevertheless, Tim Witham the lab director of the Open Source Development Labs (OSDL), the precursor of the Linux Foundation [13] had already established a system whereby Intel engineers could develop personal open source projects with a full copyright disclaimer and this proposal was accepted, and therefore Hammerora was now in development under a GPLv2 license.

2.2 Architectural and Development Language Decisions

Heavily influenced by the interface of the Mercury LoadRunner tool, the decision was made to develop a benchmarking solution with a graphical user interface and a scripted component for building custom workloads. Drawing on extensive experience in database testing, it was clear from the outset that the tool needed to be multi-threaded and highly scalable, capable of generating parallel workloads to stress the database engine's concurrency, rather than being limited by the concurrency model of the implementation language.

Java was initially considered; however, its heavy resource footprint, lack of an integrated scripting language, and ongoing concerns over thread scalability deemed it unsuitable [14]. Python was also evaluated, offering a scripted, programmable interface for test automation, Oracle connectivity, and a graphical user interface via Tkinter. Its major drawback, however, was the Global Interpreter Lock (GIL) in its threading implementation, which prevents multiple threads from executing Python bytecode in parallel. This concurrency limitation significantly constrained Python's performance at the time, and the GIL remains a notable restriction to Python scalability to this day.

While all of the researched TPC benchmark full disclosure reports were based on implementations written in C, this approach was not well suited to creating an easy-to-use benchmarking kit. A more accessible solution required a higher-level language and integrated interface, enabling users to configure and run complex workloads without compiling or modifying low-level code.

2.3 Tcl/Tk

Tcl was ultimately selected as the implementation language due to its exceptional simplicity, lightweight footprint, and strong support for database connectivity. It offered an advanced C-level Oracle interface in the form of Oratcl, enabling direct use of the Oracle Call Interface (OCI) for high-performance connectivity, and was easily extensible in C for adding custom functionality when required. Using Tcl also enabled the direct use of the Tk toolkit to deliver a capable and responsive graphical interface. Most importantly as shown in Fig. 2. Tcl included a robust and highly scalable native threading model [15], allowing the same language to be used both for the user's benchmark scripts and the tool's back-end engine. This unified approach enabled the creation of a benchmark driver that was not only simple, programmable and robust but also capable of generating massive parallel workloads to fully exercise database concurrency.

An additional advantage was full cross-platform compatibility, with the same code running unmodified on both Linux and Windows on the x86 and x86–64 platforms. A key design decision was that all features and functionality would fully support both Windows and Linux in marked contrast to other tools with all any extensions being updated to compile with gcc on Linux and MSVC on Windows. The Tcl language was also itself fully open source, aligning with the ethos of open benchmarking through all layers of the test software stack.

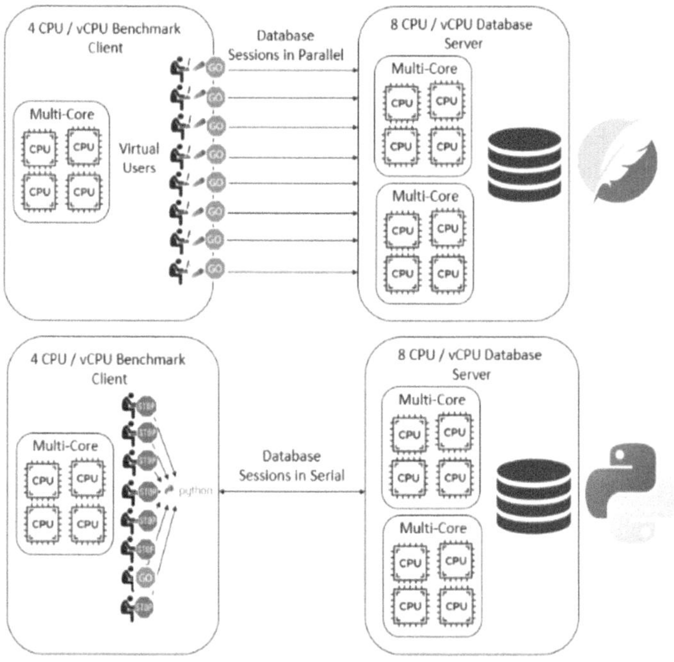

Fig. 2. Tcl vs Python Thread Scalability

The first release of Hammerora was published on the SourceForge platform in 2003 supporting a feature to replay workloads against the Oracle Database captured in the form of Oracle Trace Files. This was soon followed by an implementation of the TPC-C transactional workload based upon the example stored procedures published in the TPC-C specification. Importantly this was permissible because the TPC had made their specifications freely available to implement without license restriction [16].

2.4 C, SQL & Pl/SQL

Importantly, the Hammerora Oracle TPC workloads were implemented using PL/SQL stored procedures, enabling the workload to execute entirely within the database engine and minimizing network overhead. In contrast, the Tcl Oratcl interface, being built on the Oracle Call Interface (OCI) in C, established a direct SQL-to-native interface, delivering the highest possible performance. Another key design decision was to make the workload as easy as possible to implement with a two stage methodology. Firstly, schema creation was designed to be a one click process, with table creation, data creation and loading, index creation and stored procedure creation all automated without requiring further interaction. Typically benchmark workloads, loaded data from pre-generated flat files which was a cumbersome error-prone process and therefore Hammerora used an insert based load so no additional external storage or tools were needed. Then a driver script was loaded to call the stored procedures and generate a workload against the database with the load increasing by increasing the number of threads, called Virtual Users.

2.5 UKOUG

Hammerora quickly gained traction within the Oracle community, particularly for evaluating Oracle performance on both x86 and RISC architectures, and especially for Oracle RAC. Notably, Steve Shaw authored the first published article to feature a Hammerora workload simulation, which appeared in the UK Oracle User Group magazine Oracle Scene in 2004 as shown in Fig. 3. This workload demonstrated throughput of 12,239 TPM on an x86-based Oracle RAC Cluster, illustrating the performance achievable by Oracle on Linux and validating Hammerora's design choices. Around the same time, Shaw co-authored a book on Oracle RAC, including a dedicated chapter on Hammerora, published by Apress in 2006 [17]. By this stage, Hammerora was already being recognised not only as an Oracle-focused performance and benchmarking tool, but also as a resource that underpinned professional publications, conference presentations, and industry knowledge-sharing—despite remaining a personal open-source project.

Tuning Oracle9i RAC

By Steve Shaw, Intel Solution Services

'...The big news here is that we now have a cluster technology that runs almost anything. Any application that runs on Oracle now runs on an Oracle cluster, without having to change the application at all. Fault tolerant. Scalable by simply plugging another computer into the cluster. And you don't have to do anything to the application code at all...'

It is a tempting challenge to put this to the test and investigate whether it really is possible to take a non-RAC aware application and implement it successfully on RAC, where tuning the database is permitted but 'without having to change the application at all'.

Setup

The test system is based on the following hardware and software:

Component	Configuration
Server	Two nodes 4-way with Intel® Xeon™ processors MP at 1.60GHz
Memory	2 GB of memory per node
Operating System	Red Hat Enterprise Linux* 2.1 with kernel 2.4.9-e27smp.
Oracle Version	Oracle 9.2.0.4.
Storage	EMC CLARiiON FC4700
File System	OCFS 1.0.9-9

The application used for a workload simulation is Hammerora, which includes an open source simulation of the TPC-C benchmark, http://www.tpc.org/tpcc/default.asp available from SourceForge. http://hammerora.sourceforge.net Two instances of the application are taken, running in distributed mode with fifteen user threads running against each of the database instances for a 10-minute period.

The warehouses for each user are selected at random, and no think time is used. This type of workload is useful to ensure that cache fusion is truly tested for illustrative purposes, in the expectation that any 'real-world' application will not match such limits. Being a transactional system, the success metric for measuring the level of performance is to attempt to increase the number of Oracle transactions that the system can do on average per minute, over a defined test period.

Freelists and RAC

The starting configuration for testing is taken as a database using untuned manual segment-space management. It is obvious from reading the RAC manuals that using untuned freelists without configuring additional freelist groups is clearly not to be recommended. However this starting point is useful to illustrate whether the requirements for RAC are significantly different to those of a single instance, and whether migrating from a single instance configuration to a cluster with no changes in the database layout will bring performance benefits.

After running the first test against the cluster, drilling down to the load profile within the captured statspack report shows the average transaction rate for the whole cluster as 9,734 TPM. Crucially, the transaction rate achievable for the 2 node RAC cluster is approximately 20% lower than for a single node, showing immediately that RAC is not a feature that you can just 'set and forget' without planning upfront to reap the benefits.

As expected, this simple single instance configuration is not sufficient, highlighting the first decision required when moving to a RAC environment – to manually tune the freelists by adding freelist groups, or move to automatic segment space management. Looking forward to a grid-based future, manually tuned segments require database reorganisation to accommodate new nodes, and are therefore a less practical option than automatic segment space management.

Automatic Segment Space Management

Taking advantage of automatic segment-space management simply requires specifying the following clause as part of the **create tablespace** statement:

```
SEGMENT SPACE MANAGEMENT AUTO
```

This clause selects the option to use bitmaps to manage the free space within segments. A bitmap tracks the status of the data blocks within a segment and the space left available in the block for inserts. The current state of each block is reflected in its respective bitmap, and free space is managed automatically, irrespective of the number of nodes in a RAC cluster.

For these tests the schema is redefined with automatic segment-space management for the data and index tablespaces, keeping the table definitions exactly the same. Reviewing the statspack report after running the same test again shows a 25% performance improvement over the previous manual segment-space management test, achieving an average of 12,239 TPM and a marginal improvement in scalability for the second node. For RAC automatic segment space management is the way to go.

In the statspack 'top five timed events' however, the top wait event '**buffer busy**

/ The UK Oracle User Group Journal / Issue 19 Autumn 2004 **Oracle Scene** 5

Fig. 3. Tuning Oracle9i RAC in UKOUG Oracle Scene

At the same time, Intel began running Hammerora workloads alongside official TPC-based workload kits on the same hardware platforms. It quickly became clear that Hammerora delivered performance ratios between systems that closely matched those of the official workloads, while producing results in a fraction of the time and at a significantly lower cost. In this role, Hammerora became established as a valuable component of Intel's testing methodology—used in much the same way as other external open-source tools, yet delivering insights of direct relevance to high-profile, industry-standard benchmarking.

2.6 Industry Adoption

In particular what was unique for the time was the implementation of a derived TPC-C workload without 'keying and thinking' time meaning most of the data was cached in memory and generated high throughput with a smaller number of Virtual Users. This was seen as much simpler to run, yet still delivering similar insights to the fully audited workloads. For example, the Oracle workload was featured in Intel keynote presentations at Oracle OpenWorld [18] and was later adopted by Oracle and Sun Microsystems to publish a benchmark showcasing Oracle Database performance on their SPARC T7–1 platform [19]. This was notable given that Sun Microsystems had withdrawn from participating in official TPC benchmarks. In this context, the approach demonstrated how an open-source benchmarking tool could fill the gap left by the rejection of fully audited workloads, enabling vendors to continue publishing comparative performance results outside of the formal TPC process.

Further enhancements were added to the Hammerora graphical interface using the new Tile based graphics to become Hammerora v2.0, and at this time Hammerora remained a GUI tool only. With the increased adoption of the Hammerora TPC-C workload NetApp requested an extension to add the TPC-H analytic workload, enabling Hammerora to add OLAP capabilities.

As the configuration became more complex Hammerora enhanced the XML configuration files, used since v1.31 that were parsed at startup to enable and improve the loading of additional benchmark settings.

3 HammerDB

Whilst the inspiration and initial goal for Hammerora was developing a software application to run performance benchmarks against Oracle on Linux, the Oracle community proved the inspiration for further extension of the tool through discussions at UKOUG meetings. The original architectural decisions were fully justified in enabling extensibility through 'C' extensions to interface with other databases in addition to Oracle meaning where these extensions existed they could be adopted and updated or created where they didn't.

3.1 SQL Server and MySQL

The first additional workload added to Hammerora was the TPC-C workload for MySQL, followed by both TPC-C and TPC-H for Microsoft SQL Server. Support for SQL Server significantly increased adoption on the Windows platform and marked a major milestone in shaping the tool's future direction and focus. At this stage, the project began moving away from its original Oracle-centric design. On the suggestion of a colleague at Intel, the software was renamed to HammerDB to reflect its broader mission of benchmarking multiple databases.

Driven by user requests, support was subsequently extended to additional systems, including PostgreSQL (TPC-C and TPC-H), Oracle TimesTen (TPC-C), and Redis (TPC-C). Across all platforms, the workloads followed the same methodology: automated multi-threaded schema builds combined with driver scripts to execute timed workloads for capturing performance metrics, either over a fixed interval for TPC-C or by running a defined query set for TPC-H.

3.2 NOPM and TPM

Around this time HammerDB first introduced the NOPM (New Orders Per Minute) as a primary OLTP performance metric. NOPM measured the same metric as the official tpmC, but without infringing on the copyright of the TPC by using the tpmC terminology. This move to NOPM was key as it enabled comparison of performance between different database engines that was not possible with TPM, the database specific measurement of transactional throughput. Nevertheless both metrics were retained to provide both the cross-database comparison but also the in-depth analysis of database statistics afforded by the database specific measurement recorded in performance metrics and reports.

Additionally NOPM enabled reporting to align more closely with the way official TPC-C results are published, making output easier to compare with TPC publications, in particular for the open source databases where no official TPC publications existed.

3.3 IBM DB2

HammerDB then fully updated the IBM Db2 interface for the Tcl language and added support for TPC-C and TPC-H for the IBM Db2 database completing the TPC based workloads for the three most popular commercial relational databases, Oracle SQL Server and Db2 as well as the two most popular open source relational databases, MySQL and PostgreSQL.

In addition at the request of HPE support for the Trafodion relational database on Hadoop was added. However this period of expansion provided a key learning. Although the HammerDB workload was fully implemented for Trafodion the performance of the Trafodion database itself was underwhelming and the project was later discontinued [20]. Similarly the Redis database although popular was a single-threaded NoSQL database meaning performance could not scale beyond the throughput of a single Virtual User on the Oracle database. Consequently a workload derived from TPC-C did not provide a fair comparison for Redis and eventually despite the time invested in development both workloads would become deprecated from HammerDB. Consequently the decision was made to only focus on workloads for well-established and proven relational databases that had the capability to perform well on both TPC-C and TPC-H workloads.

4 HammerDB V3.0

Up to this point HammerDB development had continued at pace adding features and functionality. However the expansion of supported databases prompted the urgent requirement for modularization breaking the individual database workloads into separate components for the ease of development.

Additionally, HammerDB remained a Windows and Linux GUI based tool. However with the increasing adoption of Cloud based environments the most requested feature was a CLI, command-line equivalent to the HammerDB GUI.

4.1 CLI

Further justifying the architectural decisions at the development stage, the CLI proved remarkably straightforward to implement with the Tcl language with the functionality being added as a 'shim' over the existing GUI functionality with the GUI calls being replaced by null functions and the majority of the code remaining unmodified. When running workloads the Virtual User threads load and run the driver script identically in the GUI and the CLI meaning performance is always the same regardless of the interface used. Implementing a CLI also enabled user based scripting to run automated workloads in bash on Linux and Powershell on Windows, enhancing the adoption of HammerDB in text-based environments.

4.2 GPLv3

V3.0 also signified a move towards standardized timed workloads as well as the adoption of the GPLv3 license. It also added a GUI Active Session History viewer for Oracle based on a modified version of the existing Ashmon tool and used with permission to include under GPLv3. HammerDB was now becoming established across the industry as a trusted and respected tool to implement workloads derived from the industry standard TPC-C and TPC-H workloads.

5 Adoption and Hosting by the TPC and GitHub

5.1 The TPC Dilemma

In 2017 the TPC was seeing a drop in officially audited TPC benchmarks as can be seen in Fig. 1. However, at the same time there was an increase in companies using TPC benchmark workloads for measurement purposes without submitting official results to the TPC. These two trends showed that the workloads in TPC benchmarks were seen as valuable data points by an increasing portion of the industry even while officially audited benchmark results were dropping. One of the main indicators to the TPC that interest in its workloads was increasing was the extra time spent informing and enforcing the TPC Fair Use rules defined in Sect. 8 of the TPC Policies document [21]. Many companies and individuals did not know about TPC Fair Use rules and published documents containing results using official TPC benchmark names and metrics. These documents and their authors were in violation of TPC Fair Use policies. So, the TPC had a dilemma. How could it effectively promote fair use implementations of its workloads while still protecting the integrity of its trademark, policies, and audited benchmark results? At the same time, the TPC was interested in becoming quicker and more flexible in developing new benchmarks. It was exploring the possibility of using a more open approach to software development and potentially open sourcing some TPC developed code.

5.2 The TPC Approach

In 2018 the TPC officially created the Open Source Software Committee (TPC-OSS) to explore options for using a more open development model. The goals of the TPC-OSS committee were defined as:

1. Promote open source as a development model within the TPC
2. Foster collaboration between the TPC and the open source community including academia
3. Identify and investigate open source projects that might be interesting to the TPC and align with the industry focus of the TPC
4. Promote open sourcing TPC source code
5. Promote fair use implementations of TPC workloads

As the committee discussed and investigated various open source projects that might help them achieve their goals there was one project that stood out. HammerDB. HammerDB had many attributes that were attractive to the TPC-OSS committee. It was already an established open source project with a growing user base, the author of HammerDB (Steve Shaw) was employed by Intel which was a member company of the TPC, the two workloads in HammerDB were based on existing TPC-C and TPC-H benchmark specifications, and the database benchmarking focus of HammerDB was aligned with the database performance goals of the TPC. The main negative attribute of HammerDB to the committee was its violation of the TPC's Fair Use Policy by using TPC copyrighted benchmark names. However, the TPC-OSS committee also saw this as an opportunity to achieve its defined fifth goal of promoting fair use implementations of TPC workloads. What if the TPC sponsored and helped curate the HammerDB project into one that met all the rules of a TPC Benchmark Standard fair use derivative work as defined in Sect. 8.3 of the TPC Policies? This would allow the TPC to promote HammerDB as an example to others in the industry of what fair use of TPC workloads looks like. So, the TPC-OSS committee was unanimously in favor of sponsoring, curating, and promoting HammerDB. HammerDB author Steve Shaw officially joined as a member of the TPC-OSS committee representing Intel to personally participate and help figure out the right next steps for HammerDB as a project sponsored by the TPC.

5.3 HammerDB as the Solution

When the TPC-OSS committee was formed, GitHub was the most popular code platform for open source projects and it still is today. So, the TPC-OSS committee decided to create a TPC GitHub repository to help promote TPC open source projects [22]. However, at the time HammerDB code and releases were hosted on SourceForge [23] The TPC-OSS collaborated with HammerDB author Steve Shaw to get the HammerDB code, issue tracking, and releases moved over to the TPC GitHub repository. GitHub provided multiple benefits to HammerDB as a project which included:

1. An integrated Discussions forum area to allow for users ask questions and maybe even find answers to their questions from prior postings
2. Easy linkage tracking between Discussion topics, Issues, and Pull Requests
3. Familiar code platform for potential open source community contributors

As the TPC worked through logistics of curating the HammerDB project [24] on GitHub it became clear that new policies needed to be put into place to facilitate the kind of release early, release often pace a popular open source project like HammerDB needed to have. So the TPC created a new Sect. 1.3 titled Open Source Development in the TPC Procedures Document [25] to allow just enough governance structure as well as the needed flexibility for open source projects like HammerDB. The TPC was fully invested in the success of HammerDB and did not want older wording targeted at private code development to get in the way.

Now all the pieces were in place for HammerDB to accelerate and evolve with new features as an industry leading database benchmark aligned with the TPC as a fair use implementation of TPC workloads.

6 HammerDB v4.0

After the transition to hosting on GitHub under the remit of the TPC, HammerDB underwent further modularization to simplify development and encourage contributions from external developers. Notably, the redesign made HammerDB 'dict'-driven, with all user-definable configuration data loaded from XML and stored in the Tcl dict (dictionary) format—a key–value data structure in Tcl that enables efficient storage and retrieval. This shift allowed the introduction of a number of common functions, simplifying the framework. Version 4.0 marked the first fully dict-based release.

6.1 TPROC Terminology

A key change at this point was the introduction of the TPROC-C and TPROC-H workloads. These designations were created to distinguish HammerDB's implementations from the official, audited TPC benchmarks, while ensuring compliance with TPC copyright. Additionally the TPC requested the removal of a spreadsheet based calculator for the TPC-H metric and instead HammerDB introduced a simpler geomean calculation for comparing query performance.

6.2 UHD Displays

Another notable enhancement was support for UHD displays in the HammerDB GUI. This was achieved by adopting scalable SVG graphics through the tksvg package for the

Tk toolkit. Earlier releases had relied on fixed-size graphics, which appeared uncomfortably small on high-resolution devices such as the Microsoft Surface PixelSense display. Users had specifically requested scalable graphics for public presentations of HammerDB workloads, and the addition of this feature demonstrated the extensibility of HammerDB in adapting to new display technologies.

6.3 Refactoring

At the same time, Steve Shaw and contributors from AWS provided significant refactoring and code improvements, further strengthening the foundation for HammerDB's future development.

A significant enhancement to HammerDB emerged through a contribution from Micron, who added the "use all warehouses" feature to drive substantially more I/O by having each virtual user operate across a broader set of warehouses rather than a single one. This was further advanced in collaboration with the AWS database performance team, which helped introduce several key capabilities: the xtprof time profiler, built directly into HammerDB, profiles all active virtual users in parallel so developers can see where time is spent across the entire workload, not just a single client; the asynchronous scaling option, implemented with Tcl's promise package and made possible by the Tcl event loop, enables HammerDB to scale to thousands of connections while sustaining a fixed-throughput workload in a manner closely aligned with the methodology of official audited TPC benchmarks. A major advantage here was HammerDB's foundation in Tcl: its parallel threading model is non-blocking, with each thread running its own interpreter. Because the Tcl interpreter is lightweight, HammerDB can scale in parallel to drive high throughput workloads. Moreover, as every interpreter includes Tcl's built-in event loop, each thread can also exploit the promise package to manage thousands of concurrent connections with keying and thinking time, combining parallelism and asynchronous execution in a uniquely powerful way. Finally, the steprun feature allowed controlled, incremental execution. Importantly, these enhancements are not mutually exclusive and can be combined to construct highly complex, bespoke workloads—one reason HammerDB has become the leading testing tool for cloud environments.

7 Cloud Collaborations

Recognition of HammerDB as a tool for testing cloud based relational database services was established when it was featured prominently in the AWS re:Invent 2020 Infrastructure Keynote, where Peter DeSantis used HammerDB to demonstrate the performance of PostgreSQL on Graviton processors as illustrated in Fig. 4. This marked the first time HammerDB was presented in a major cloud vendor keynote, underlining its role as the de facto standard for open-source database benchmarking at scale [26].

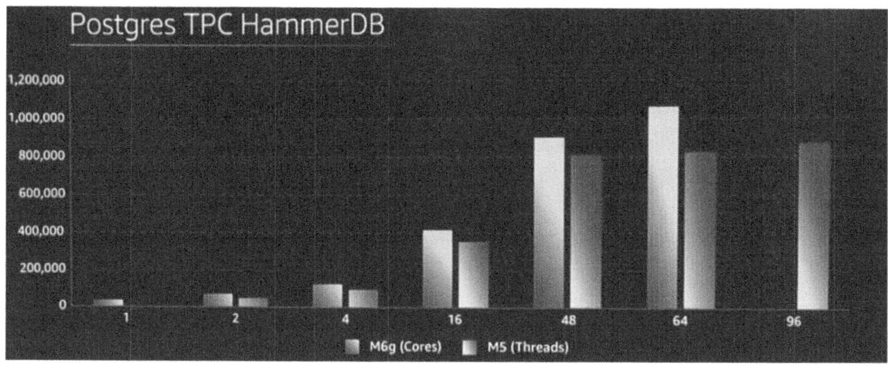

Fig. 4. Postgres TPC HammerDB at AWS re:Invent 2020

7.1 SQLite

Subsequently, cloud collaboration and usage drove further enhancements to HammerDB. In particular up to this point data and results were stored in text file format. However HammerDB using the Tcl language had a unique advantage that the SQLite database originated as a Tcl extension and is built into every Tcl build and fully integrated into the Tcl language and therefore by definition already included in every HammerDB installation.

7.2 Web Service

Previously from version 3, HammerDB had introduced a REST/HTTP based web service interface to support cloud-oriented usage, with benchmark output stored in a SQLite repository. However in a typical open source approach of release early, release often, this feature did not gain traction compared to the existing GUI and CLI interfaces. Nevertheless this functionality provided the pathfinding for rewriting and extending the web service with both GUI and command-line integration and enhanced querying features, enabling configuration, results, and timing data to be retrieved in both JSON format as well as HTTP through a browser. Using the WAPP extension from Dr Richard Hipp the author of SQLite [27], these developments provided a persistent SQLite based benchmark repository and improved the ability to integrate HammerDB within service-based cloud environments. The HTTP based web service also provided the ability to automatically generate charts from benchmark data using Apache ECharts via the ticklecharts package to provide visual diagnosis of HammerDB workloads, illustrated in Fig. 5. The HammerDB webservice also has the ability to run as an SCGI application under the NGINX web server to front the service with a production-grade web server making it robust enough for public-facing sites.

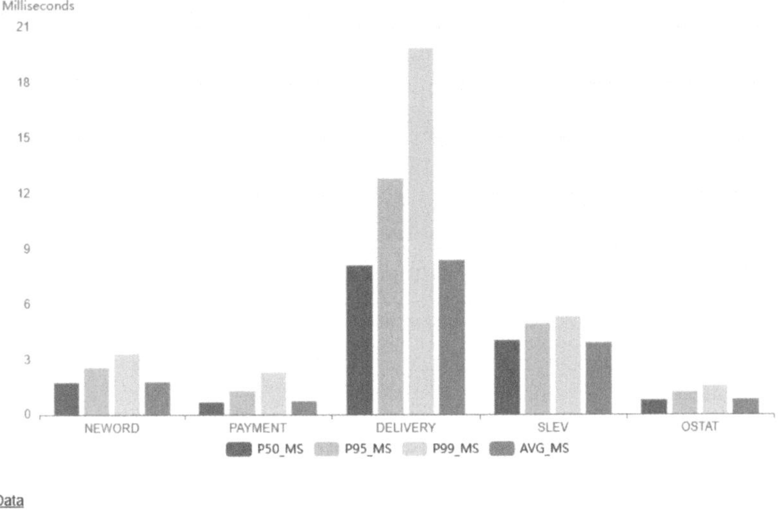

Fig. 5. Web Service Data Visualization

7.3 MariaDB

By this stage HammerDB supported all of the major relational databases offered by the leading cloud providers—AWS, Microsoft Azure, Google Cloud, and Oracle Cloud. This included the commercial systems Oracle, Microsoft SQL Server, and IBM Db2, as well as the widely adopted open-source databases MySQL and PostgreSQL. MariaDB, initially covered by the MySQL workload, was a partial exception. As MariaDB diverged from MySQL over time, HammerDB introduced MariaDB as a distinct database option to enable use of features unique to MariaDB, such as running analytic workloads against MariaDB ColumnStore, which had no MySQL equivalent. Around this time, HammerDB also began accepting external contributions extending support for cloud-based databases derived from MySQL and PostgreSQL, most notably the distributed PostgreSQL extension Citus Data from Microsoft.

7.4 Automation with Docker, Example Scripts and Python

The addition of Docker support to HammerDB began with community members publishing their own images, as users sought a simpler and more reproducible way to run benchmarks in cloud and CI/CD environments before any official container was available. Docker is an open-source platform that packages software and its dependencies into portable 'containers', ensuring that applications run consistently across different environments. To formalize this capability, Intel contributed an official Dockerfile together with example TPROC-C scripts for schema creation and workload execution [28]. From this point forward, HammerDB provided a reliable, versioned container image aligned with each release, enabling benchmarks to be launched in cloud and CI/CD environments with a single command.

The bundled example scripts offered users a ready-to-run workflow, further simplifying adoption and lowering the barrier to integrating HammerDB into automated pipelines with the scripts supporting both bash/Linux and PowerShell/Windows environments. The Docker images also included a CloudTk image, allowing the existing Tk based GUI environment to be deployed through a web browser enabling both CLI and GUI functionality in Cloud environments. This change demonstrates the unique flexibility of leveraging the Tk toolkit for graphics in that the GUI could be deployed on a desktop or through a browser with no code changes needed.

With the addition of automated scripted workloads, the requirement for additional functionality in the core workloads was clear. Firstly the ability to delete the generated schema from within HammerDB was added. This enabled all of the steps of setup, test, report and delete to be done in the self-contained HammerDB environment. Also the TPC specifications included queries for schema consistency checks and therefore an additional command in both GUI and CLI was added to run these checks.

We have seen how HammerDB was originally built on Tcl for its high performance threading capabilities and extensibility. However, although designed as a simple to learn and highly accessible language, Tcl had a reputation as a tool for highly expert and experienced engineers in areas such as database, networking, or electronic design. By contrast, although still lacking the threading capabilities for high performance database testing Python more cloud based engineers had scripting language knowledge in Python.

To make HammerDB more accessible to this wider audience, a Python extension was added to the CLI. The design took inspiration from Tkinter, which embeds Tcl inside Python. Instead of rewriting HammerDB, the existing Tcl interpreter was embedded into Python, keeping the Tcl engine with its threading and performance intact while allowing Python to act as a front end. From the user's perspective, HammerDB could now be driven directly from Python. The example scripts were provided with both Tcl and Python equivalents with both maintaining Tcl at the core for extensibility, scalability and performance, with a Python alternative at the interface for accessibility and integration.

8 Build Automation with Bawt

Despite the increased complexity and broad database support, HammerDB was still being compiled manually for Linux (gcc) and Windows (MSVC). Although all extensions used were open source and available on GitHub, the build process was not public. Consequently HammerDB moved to make the full build process automated and transparent. This was achieved by adopting and modifying the Bawt system by Paul Obermeier. [29] Using Bawt, now HammerDB could be built on both Linux and Windows by downloading the HammerDB source from GitHub, navigating to the Build directory and executing a single command. This process would then pull the HammerDB Tcl and Tk packages and all necessary extensions from the HammerDB website, compile them in the correct order and produce an executable package for the build platform. Running a build would enable the user to be able to see all of source code used in a HammerDB deployment.

Where extensions were updated by HammerDB maintainers such as Mariatcl, the modified source was also updated on GitHub. Adopting the Bawt system also allowed for a more streamlined HammerDB release cycle with the same process now used to build the executable packages available on GitHub.

9 Performance Profiles and System Metrics

HammerDB had always encouraged the development of performance profiles, running a series of benchmarks with an increasing number of virtual users to show how throughput changes as load rises. This produces a curve that reveals both the peak performance point and the point where additional load no longer improves, or more likely reduces throughput, through increased contention. This point in the curve most often provides a key point for analysis in identifying performance bottlenecks. Earlier releases supported this concept in the GUI with the autopilot feature, which could automatically step through different virtual user counts, added at user request to automate the repetitive nature of benchmarking. The CLI with scripted Tcl and Python support made generating performance profiles easy by adding for or while loops around increasing Virtual User counts. However, in the web service each Job was individually recorded, EnterpriseDB, a PostgreSQL vendor proposed grouping multiple jobs under a shared id which would enable viewing of the grouped jobs under a performance profile. This functionality was added for both the GUI with autopilot and CLI with scripting to view the relationship of multiple jobs with no manual collation of results required.

The advancement of the WAPP-based HammerDB web service, with browser-based viewing of jobs, laid the foundation for further development in workload analysis through enhanced system and database metrics. HammerDB already included a CPU metrics viewer in the GUI for both Linux and Windows, aimed at identifying active cores and breaking down utilization into user and system components. This proved particularly useful for diagnosing fully utilised cores handling interrupts on Linux, or for validating processor group configuration on Windows. The same capability was subsequently extended to the CLI, allowing total user and system CPU utilization to be reported consistently across workload runs. With these enhancements active, CPU metrics could now also be visualised graphically within the web service, giving users a unified view of database performance alongside underlying system behaviour.

10 HammerDB v5.0

The next major breakthrough came with HammerDB at v5.0, enabling the building of the release of HammerDB that had always been envisioned from the outset. This was realised by the release of Tcl 9.0, the first major release of Tcl in twenty-seven years, enabled a significant upgrade to HammerDB by modernizing both the runtime and the deployment model. Among its most impactful features was the introduction of a native zip-filesystem, which allowed HammerDB to be packaged as a self-contained single-file executable. This capability simplified distribution and installation across platforms, removing the need for multiple external dependencies and ensuring a consistent runtime environment. Additionally, having already adopted the Bawt build system the complexity in building the single-file executables requiring both static and dynamic builds could be removed with the entire process updated in the Bawt system.

However there was major development to be done as an upgrade to Tcl 9 required updating all of the C extensions for both Linux and Windows, a non-trivial task. At this time Steve Shaw took the decision to leave Intel and work full-time on HammerDB founding HammerDB Ltd to both own and manage the project going forward. This enabled the time to be dedicated to the full Tcl 9 update whilst maintaining the open source ethos on which HammerDB was established by contributing all of the Tcl 9 package updates back to the Tcl community. This also could not have been possible without the extensive support and guidance from the Tcl community itself, notably one of the core developers Ashok Nadkarni who both provided guidance on the building of the single file executables whilst also providing core Tcl functionality improvements such as the threading model and character set handling for different databases running on Windows.

In contrast to the 12,000 TPM demonstrated in the very first HammerDB publication in an enterprise server clustered environment in 2004, HammerDB can now run workloads in the millions of TPM on a single desktop system and tens of millions on a single server, as seen in Fig. 6. Further illustrating that the tool has been able to scale to reflect the advancements in both hardware and database software to orders of magnitude levels of performance improvements.

With the package updates HammerDB v5.0 was released in April 2025 and was now able to support multiple Linux installations such as RPM for RedHat and the Debian Binary Package format Ubuntu and a Windows installer.

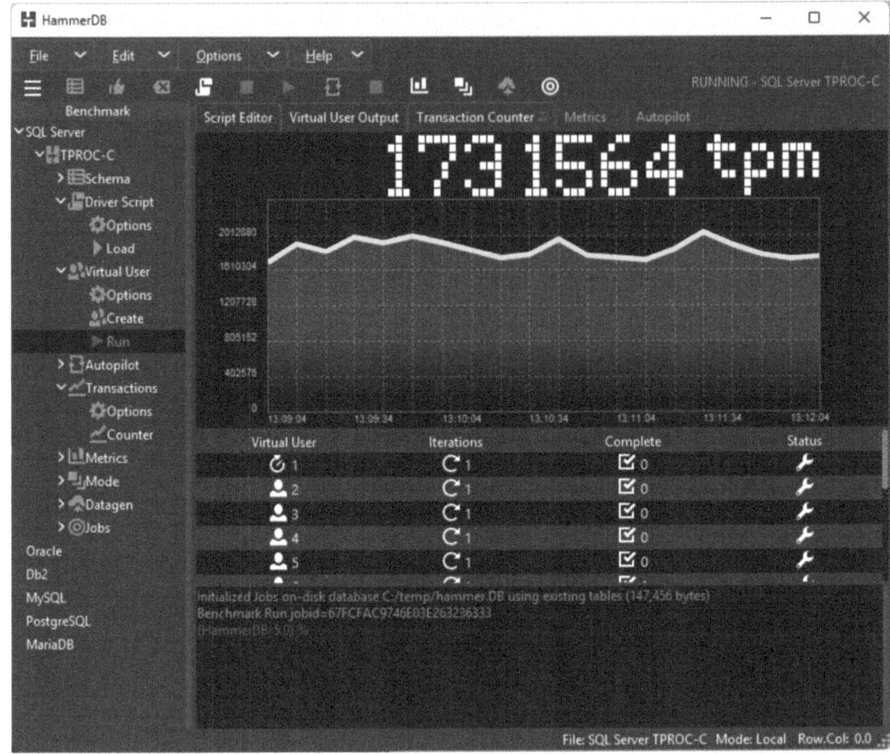

Fig. 6. HammerDB v5.0 on Windows

At the time of writing there has been over 593,000 downloads of HammerDB since TPC adoption as well as over 93,000 downloads of the provided Docker images. There are currently over 34 contributors to HammerDB on GitHub right across the global database community and HammerDB is ranked in the top 10 GitHub repositories for the Tcl language ranked by GitHub stars out of more than 24,000 repositories. [30] The collaboration between the TPC and HammerDB has been an incredible success in taking database benchmarking open source, Free and accessible to all.

11 Future Steps

The success of the TPC/HammerDB collaboration continues with regular meetings and updates with the TPC-OSS subcommittee to decide on future steps. Key planned developments are to build on the v5.0 foundation with further CI developments to integrate HammerDB into a CI pipeline, enabling HammerDB to listen to GitHub webhooks and trigger benchmarking actions. Additionally, the same approach of listening and responding to community feedback is being taken with plans to extend support of HammerDB to the ARM platform for both Windows and Linux. Finally and most importantly there are plans within the TPC for the submission of open source benchmarks with HammerDB further lowering the barrier to sharing database performance data across the industry and maintaining the TPC as the key reference for trusted database performance data.

References

1. Gray, J.N.: Database systems: A textbook case of research paying off. https://homes.cs.washington.edu/~lazowska/cra/database.html. Accessed 8 Aug 2025
2. Mordor Intelligence: Database Market Size & Share Analysis - Growth Trends & Forecasts (2025–2030).https://www.mordorintelligence.com/industry-reports/database-market. Accessed 8 Aug 2025
3. Grand View Research: Enterprise Software Market Size, Share & Trends Analysis Report By Type, By Organization, By Deployment, By Function, By End-use, By Region, And Segment Forecasts, 2024–2030. https://www.grandviewresearch.com/industry-analysis/enterprise-software-market. Accessed Aug 2025
4. Anon, et al.: A measure of transaction processing power. Datamation **31**(7), 112–118 (1985). https://jimgray.azurewebsites.net/papers/ameasureoftransactionprocessingpower.pdf. Accessed Aug 2025
5. DeWitt, D.J., Levine, C.: Not just correct, but correct and fast: a look at one of Jim Gray's contributions to database system performance. SIGMOD Record **37**(2), 45–49 (2008). https://doi.org/10.1145/1379387.1379403
6. Transaction Processing Performance Council (TPC): TPC History. https://www.tpc.org/information/history.asp. Accessed Aug 2025
7. Poess, M., Nambiar, R.O., Walrath, D.: Why you should run TPC-DS: a workload analysis. In: Proceedings of the 33rd International Conference on Very Large Data Bases (VLDB 2007), University of Vienna, Austria, 23–27 September 2007. ACM (2007)
8. Taheri, H. R.: Does the TPC still have relevance? In: Proceedings of the 11th Conference on Hot Topics in Storage and Filesystems (HPTS 2017), 9 October 2017. VMware Inc. (2017). https://hpts.ws/papers/2017/tpc-relevance.pdf
9. Regan, K.: Sun Declares War on TPC. The Register (2001). https://www.theregister.com/2001/09/26/sun_declares_war_on_tpc/
10. Shakshober, J., Trehan, V.: Understanding the Performance of enterprise applications on x86 systems. In: Proceedings of Red Hat Summit 2009 (2009).https://www.insight.com/content/dam/insight/en_US/pdfs/redhat/whitepapers/red-hat-clear-leader-for-enterprise-web-applications-whitepaper.pdf
11. Poess, M., Othayoth Nambiar, R.: Large scale data warehouses on grid: oracle database 10g and HP proliant systems. In: Proceedings of the 31st International Conference on Very Large Data Bases (VLDB 2005), Trondheim, Norway, 30 August–2 September 2005. ACM (2005)
12. Oracle and Open Source – Tools and Applications: Includes Perl, Linux, Tcl, Python, Apache, Java and More. https://www.oreilly.com/library/view/oracle-and-open/0596000189/
13. Open Source Development Labs. https://en.wikipedia.org/wiki/Open_Source_Development_Labs
14. Ogasawara, T.: Scalability Limitations when Running a Java Web Server on a Chip Multiprocessor. SYSTOR 2010, IBM Research – Tokyo (2010). https://research.ibm.com/haifa/conferences/_systor2010/present/1_2_2_presentation.pdf
15. Welch, B.: Threads Done Right… with Tcl. ActiveState blog (2016). https://www.activestate.com/blog/threads-done-right-tcl
16. Contact the TPC. https://www.tpc.org/information/about
17. Dyke, J., Shaw, S.: Pro Oracle Database 10g RAC on Linux: Installation, Administration, and Performance, 1st edn. Apress (2006). https://doi.org/10.1007/978-1-4302-0214-1

18. James, R.J.: Silicon Photonics demonstration—Oracle OpenWorld 2014 keynote. In: Oracle OpenWorld 2014, Moscone Center, San Francisco, USA. Oracle Corporation (2014). http://medianetwork.oracle.com/video/player/3811144032001. Accessed 15 Aug 2025
19. Whitney, B.: OLTPbenchmark (TPC-C) Workload, Open-Source Benchmark: SPARC T7–1 Performance Beats IBM S824, Beats x86 E5–2699 v3. Oracle Advanced (Oracle Corporation) (2016). Accessed 17 Mar 2016
20. Apache Software Foundation Board of Directors: Board Meeting Minutes—April 21, 2021: Special Order 7H, Terminate the Apache Trafodion Project. https://whimsy.apache.org/board/minutes/Trafodion.html
21. TPC Policies Document. https://www.tpc.org/TPC_Documents_Current_Versions/pdf/Policies_v6.19.pdfSee. Also TPC Fair Use Quick Reference Document. https://www.tpc.org/TPC_Documents_Current_Versions/pdf/Fair_Use_Quick_Reference_v1.0.0.pdf
22. TPC GitHub Repository. https://github.com/TPC-Council
23. Archived HammerDB SourceForge project. https://sourceforge.net/projects/hammerdb/
24. HammerDB GitHub Repository. https://github.com/TPC-Council/HammerDB
25. TPC Procedures Document. https://www.tpc.org/TPC_Documents_Current_Versions/pdf/Procedures_v1.0.0.pdf
26. DeSantis, P.: AWS re:Invent 2020 Infrastructure Keynote. Amazon Web Services (2020). https://aws.amazon.com/blogs/aws/reinvent-2020-liveblog-infrastructure-keynote/
27. Hipp, D.R.: Wapp – a super-simple yet powerful, secure, and robust framework for writing web applications in Tcl. In: Proceedings of the 26th Annual Tcl/Tk Conference (Tcl'2019), Houston, Texas, USA, 5–8 November 2019. Tcl Community Association (2019). https://www.tcl-lang.org/community/tcl2019/assets/talk159/Paper.html. Accessed 20 Aug 2025
28. Jain, P.: Added Dockerfile to build a HammerDB container and TPROC_C sample scripts to build schema and run tests. Pull Request #339, TPC-Council/HammerDB (GitHub) (2022). https://github.com/TPC-Council/HammerDB/pull/339
29. Obermeier, P.: BAWT – Build Automation With Tcl. User Manual version 2.0.0, 22 August 2021, Copyright 2016–2021 by Paul Obermeier
30. https://www.tcl3d.org/bawt/download/BawtManual-2.0.0.pdf. Stardev.io: Top Tcl Repositories by GitHub Stars. https://www.stardev.io/languages/tcl

Delivering MLPerf Submissions on AMD Instinct GPUs: Journey to Leadership Performance

Miro Hodak[1(✉)] and Meena Arunachalam[2]

[1] AMD, Artificial Intelligence Group, Austin, TX 78735, USA
Miro.Hodak@amd.com

[2] AMD, Artificial Intelligence Group, Santa Clara, CA 95054, USA

Abstract. MLPerf is the best-known industry standard AI benchmark. With buy-in from key industry players, fully defined performance and accuracy metrics it stands alone as the de facto standard AI benchmark. At the same time, submissions to MLPerf on new platforms are very difficult. A significant investment is needed for a new organization to generate results competitive with established submissions. In this contribution, we show how AMD was able to publish competitive and even leadership performance in the space of 1 year covering both MLPerf Inference and MLPerf Training on several Instinct GPU platforms. Focusing on a few sub-benchmarks and extensive optimizations enabled the initial submissions. Overall, we find that MLPerf has a high barrier to entry and cross-company alignment is necessary for successful submissions.

Keywords: AI · Benchmark · MLPerf

1 Introduction

Benchmarking Artificial Intelligence (AI) workloads is a difficult task. The field moves very fast while benchmarking values stability and predictability. It is hard to identify the right models to use and model execution depends on many techniques and parameters that substantially affect performance. In addition, accuracy of the results needs to be considered alongside the performance.

Given the number of parameters and choices, AI benchmarking needs to be a collaborative project to arrive at a fair evaluation of the field. Currently, MLPerf benchmarks [1] administered by MLCommons consortium [2] are the only collaborative benchmarks covering cutting edge AI. As such, they are the *de-facto* standard for measuring AI performance. Established in 2018, the benchmark suite covers multiple areas of AI workloads including inference, training, storage, and safety.

One of the key features of MLPerf benchmarks is that they allow a wide variety of modifications and optimizations as long as rules of mathematical equivalency [3] are satisfied. These include a complete reimplementation of reference code and quantization to any numerical precisions. These rules make the benchmarks very flexible and allow

R. Nambiar and M. Poess (Eds.): TPCTC 2025, LNCS 16261, pp. 155–169, 2026.
https://doi.org/10.1007/978-3-032-18070-4_10

submitters showcase newly supported numerical formats such as FP4 for established benchmarks. The downside is that competitive submissions require significant development time and resources and as a result many smaller AI chip vendors decided not to participate [4].

This article summarizes experience and learnings to deliver competitive MLPerf benchmark publications on AMD Instinct accelerators. With MLPerf being very different from traditional benchmarks where code is provided, a different approach that combines development, optimization, and cross-team collaboration is needed. Even with this approach, delivering each benchmark in MLPerf suite is a time-consuming effort that requires executive level prioritization and alignment between multiple teams. Over the course of this, now a year old, effort we were able to deliver submissions in both MLPerf Inference and Training and continue to work on expanding our benchmark coverage.

The article is structured as follows: Second section gives overview of MLPerf benchmarks, Sect. 3 gives timeline and results of authors efforts to deliver MLPerf submissions while Sects. 4 and 5 give overview of optimizations that made the publications possible. Section 6 describes the value of MLPerf beyond publications and Sect. 7 summarizes learnings throughout this process. Section 8 discusses future steps in the project and Sect. 9 provides a summary.

2 MLPerf Overview

Founded in 2018, MLPerf built on previous AI benchmarking effort DAWNBench [5]. The very first results were published in late 2018 for MLPerf Training with MLPerf Inference added in 2019. MLCommons was founded the following year as an organization overseeing the MLPerf benchmarks and other activities. Since then, MLPerf has steadily grown to include storage, safety, client and mobile devices and other aspects of AI usage.

Key aspects of MLPerf success are: (i) collaborative engineering, (ii) fast pace of change, and (iii) flexibility. First, MLPerf brings together companies that compete in the AI marketplace to define fair benchmarks. Second, MLPerf benchmarks are rapidly updated often to keep pace with the field. Finally, flexibility allows submitters to re-implement the benchmarks in their framework of choice and use any numerical precision. The guardrails are that the new code needs to be mathematically equivalent to the original and that the accuracy targets must be met.

Here we are concerned with MLPerf Inference for Datacenter and MLPerf Training. Both benchmark suites have two submission windows in a year. Submitters are free to pick and choose which sub-benchmarks they want to submit. Currently, as of v5.0, MLPerf Inference Datacenter has 10 benchmarks, while MLPerf Training has 7. Submissions are followed by a peer review period of several weeks during which results can be withdrawn. Following the review period, results are published on MLCommons website. The publication includes code and logs so that published scores can be verified by the public after publication.

Most of MLPerf submissions come from server manufacturers. They partner with accelerator vendors who provide optimized implementations of the benchmarks for their chips. Therefore, it is the accelerator vendors who do most of development and optimization work, while server OEMs focus on platform level tunings. The accelerator vendors also publish their own results, so in each MLPerf round there are results for systems with the same (or very similar) configurations from multiple sources.

Currently, as of June 2025, both MLPerf Inference and Training are at v5.0 with v5.1 rounds coming later in the year. In v5.0, Inference had 20 submitting organizations and Training 19. Inference had 4 different accelerator vendors: AMD, Nvidia, Google, and Intel (CPU only). For Training v5.0 it was AMD, Nvidia, and Google.

MLPerf Inference submissions typically require two scenarios: Offline and Server. In the former, a single query containing all of the data is sent to the System Under Test (SUT) and the time to process the data is recorded. This is the simplest scenario covering batch processing and the metric is throughput in samples per second. Server scenario represents online processing of requests. Samples are sent with certain frequency according to a Poisson distribution. The maximum frequency at which responses can be returned within a pre-defined latency is the performance result expressed as queries per second. For LLMs, both scores are displayed in tokens/sec.

MLPerf Training metric is time-to-train, that is the time it takes to reach a predefined convergence criterion when starting from a randomized model or from a model checkpoint as defined for each benchmark.

3 Timeline of the Effort and Results

The effort that led to the inaugural AMD MLPerf submission in MLPerf Inference 4.1 due in July 2024, started in late spring 2024 as a feasibility effort led by the authors with participation of members of different teams and several contractors. We have decided to focus on a single model, Llama2-70b benchmark [6], one of nine MLPerf Inference Datacenter v4.1 workloads. The reason for selecting this benchmark was the popularity of Llama models and the field and an overlap with customer optimization requests for this model.

The hardware target was an AMD Instinct MI300X GPU that natively supports FP8 data type format. The performance goal was for an 8xMI300X server to match the performance of 8x Nvidia H100 GPU server, which in the v4.0 round achieved performance of about 22,000 tokens/sec (submission ID 4.0-0062). Initial performance was much lower, at about 6,000 tokens/sec, indicating that substantial performance improvements were needed. Utilizing FP8 quantization, GEMM tunings and other optimizations described in the next section, we were able to exceed the target and achieve the Offline performance of 23,515 tokens/second (submission ID 4.1-0002) in the space of about 6 weeks. Figure 1 shows performance improvements leading to the submission.

In addition to AMD's own publication, we shared the optimized code with Dell who published their own score on their AMD MI300X server and achieved a similar score.

Building on the success in the MLPerf Inference v4.1, a new team focused on MLPerf optimizations and publications has been created under the leadership of one of the authors (MA). The team took on MLPerf Inference v5.0, due in February 2025, and delivered publication on of Llama2-70b and SDXL on MI325X. The Llama2-70b score increased by 45% from the previous round to 33,928 Offline tokens/sec, submission ID 5.0-0001. Platform partners increased to 4: ASUSTeK, GigaComputing, MangoBoost,

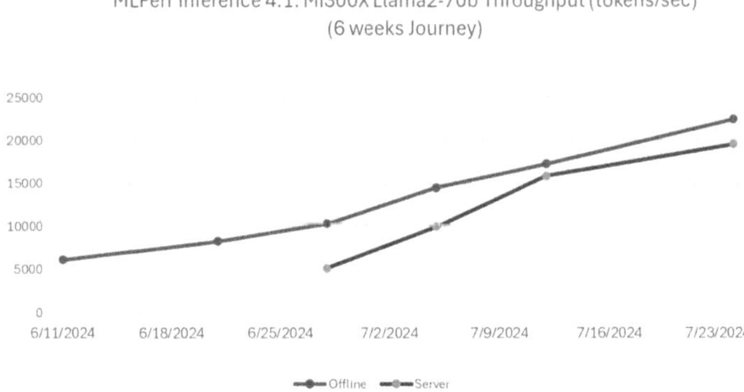

Fig. 1. Performance improvement over the initial effort to deliver MLPerf Inference 4.1.

and Supermicro. The progression of the performance results for Llama2-70b Inference benchmark is shown in Fig. 2.

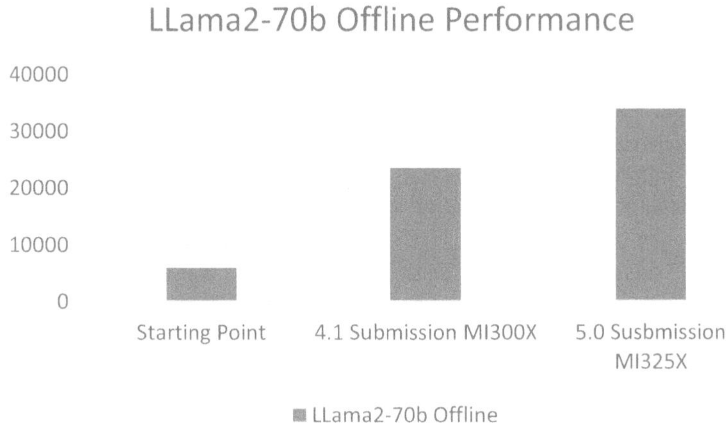

Fig. 2. Performance improvements across MLPerf Inference submission for Llama2-70b Offline.

The team has extended its focus to MLPerf Training and delivered the first ever MLPerf Training submission in the v5.0 round in May 2025. The submission utilized MI300X and MI325X in Llama2-70b Lora fine-tuning benchmark on a single node. The results relative to the competition are shown in Fig. 3. The base for comparison to MI300X (5.0-0026) is Nvidia H100 result from the 4.1 round – the latest available for that GPU, 4.1-0050. The base for comparison to MI300X (5.0-0027) is the average of all available H200 submissions in v5.0: 5.0-0034, 5.0-0045, 5.0-0050, 5.0-0078, 5.0-0081 and 5.0-0090, which is 24.02 min.

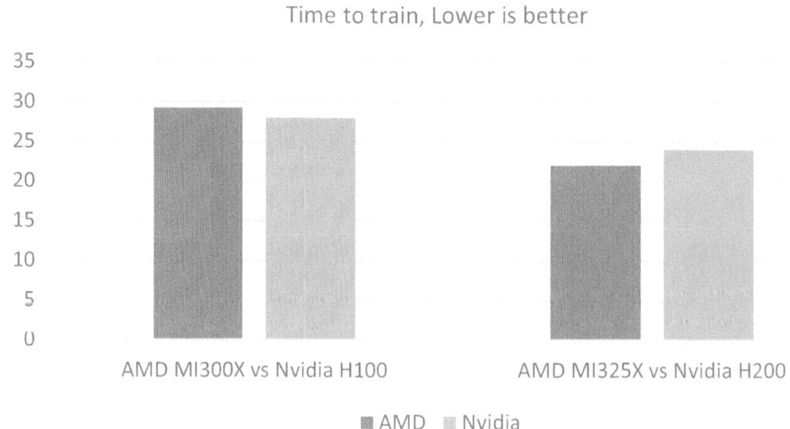

Fig. 3. Comparison of AMD vs Nvidia MLPerf Training results. AMD result IDs are 5.0-0026 for MI300X and 5.0-0027 for MI300X.

Once again, partnerships with server OEMs and cloud providers were part of this effort and we have submitted with 6 partners: Dell, GigaComputing, MangoBoost, Oracle, QCT, and Supermicro.

An engineering partnership with MangoBoost, an AI startup, produced a multi-node training submission, extending our single node submission to up to 4 nodes. Scale-out is an important part of AI training and this collaboration enabled first ever multi-node submission on AMD Instinct GPUs.

Most recently, MLPerf has been used to generate data for the launch of a new Instinct GPU, MI355X. Building on MLPerf Training v5.0 submission, the Llama2-70 Lora benchmark was ported to the new MI355X GPU and achieved an unofficial MLPerf score better than competing GPUs in v5.0. This datapoint was part of AMD Advancing AI event and was presented by AMD CEO, Lisa Su [7]. The slide from the presentation is shown in Fig. 4. Including MLPerf in such a high-profile event demonstrates growing adoption of MLPerf as an industry standard performance measurement within the company.

Table 1 below summarizes the MLPerf publications delivered by our team. While clearly in the early stages, it shows progression going from no publications prior to 2024, to publications in both MLPerf Inference and Training and even public events within a space of a year. At the same time, the number of publication partners increases as does the coverage of benchmarks and GPUs.

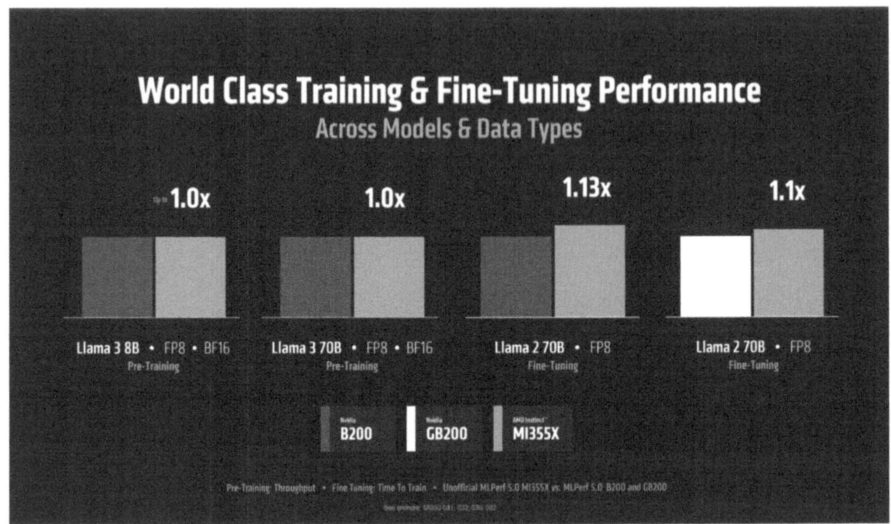

Fig. 4. A slide from AMD Advancing AI 2025 event showing MLPerf data labeled as "Llama2 70B FP8 Fine-Tuning" on the right-hand side.

Table 1. Summary of MLPerf Data Publications

Event	Date	Models	GPU	Partners
MLPerf Inference 4.1	July 2024	Llama2-70b	MI300X	1
MLPerf Inference 5.0	February 2025	Llama2-70b SD-XL	MI325X	4
MLPerf Training 5.0	May 2025	Llama2-70b Lora	MI300X, MI325X	6
Advancing AI	June 2025	Llama2-70b Lora	MI355X	N/A

4 MLPerf Inference Optimizations

Our Inference submissions for LLMs have been implemented within the vLLM inference framework [8]. The following optimizations areas were most impactful.

4.1 vLLM Optimizations

Scheduling in the vLLM inference engine is a key factor that impacts efficiency. Scheduling can introduce CPU overhead that can lower GPU utilization and throughput. Using *num_scheduler_steps*, N decode steps at once can be scheduled, thus executing N forward steps consecutively without waiting for CPU instructions. Two key hyperparameters need to be tuned as well: *max_num_batched_tokens* and *max_num_seqs*, which determine maximum batch sizes for prefill and decode, respectively.

To further enhance performance, we batch as many queries as possible, minimizing the overhead of end-to-end kernel calls and maximizing GPU throughput. In the offline scenario, we consistently achieve batch sizes close to the maximum for both prefill and decode phases. In the server scenario, while adhering to TTFT constraints, we avoid prefill when the number of queries that are waiting to be prefilled is low, ensuring efficient GPU utilization.

4.2 MLPerf Harness Optimizations

LLM serving typically uses multiple GPUs with multiple vLLM instances to serve the user queries. It is essential that we distribute the load on each GPU equally, as imbalance in loads can cause significant queueing delays. The problem is further complicated by the variations in input sequence length (ISL) and output sequence length (OSL) of each query. To address this problem, we have developed a load balancing algorithm that chooses the GPU with the minimum load, based on the number of queries and size of queries in each GPU, to assign an incoming query.

4.3 Quantization

Using AMD Quark, we quantize the model using the Open Compute Project (OCP) FP8-e4m3 format. For calibration, we used the calibration dataset provided by MLPerf for the Llama2-70b model. All linear layers in the decoder blocks are quantized, covering both inputs and weights. The quantization scales for inputs and weights are computed during calibration. The weights for query (Q), key (K), and value (V) share one common scale, which is the highest of their individual scales. We also apply the AutoSmoothQuant algorithm in AMD Quark to reduce errors. The KV cache entries are also quantized. We experimented with several quantization recipes, such as FP8 Attention quantization to produce the best performing model that satisfies MLPerf accuracy criteria.

4.4 GEMM Tuning

In the Llama 2 70B model, GEMM accounts for over 70% of the total end-to-end computation cost as shown in Fig. 5. We identified the most performance-critical FP8 GEMMs and optimized them with hipBLASLt offline GEMM tuning to pick appropriate tile sizes to reach high compute efficiencies. As a result of this work, prefill and decode phases on MI325X achieve 1.5K TFLOPs and 1.4K TFLOPs, respectively. We repeat GEMM tuning runs as we optimize and improve performance for the other phases of the benchmark that enable the GPU to handle larger batch sizes while keeping within the TTFT and TPOT latency thresholds.

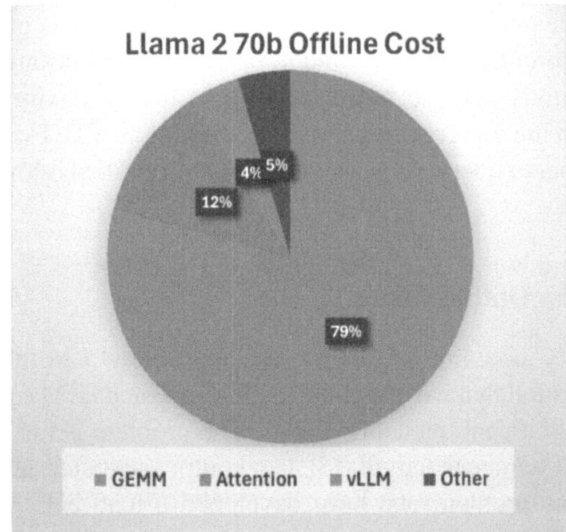

Fig. 5. Breakdown of Llama2-70b Inference Computational Cost.

5 MLPerf Training Optimizations

In MLPerf Training Llama 2 70B LoRA fine-tuning benchmark only a small subset of the model's parameters are trained by injecting trainable low-rank matrices into specific layers of the transformer architecture. This approach significantly reduces memory consumption and computational overhead compared to full fine-tuning, enabling faster training and lowering resource requirements without compromising model accuracy. The following optimization techniques were most important for achieving optimal performance.

5.1 Utilizing Large Memory Capacity

AMD Instinct accelerators offer industry-leading memory sizes, and we took advantage of this feature to improve our performance. When using MI325X with 256GB of HBM3e we were able to fit the entire model into the memory of a single GPU thus dramatically decreasing networking communication and improving training performance. The same thing is possible on MI300X with 192GB of HBM3, but activation checkpointing (recomputing all 21 transformer blocks during the backward pass) has to be used. This introduces an overhead, but it is still preferable relative to the communication cost and improves training throughput by over 20%.

5.2 Flash Attention Optimization

Using Flash Attention implemented within AMD's Composable Kernel for backend the FAv3 backward pass helped reduce the time-to-train score ~23%. In this setup, BF16 Flash Attention was leveraged through the ROCm Transformer Engine, using Composable Kernel as the backend.

5.3 GEMM Tuning Optimizations

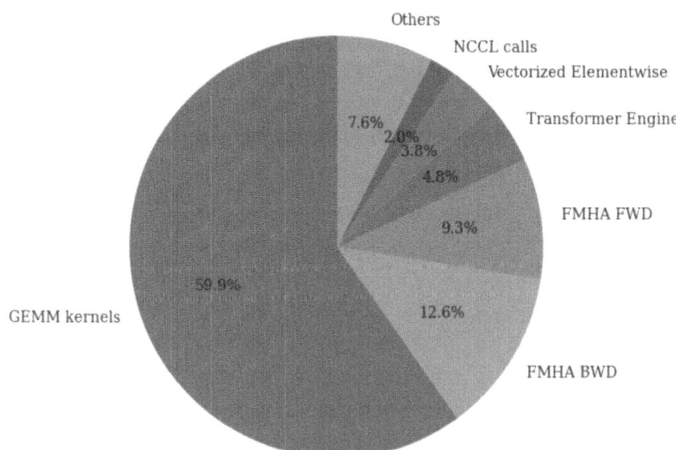

Fig. 6. Breakdown of Computational Kernels for Llama2-70b Lora fine-tuning

The distribution of time spent on different kernels (see Fig. 6) shows that GEMMs make up 60% of the end-to-end latency and therefore, it is critical to optimize their performance. GEMM tuning allows picking the most optimal kernels for GEMM computations. Using offline GEMM tuning, we were able to achieve about 10% improvement in GEMM performance.

5.4 Transformer Engine Improvements

Several non-GEMM kernels were optimized by developing forward and backward implementations. Improvements to RMSNorm, SwiGLU and Elementwise cast transpose operations brought about 5% improvement in training throughput.

5.5 System Tuning

While the majority of performance gains came from optimizing GPU kernels and exploiting high-throughput memory, CPU configuration and OS-level settings contribute as well. We have found that the following system settings provide best performance

- Clearing the file system cache avoiding stale cache effects
- Disabling low-power sleep states to prevent CPUs from going to sleep between kernel launches
- Setting the CPU frequency to performance mode to keep CPUs at max clock speed
- Disabling NUMA balancing, address space randomization, and watchdog timers to reduce runtime overhead and variability
- Enables Transparent Huge Pages (THP) and defragmentation to improve memory access efficiency

6 Value of MLPerf Beyond Submissions

One of the most important learnings throughout this process is that MLPerf has significant value beyond generating benchmarking scores for public submissions. Below are some of the most important areas.

6.1 Improving Relationships Between GPU/Accelerator Makers and Server OEMs/Cloud Providers

As mentioned above, chip vendors optimize MLPerf workloads for their chips and share the code with server OEMs and cloud providers. This is a mutually beneficial relationship: a chip vendor gets a larger presence in MLPerf publications while platform makers/providers get public validations of their platforms.

These are highly valued by OEMs because the data is often used in customer conversations and support sales. In addition, the OEMs engineering teams gain experience executing workloads and optimizing performance for new platforms. Finally, it gives those entities directly comparable data they can bring to their customers so that they can evaluate value propositions of different accelerated systems.

Overall, we did find the server OEMs response overwhelmingly positive and most of OEMs building AMD Instinct GPU-based servers have actively asked for optimized MLPerf code and have been encouraging us to increase our coverage of optimized MLPerf workloads. The collaboration improved relationships between engineering teams on both sides and has enabled OEMs to better understand performance tuning on AMD Instinct GPUs.

6.2 Publicly Available Reproducible Performance

Reproducibility is one of the key principles of MLPerf publications. This is ensured by releasing the code that was used to generate scores as a part of results publication. Reproducibility makes MLPerf publications uniquely useful because many other public performance claims such as product launches, marketing materials or blogs, only provide disclosures while the code itself remains unavailable.

We have embraced this aspect of MLPerf and went beyond the basic requirements. In practice, MLPerf publications are hard to reproduce: the instructions are often hard to follow and setup procedures for models and datasets are tedious and complicated. To improve on this, we have released blogs aimed at easy reproduction of our submissions [9–11]. For example, for MLPerf Inference v5.0 we have simplified the procedure by releasing prebuilt docker container on dockerhub [12], quantized Llama2-70b model on HuggingFace [13] and created a script that downloads the preprocessed dataset. Therefore, the reproduction procedure is as follows [10]:

1. Pull and start docker container
2. Get quantized model from Hugging Face
3. Download pre-processed dataset
4. Apply optional system/GPU tuning scripts
5. Run inference benchmark in Offline or Server scenario

While this procedure still takes time – the quantized model is about 70 GB, the manual steps are kept to a minimum. Once the prerequisites are in place, the procedure can be easily integrated into CI/CD testing pipelines making MLPerf useful for regression testing. These efforts have been lauded by Semianalysis [14] who said: "AMD has started posting easy-to-follow instructions that allow users and developers to replicate their benchmarking runs instead of publishing unrealistic or biased performance claims that can't be verified."

6.3 Generating Data for RFPs and Customers Asks

MLPerf is part of many public RFPs as well as requested by individual customers to evaluate performance of competing solutions. While using MLPerf for purchasing decisions makes sense as it is a *de facto* industry standard, the fact that generating competitive MLPerf scores is extremely time and resource intensive effectively locks out vendors that do not already have performant MLPerf implementations.

The publications performed as a part of this effort have enabled AMD participation in additional public tenders, which further underscores the value of this work.

6.4 Technical Marketing

Marketing is an important aspect of MLPerf publications. Every release is preceded by the MLCommons-organized press meeting where finalized results are shared with technical journalists who have the opportunity to ask questions. In addition, every organization can organize their own press meetings giving the press their side of the story. These press briefings serve as a basis for articles covering MLPerf releases. Therefore, each submission brings press exposure to participating companies.

We have actively participated in this process by attending MLCommons press briefings and organizing our own ones. With MLPerf results published as a long spreadsheet and multiple results for each GPU, the interpretation of the results is always obvious. Our own briefings have focused on our competitive standings compared to competing GPUs of the same generation. In addition, we have highlighted our partners and their submissions on AMD Instinct GPUs. An example of our messaging showing performance leadership in gen-on-gen comparison, which made its way into several press articles [15] for MLPerf Training v5.0 is shown in Fig. 7.

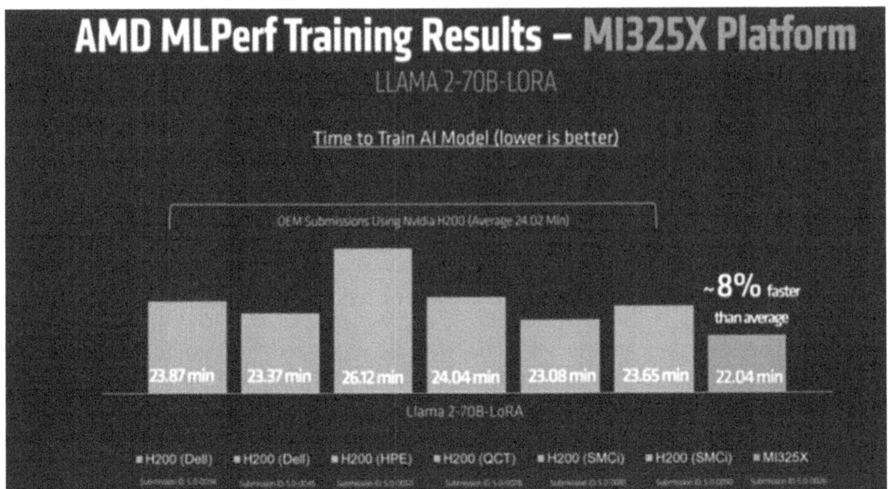

Fig. 7. A slide from AMD Press Briefing for MLPerf Training v5.0 publication.

7 Learnings

7.1 High Cost of Delivering MLPerf Benchmarks

The most important lesson has been that optimizing each sub-benchmark takes a lot of resources – both engineering and computational – and time. So far, in one year of existence, our team has published 2 MLPerf Inference benchmarks (out of 10 possible) and 1 Training benchmark out of a total of 7. More benchmarks have been attempted but they have not been fully optimized for our hardware targets.

The high cost of MLPerf benchmarks stems from the fact that existing submissions are highly optimized and utilize accelerators close to 100% throughout the workload execution. Therefore, new submissions need to be optimized as well, otherwise the results will not reflect hardware capabilities. This makes MLPerf an optimization benchmark: any inefficiency needs to be identified and improved until the workload performance is close to its roofline limit.

7.2 Alignment with Other Teams is Critical

Another important realization has been that MLPerf delivery cannot be contained within a single team. Alignment and prioritization are needed across multiple teams spanning both software and hardware components. On the software side, alignment with frameworks and libraries teams is critical. All the necessary features need to be supported in the framework and all the computational kernels need to be highly performant by the submission deadline.

On the hardware side, collaboration with firmware and platform optimization teams brought additional performance improvement. In particular, adjusting GPU frequency and power settings gave us an additional performance boost. The settings have been propagated into publicly released firmware. We have found that using high-frequency

CPUs improves performance for CPU-bound parts of the execution pipeline. Finally, early access to new systems is critical to have sufficient time to publish MLPerf on new platforms in line with MLPerf schedule.

For this collaboration to work, we needed executive prioritization and have created a virtual cross-functional team to make sure that all features are delivered on time.

7.3 MLPerf Publications are Highly Competitive

Because MLPerf facilitates direct comparison between platforms, publications are highly competitive. With only 2 opportunities per year to submit, there is a pressure to submit as optimized scores as possible at the deadline.

Our goal has been to match the performance of GPUs with similar specs to our own GPUs. The benchmarks that did not match this criterion were not published as this would create a false picture of performance. Because of this, our approach has been to deeply optimize a narrow set of MLPerf benchmarks rather than targeting a wide range of benchmarks.

7.4 Fast Pace of Performance Improvement

With constant improvements in AI algorithms, numerical techniques, and other optimizations, MLPerf results improve from round to round even on the same hardware. It is not unusual to see round-to-round performance improvements of more than 10% for the same system.

That means that the benchmark code needs to be constantly optimized and improved to keep pace with the field and competition even for platforms that have already have an existing score.

The improvements need to be considered when trying to match a competitor's score: Meeting the score from the previous round is not sufficient, a performance improvement needs to be estimated to get a performance target.

7.5 Support for Low Numerical Precisions is a Must

MLPerf does not separate results according to numerical precisions. All the results are equal as long as they satisfy accuracy criteria. This encourages using low numerical precisions. While MLPerf accuracy targets are quite strict, it has turned out that these can be satisfied by with low numerical precisions – FP8 for training and, remarkably, FP4 for Inference.

Because these precisions offer significant performance improvement, using higher precision would put submitters at a competitive disadvantage. Therefore, hardware and software support for state-of-the art numerical precisions is a must. The downside of this approach is that higher precisions, which are still commonly used for practical applications, are not being submitted to MLPerf because there is no way to convey within MLPerf results display that the results have been obtained using higher precision.

8 Future Steps

The results and progress presented here are a snapshot of this effort as of June 2025. Going forward our plan is to increase benchmark coverage and support upcoming Instinct GPUs. Generally, adding a new benchmark for each Inference and Training round is desirable. With 10 benchmarks in the MLPerf Inference suite and 7 in MLPerf Training, there is still a need to increase the benchmark coverage. For Training, expansion needs to be both in scope and scale because AI training is a scale-out problem so networking and convergence at scale need to be considered as well.

Supporting new GPUs will require support for new numerical precision. The upcoming MI355X GPU will support FP4 in hardware and thus performance needs to be optimized for the FP4 datatype while preserving accuracy. In addition, timing needs to be considered as well. Because MLPerf allows for Preview submissions on unreleased hardware, early access is important to showcase new GPUs. This needs to be accompanied by library optimizations for MLPerf workloads, which can be a challenge given competing priorities in supporting customer workloads.

9 Summary

MLPerf is different from traditional benchmarks. Its setup reflects a highly moving field and allows a high degree of flexibility. This makes it a benchmark with a high barrier to entry. With established submitters already spent time optimizing the many sub-benchmarks in MLPerf Training and Inference suites, it is difficult for the new entrants to get to the same level of software optimization even for GPUs and accelerators with equivalent performance.

Based on these considerations, our approach has been to go narrow and deep – that is, to focus on a few benchmarks for our initial publications. This has been met with success as we were able to publish competitive MLPerf Inference and Training submissions. Getting alignment with software teams responsible for frameworks and libraries has been crucial because support for the latest algorithms and highly tuned computational kernels is a must and needs to be delivered on time to meet submission deadlines.

Overall, we find that the investment in MLPerf brings significant benefits beyond publications. It opens new potential revenue streams for RFPs that require MLPerf scores. It provides a clear view of the gaps in capabilities in benchmarks that cannot achieve the expected performance. Also, it improves collaboration with partners and public code release allows 3rd parties to reproduce and validate performance claims.

Disclosure of Interests. The authors have no competing interests to declare that are relevant to the content of this article.

References

1. MLPerf Benchmarks. https://mlcommons.org/benchmarks/. Accessed 23 June 2025
2. MLCommons. https://mlcommons.org/about-us/. Accessed 23 June 2025

3. MLPerf Training Rules. https://github.com/mlcommons/training_policies/blob/master/training_rules.adoc. Accessed 23 June 2025
4. ZDNet Article. https://www.zdnet.com/article/cerebras-did-not-spend-one-minute-working-on-mlperf-says-ceo/. Accessed 23 June 2025
5. DAWNBench. https://dawnd9.sites.stanford.edu/dawnbench. Accessed 23 June 2025
6. Llama 2 70B: An MLPerf Inference Benchmark for Large Language Models. https://mlcommons.org/2024/03/mlperf-llama2-70b/. Accessed 23 June 2025
7. Advancing AI 2025 Keynote. https://www.amd.com/en/corporate/events/advancing-ai/keynote-2025.html. Accessed 23 June 2025
8. vLLM: Easy, fast, and cheap LLM serving for everyone. https://docs.vllm.ai/en/latest/. Accessed 23 June 2025
9. ROCm Blogs: Benchmarking Machine Learning using ROCm and AMD GPUs: Reproducing Our MLPerf Inference Submission. https://rocm.blogs.amd.com/artificial-intelligence/mlperf-inf-4-1/README.html. Accessed 23 June 2025
10. ROCm Blogs: Reproducing the AMD Instinct™ GPUs MLPerf Inference v5.0 Submission. https://rocm.blogs.amd.com/artificial-intelligence/reproducing-amd-mlperf-inference-submission/README.html. Accessed 23 June 2025
11. ROCm Blogs: Reproduce AMD's MLPerf Training v5.0 Submission Result with Instinct™ GPUs. https://rocm.blogs.amd.com/artificial-intelligence/reproduce-mlperf-training-v5.0/README.html. Accessed 23 June 2025
12. Docker Repository of AMD Optimized Containers for MLPerf Inference and Training. https://hub.docker.com/r/rocm/amd-mlperf. Accessed 23 June 2025
13. HuggingFace: amd/Llama-2-70b-chat-hf_FP8_MLPerf_V2. https://huggingface.co/amd/Llama-2-70b-chat-hf_FP8_MLPerf_V2. Accessed 23 June 2025
14. Semianalysis: AMD 2.0 – New Sense of Urgency. https://semianalysis.com/2025/04/23/amd-2-0-new-sense-of-urgency-mi450x-chance-to-beat-nvidia-nvidias-new-moat/. Accessed 23 June 2025
15. Forbes. https://www.forbes.com/sites/karlfreund/2025/06/04/latest-mlperf-shows-how-amd-compares-with-nvidia-sort-of/. Accessed 23 June 2025

Tabular Data Augmentation for Database Scalability Testing – A Case Study with Medical Insurance Claims Analytics Workloads –

Taro Fujimoto[1(✉)], Shinji Fujiwara[1], Jumpei Sato[1,2], Yuto Hayamizu[2], and Kazuo Goda[2]

[1] Hitachi, Ltd., Yokohama, Kanagawa, Japan
taro.fujimoto.co@hitachi.com
[2] The University of Tokyo, Meguro-ku, Tokyo, Japan

Abstract. Scalability testing is a critical step in preparing a database system for deployment in production environments. However, developers are rarely granted access to full-scale real-world datasets due to privacy and security constraints. Instead, they must often rely on small, and sometimes redacted, samples. To conduct meaningful scalability evaluations, developers must interpret the semantics of the available data and generate large-scale synthetic datasets that faithfully preserve their statistical and structural properties. This paper proposes a tabular data augmentation method based on Generative Adversarial Networks (GANs), which enables the expansion of input tabular datasets to much larger scales while maintaining their original statistical characteristics and inter-table relationships. We have applied the proposed method to Japanese medical insurance claims data and demonstrate that the augmented datasets closely preserve the statistical distributions of the original records. Furthermore, we have conducted a scalability test using a commercial database engine, assessing both capacity utilization and query performance. Our findings suggest that GAN-based tabular data augmentation provides a viable path toward realistic and scalable database benchmarking in data-restricted environments.

Keywords: Tabular Data Augmentation · Generative Adversarial Networks · Database Benchmark · Medical Insurance Claims

1 Introduction

Scalability testing is a critical step in preparing a database system for deployment in production environments. In particular, understanding the potential impact on performance and resource consumption caused by the data growth is a must for system design and tuning. Yet, developers are rarely granted access to full-scale real-world datasets due to privacy and security constraints. Instead, they must often rely on small, and sometimes redacted, samples. To conduct meaningful

R. Nambiar and M. Poess (Eds.): TPCTC 2025, LNCS 16261, pp. 170–185, 2026.
https://doi.org/10.1007/978-3-032-18070-4_11

scalability evaluations, developers must interpret the semantics of the available data and generate large-scale synthetic datasets that faithfully preserve their statistical and structural properties. Traditional data augmentation methods have struggled to achieve both scalability and fidelity when applied to tabular data that includes a mix of categorical and numerical variables and exhibits relational structures across multiple tables.

To address these challenges, this paper presents a tabular data augmentation method based on Generative Adversarial Networks (GANs). This method learns the statistical distributions and inter-table relationships of the input samples and generates synthetic datasets that can be scaled to arbitrary sizes while preserving these original characteristics.

This paper presents our experiment in which we have applied the GAN-based augmentation to Japanese medical insurance claims, and it demonstrates that the augmented dataset can reproduce the statistical property and the inter-table relationship that the original dataset holds. This paper also presents a scalability test that we conducted using the generated synthetic data on Hitachi's commercial database engine, demonstrating that the GAN-based augmentation potentially plays a vital role for many database scalability tests.

The contributions of this paper can be summarized as follows.

1. This paper presents a GAN-based augmentation method for tabular data that achieves both statistical fidelity and structural consistency.
2. This paper experimentally demonstrates that this augmentation method can well reproduce the statistical property.
3. This paper reports a case study of scalability evaluation with a commercial database engine.

The remainder of this paper is organized as follows. Section 2 reviews known methods for tabular data augmentation. Section 3 presents Japanese medical insurance claims data and presents our augmentation design. Section 4 presents our experiments for evaluating the augmentation accuracy and then reports a case study of scalability evaluation with a commercial database engine. Section 5 reviews related work and finally Sect. 6 concludes the paper.

2 Tabular Data Augmentation

Tabular is a standard format in real-world business systems for managing business data. Tabular data often contains categorical variables and numerical variables, along with relational structures spanning multiple tables. Hence, tabular data has traditionally been considered more challenging to augment using generative models compared to other data formats such as images or text [22].

Yet, recent advances in deep learning technologies are enabling a variety of data augmentation approaches specifically designed for tabular data [22]. They learn the distribution of real-world samples using generative models, enabling the generation of much larger synthetic data with high fidelity.

This section groups major tabular data augmentation methods into four approaches and reviews their technical properties (Table 1). From a practical standpoint, it is essential to thoroughly understand the statistical properties and structural constraints of the input sample in data expansion and to select a data expansion approach appropriate to those properties. Additionally, practical requirements such as privacy protection and generative efficiency must also be considered when choosing suitable methods.

Table 1. Major work on tabular data augmentation.

Category	Models (Year)
Statistical machine learning approach	SMOTE (2005) [8], SMOTE-ENC (2021) [16], SMOTE-CDNN (2023) [24]
GAN-based approach	TableGAN (2018) [18], CTGAN (2019) [25], RC-TGAN (2023) [7], CTAB-GAN+ (2024) [26]
Diffusion model approach	TabDDPM (2023) [13], TabDDPM-EHR (2023) [2], TABDIFF (2024) [21]
LLM-based approach	GReaT (2023) [1], EPIC (2024) [12]

2.1 Statistical Machine Learning Approach

Even before the advent of deep learning, statistical machine learning techniques had been applied to generate extended data from existing samples. In particular, oversampling methods have been studied as a way to address class imbalance problems by increasing the number of samples in minority classes [6,11].

SMOTE (Synthetic Minority Over-sampling Technique) is a representative example, which generates new samples by performing linear interpolation between minority class data points and their nearest neighbors [8]. While this algorithm is relatively simple and computationally efficient, it has been noted to have limitations, such as generating samples that deviate from the original distribution or amplify noise. In recent years, several complementary methods have been proposed, such as SMOTE-ENC [16], which supports categorical variables, and SMOTE-CDNN [24], which integrates deep learning techniques in part.

2.2 GAN-Based Approach

Generative Adversarial Networks (GANs) are a machine learning framework for generative modeling, specifically for creating new data instances that resemble a training dataset. They have two neural networks, a generator and a discriminator, which compete against each other in a game-like setting, leading to the generation of increasingly realistic data. While this approach has achieved remarkable success in domains such as image and audio generation, recent developments have extended its application to tabular data.

TableGAN is known as one of the early applications of GANs to tabular data [18]. It uses convolutional neural networks (CNNs) for both the generator and discriminator. By applying preprocessing to the training dataset, it enables the generation of tabular data that includes both numerical and categorical features. Training becomes unstable when categorical variables exhibit skewed frequency distributions, and there are limitations in faithfully reproducing the distribution of real-world data [25].

CTGAN (Conditional Tabular GAN) addresses the limitations of TableGAN by introducing a conditional GAN framework to handle imbalanced categorical variables [25]. It also adopts a training-by-sampling strategy, which considers data imbalance during training and improves the generation quality of minority categories, successfully mitigating mode collapse. Mode collapse refers to a phenomenon in which a generative model fails to produce diverse outputs and repeatedly generates only a limited set of patterns. CTGAN is now widely used as a baseline method for tabular data augmentation.

RC-TGAN (Relational Conditional Tabular GAN) extends CTGAN by enabling data generation that accounts for relational structures across multiple tables [7]. While CTGAN focuses on single-table generation, RC-TGAN supports the preservation of relationships defined by primary and foreign keys, making it applicable to databases with complex real-world schemas.

CTAB-GAN+ balances high expressiveness and privacy protection in tabular data synthesis [26]. By considering differential privacy, this approach theoretically reduces the risk of inferring original personal information from the synthetic data.

2.3 Diffusion Model Approach

Diffusion models, specifically Denoising Diffusion Probabilistic Models (DDPM), have recently gained significant attention as generative models. These models learn to generate data through two processes: a forward process that gradually adds noise to the original data, and a reverse process that removes the noise to reconstruct the original data. Compared to GANs, diffusion models offer more stable training and are less prone to issues such as mode collapse.

However, due to the nature of diffusion models, data generation requires a large number of iterative denoising steps. As a result, generating large-scale datasets can be time-consuming, posing practical limitations for real-world applications.

TabDDPM is a pioneering method that applies diffusion models to tabular data [13]. It introduces an encoding strategy that enables unified handling of numerical and categorical variables, and has been reported to generate synthetic data of higher quality and greater diversity compared to GAN-based approaches. More recently, extended methods such as TABDIFF have been proposed, which incorporate conditional generation and structural constraints into the diffusion process [21].

Furthermore, domain-specific applications are also advancing, with particular attention in the healthcare field. TabDDPM-EHR applies TabDDPM to

Algorithm 1: Hybrid Tabular Data Augmentation

Input: Original tables
$\mathcal{T} = \{\texttt{MED\_HO}, \texttt{MED\_IR}, \texttt{MED\_IY}, \texttt{MED\_RE}, \texttt{MED\_SI}, \texttt{MED\_SY}, \texttt{MED\_TO}\}$

Output: Synthetic tables $\mathcal{T}'$

Step 1: Generate `claim_id` using RC-TGAN
Train RC-TGAN on all `claim_id` columns from $\mathcal{T}$
Generate synthetic `claim_id` values for each table in $\mathcal{T}$
Step 2: Generate attribute columns using CTGAN
foreach $T \in \mathcal{T}$ **do**
  Train CTGAN on T excluding `claim_id`
  Generate synthetic attribute columns
end
Step 3: Merge synthetic `claim_id` and attributes
foreach $T \in \mathcal{T}$ **do**
  Concatenate synthetic `claim_id` with synthetic attributes
  Store as final synthetic table T'
end

the generation of electronic health records (EHRs), and empirical evaluations have demonstrated its ability to produce high-quality synthetic EHR data while preserving the statistical characteristics of the original dataset [2].

2.4 LLM-Based Approach

Recently, there has been growing interest in applying Large Language Models (LLMs) to the generation of tabular data. This approach involves converting each row of a table into a text format following a specific structure, inputting it into an LLM, and generating new row-level text that reflects contextual relationships. The generated text is then parsed back into tabular format for use as synthetic data.

GReaT (Generalized Retrieval-Augmented Tabular data generation) addresses challenges such as information loss during preprocessing and lack of contextual relationships between features by converting each row into a text representation that reflects the semantics of the tabular data [1]. EPIC (Entity-based Prompting for Informative and Controllable tabular data generation) enables more informative and controllable tabular data generation through prompt engineering [12], improving the representation quality of minority classes by designing prompts that focus on specific classes or entities.

Although LLM-based methods are still in the early stages of development, they offer a novel approach to tabular data augmentation that differs from traditional generative models and represent a promising direction for future research.

Table 2. Major record types for medical insurance claims in Japan. This example illustrates a case of MED (fee-for-service) medical claims. Each claim is supposed to have one record of the IR, RE, and HO record types, and it may have one or more records of the SY, SI, IY, and TO record types.

Identifier	Record type	Information to be described
IR	Medical institution	Medical institution information (e.g., institution code, institution name, and location)
RE	Basic information	Patient and consultation information (e.g., name, gender, age, and consultation date)
HO	Insurance	Insurance information (e.g., insurance identifier code, consultation days, and total expense)
SY	Diagnosis	Disease information (e.g., disease code, and first diagnosing date)
SI	Medical service	Medical treatment information (e.g., treatment code, and quantity)
IY	Drug prescription	Prescription information (e.g., medication code, and quantity)
TO	Medical instrument	Instrument usage information (e.g., instrument code, and quantity)

3 A Case for Medical Insurance Claims in Japan

Japan has employed the universal service policy for its health system, in which all citizens are enrolled in any public medical insurance programs, and necessary medical services are financially supported by those insurance programs. Medical insurance claims are a platform data format for exchanging information on medical service provision between medical service providers (e.g., hospitals, clinics, and drug stores) and medical insurance operators, allowing the medical insurance operator to pay the medical service provider for the compensated portion of the medical expense. In addition, the claims data is collected and accumulated by the government, serving as a critical source of information for analyzing healthcare costs, understanding disease trends, and supporting policy development [9,19].

The claim format is standardized by the Japanese government. Each claim is composed of multiple snippets (i.e., records). Table 2 shows a case of MED (fee-for-service) medical claims. Typically, each MED claim is supposed to have one record of the IR (medical institution), RE (basic information), and HO (insurance information) record types, and it may have one or more records of the SY (disease information), SI (medical treatment information), and IY (prescription information), TO (instrument usage information) record types. When being exchanged between medical service providers and insurance operators, the

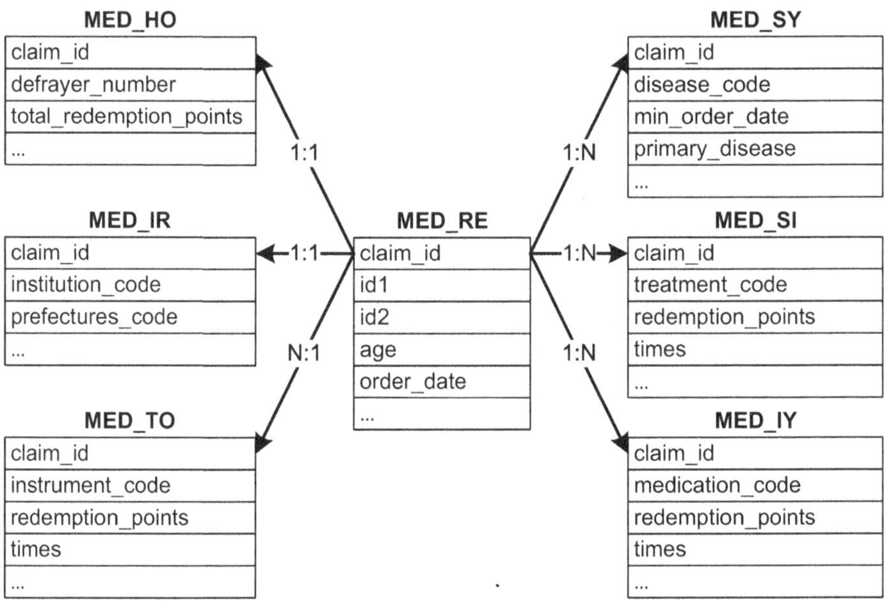

Fig. 1. Relational schema for medical insurance claims data. Records are stored in separate tables associated with their record types, and `claim_id` is appended to each record to allow for the reproduction of the original claim. For example, the RE record is stored in the table `MED_RE` and the SY record is stored in the table `MED_SY`. `claim_id` is a join key that associates the RE record and the SY record that are stored in the identical claim.

claims are stored in the CSV file in the nested-tuple format. However, they are often stored and managed in the schema illustrated in Fig. 1 since the relational schema is convenient for software developers and operators.

Here, let us summarize two major properties that medical insurance claims data hold to think about how to augment the claims data. First, the majority of variables appearing in the claims data are categorical, and their values are significantly skewed. This is a natural consequence of medical science; for example, the diseases that medical doctors see in the practice setting are wide-ranging, with a marked bias from common diseases to rare diseases, providing a corresponding bias in the treatments and medications. One technical challenge is to reproduce such imbalanced distributions for categorical variables accurately. Second, the claim is composed of different record types, which are stored in separate relational tables. Known practices designed for single-table data are not perfect. Another technical challenge is to preserve these inter-table relationships during data augmentation.

This paper presents a hybrid solution of tabular data augmentation that combines RC-TGAN and CTGAN. Algorithm 1 shows the pseudocode. Specifically, RC-TGAN generates the join key attribute (`claim_id`) to preserve the inter-table relationship, while CTGAN is in charge of generating the remaining attributes (including numerical and categorical variables). This combination works well to achieve both structural consistency and statistical fidelity. During the data generation process using CTGAN, we encountered memory limitations. To address this, the generation process was divided into multiple segments. We confirmed that even when the process is split, the generated data maintains a comparable level of fidelity and diversity. Note that, although we have also considered the possibility of using diffusion models, they have been excluded from this study due to their impractically long processing time for large-scale data generation.

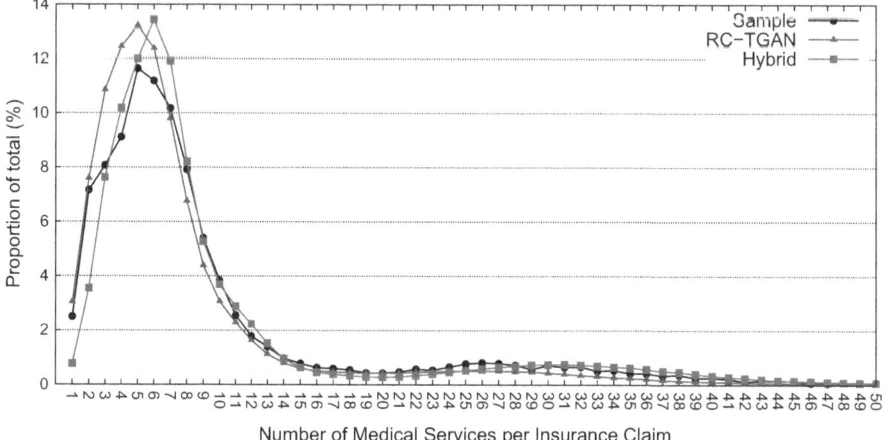

Fig. 2. Distribution of the number of SI records per claim. The horizontal axis represents the number of SI records associated for each claim, and the vertical axis indicates the proportion of the total. The generated synthetic data shows a similar distribution to the original data, confirming that the structural characteristics at the claim level are appropriately reproduced.

The next section presents a comparative study of the hybrid solution and the existing RC-TGAN solution.

4 Experiments

We conducted experiments using sample data from medical insurance claims in Japan to evaluate the effectiveness and practicality of the proposed augmentation approach. First, data augmentation was performed using the proposed method, and the generated synthetic data was evaluated to determine how well it preserved the statistical characteristics of the original data and the relational structure between tables. Additionally, scalability tests were conducted using a commercial database engine, assessing both capacity utilization and query performance.

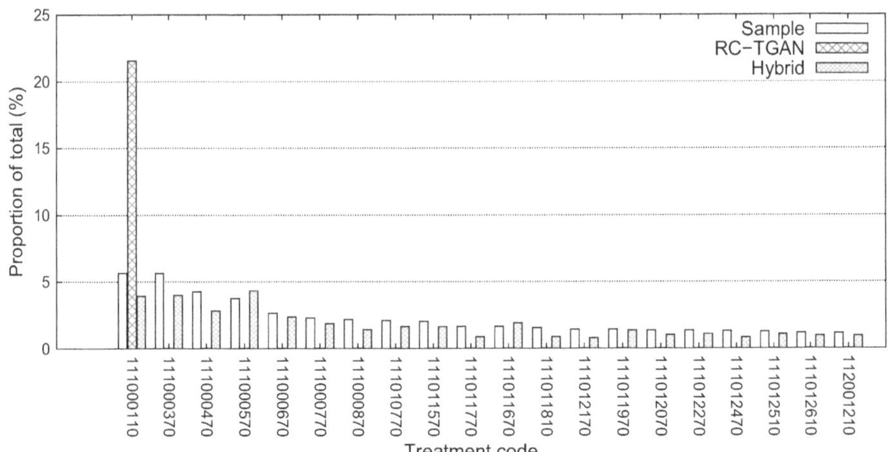

Fig. 3. Distribution of the occurrence of medical treatments. The horizontal axis represents medical treatment codes (in the descending order of the occurrence), and the vertical axis indicates the occurrence ratio. The RC-TGAN solution yielded significant errors (e.g. in the case of "111000110" indicating "initial consultation fee"). In contrast, the Hybrid solution produces a successful similarity to the training dataset, demonstrating its superior ability to reproduce categorical variable distributions.

4.1 Experimental Setup

We conducted all experiments on a modern enterprise-grade server, specifically Hitachi HA8000V/DL380 Gen10 with two Intel Xeon Gold 6240R CPUs (24 cores each, with hyper-threading enabled) plus 768 GB of memory. For both training and generation, we utilized an NVIDIA Tesla T4 GPU with 16 GB of GDDR6 memory. The operating system used was Red Hat Enterprise Linux 8.3. We used Hitachi's commercial database engine (HADB) [10] for a case study of scalability test.

A sample of 12,000 medical insurance claims in Japan (1,000 claims per month over 12 months) was used for the experiments. This sample was created by the authors based on publicly available information, including the number of claims and sample data [15]. Using this sample, a dataset of approximately 10 million claims was generated with RC-TGAN.

We used the publicly available RC-TGAN [3] and CTGAN [20] libraries for our experiments. To enable scalability testing in this paper, we modified the generation function in the RC-TGAN library to allow specification of an arbitrary number of output claims.

4.2 Evaluation of Data Augmentation Characteristics

The statistical fidelity of the synthetic dataset, consisting of approximately 10 million claims generated using the modified RC-TGAN, was evaluated from

Table 3. Comparison of Jensen-Shannon Divergence (JSD) values for the join key attribute (`claim_id`) in each child table related to the parent table MED_RE, using data generated by the RC-TGAN and Hybrid approaches. This table quantitatively evaluates the similarity of the duplication degree distribution of foreign keys in each child table to the training data using JSD values. Overall, the JSD values are very small, indicating that both methods achieve high reproducibility of relational structure. Since MED_HO and MED_IR have a one-to-one relationship with MED_RE, their JSD values are zero. On the other hand, MED_IY, MED_SI, and MED_SY have one-to-many relationships, but their JSD values remain low, indicating that structural reproducibility is maintained.

Parent Table	Child Table	JSD	
		RC TGAN	Hybrid
MED_RE	MED_HO	0.000	0.000
	MED_IR	0.000	0.000
	MED_IY	0.011	0.012
	MED_SI	0.009	0.010
	MED_SY	0.006	0.008
	MED_TO	0.000	0.000

the following two perspectives. The first perspective is the reproducibility of relational structure. We calculated the Jensen-Shannon Divergence (JSD) [14] between the distribution of duplication degrees in the column used for table joins (`claim_id`) and that of the original data. The second perspective is the reproducibility of variable distributions. For categorical and numerical variables contained in each table, we similarly evaluated the frequency distributions using JSD.

The evaluation was conducted on the following three types of data based on the criteria described above:

- **Sample:** Refers to the sample data used for training.
- **RC-TGAN:** Refers to the synthetic data generated solely by RC-TGAN. In this paper, we refer to this generation method as the RC-TGAN approach.
- **Hybrid:** Refers to the synthetic data generated using the Hybrid approach (RC-TGAN for join key columns and CTGAN for attribute columns). In this paper, we refer to this generation method as the Hybrid approach.

Figure 2 shows the duplication degree distribution of the join column (`claim_id`) for each dataset, used to evaluate the reproducibility of relational structure. Similar distributions were obtained across all datasets, confirming that both approaches effectively reproduce relational structure in the synthetic data.

Figure 3 shows the frequency distribution of a specific categorical variable (`treatment_code`) to evaluate the reproducibility of variable distributions. In this graph, it can be observed that the RC-TGAN approach fails to reproduce the variable distribution. On the other hand, the Hybrid approach, which combines

Table 4. Comparison of JSD values for numerical and categorical variables in the data generated by the RC-TGAN and Hybrid approaches. The table shows the average JSD values for numerical and categorical variables contained in each table. The best results in each category are highlighted in bold and underlined. For numerical variables, the RC-TGAN approach generally shows lower JSD values, indicating higher fidelity to the original data distribution. On the other hand, for categorical variables, the Hybrid approach consistently shows lower JSD values across all tables, demonstrating superior reproducibility of categorical distributions.

Table Name	JSD (Numerical Variables)		JSD (Categorical Variables)	
	RC-TGAN	Hybrid	RC-TGAN	Hybrid
MED_HO	**0.030**	0.074	0.015	**0.004**
MED_IR	**0.010**	**0.010**	0.011	**0.008**
MED_IY	0.251	**0.197**	0.196	**0.012**
MED_RE	**0.021**	0.028	0.176	**0.080**
MED_SI	**0.036**	0.203	0.154	**0.019**
MED_SY	**0.026**	0.042	0.153	**0.009**
MED_TO	**0.214**	0.229	0.115	**0.005**

CTGAN for categorical attributes, yields a distribution similar to the sample data, confirming that it outperforms the RC-TGAN approach in reproducing categorical variable distributions.

Tables 3 and 4 show the comparison of JSD values [14] for the datasets generated by the RC-TGAN and Hybrid approaches. A JSD value closer to 0 indicates a higher similarity to the distribution of the original data. The results show that while the RC-TGAN approach achieves slightly higher fidelity for numerical variables, the Hybrid approach significantly outperforms it in reproducing categorical variable distributions.

In particular, for analytical queries on medical insurance claims data, the distribution of categorical variables significantly affects query selectivity and aggregation results. Therefore, accurately reproducing the distribution of categorical variables is crucial. From this perspective, the dataset generated by the Hybrid approach is effective for realizing more practical database benchmarks.

4.3 Database Benchmarking and Scalability Testing

We conducted a database benchmarking experiment using synthetic data. To evaluate the synthetic data generated by the Hybrid approach from a scalability perspective, we created three datasets of different scales: small (100,000 claims), middle (1 million claims), and large (10 million claims). The number of records in the medical insurance claims tables for each scale is shown in Fig. 4.

Each generated dataset was loaded into a commercial column-oriented out-of-order database engine [5] for evaluation. This engine uses a column-store format, which enables efficient compression at the column level. As a result, the database

Table 5. Comparison of synthetic datasets generated at different scales. This table compares the number of claims, number of records, text file size, and database size across three scales: small, middle, and large. As the data scale increases, each value shows a progressive increase. Additionally, due to the use of a column-store database engine, efficient column-level compression is achieved, resulting in a database size that is approximately half that of the original text files.

	Small Scale	Medium Scale	Large Scale
Number of claims	100,000	1,000,000	10,000,000
Number of records	3,351,101	33,512,082	335,276,427
Total size in text files	0.6 GB	6.0 GB	60.0 GB
Total database size	0.3 GB	2.8 GB	27.6 GB

Table 6. Overview of 10 benchmark queries designed to reflect analytical needs for medical insurance claims data. This query set covers representative use cases in actual medical data analysis tasks, including cost aggregation, identification of patients with specific diseases and their treatments, and analysis of the usage of pharmaceuticals and medical devices.

No.	Description
Q1	This query reports monthly medical expenditure
Q2	This query reports medical expenditure that medical organizations claimed to care for outpatients diagnosed with specific diseases
Q3	This query reports monthly utilization of specific medical instruments performed at outpatient departments and medical expenditure claimed for the utilization
Q4	This query reports the number of patients diagnosed with specific diseases and overall medical expenditure claimed to care for the patients within one year
Q5	This query reports disease escalation in a group of patients diagnosed with specific diseases
Q6	This query reports monthly utilization of specific medicines
Q7	This query reports nation-wide monthly utilization of specific medicines dispensed for outpatients diagnosed with specific diseases
Q8	This query reports medical expenditure claimed to perform specific medical intervention actions
Q9	This query reports specific intervention actions for patients diagnosed with specific diseases
Q10	This query reports specific intervention actions for patients diagnosed with specific diseases

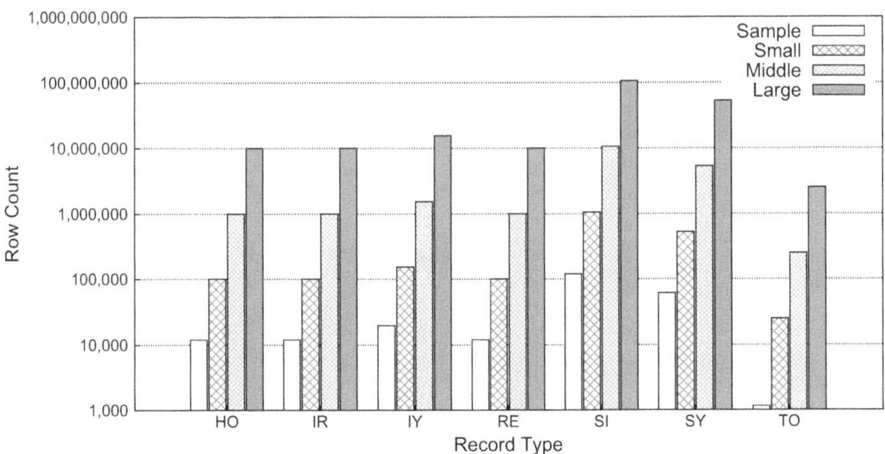

Fig. 4. Number of records per table in the generated medical insurance claims data for each scale. This figure was created to evaluate the scalability of synthetic data generated by the Hybrid approach. In all tables, the number of records increases approximately 10-fold and 100-fold in proportion to the scale, confirming the scalability of the data generation process.

size tends to be smaller than the original text file size. Details of storage usage for each scale are shown in Table 5. As the data scale increases, the database size also increases progressively.

For performance evaluation, we used a query set consisting of 10 queries designed based on actual analytical requirements. The business objectives of each query are listed in Table 6, and the measured execution times are shown in Fig. 5.

The evaluation results show that the dataset generated by the Hybrid approach exhibits a tendency for query execution time to increase with data scale. This indicates that synthetic data generated by the Hybrid approach is a valid option for database benchmarking purposes.

5 Related Work

Traditionally, database benchmarks have two main categories: transactional processing and analytical processing. There are several well-known benchmarks: TPC-C and TPC-E are for transaction processing; TPC-H, TPC-DS and Star Schema Benchmark [17] for analytical processing.

In recent years, as database usage has diversified, domain-specific and application-specific benchmarks have emerged. Examples include TPC-W for web commerce, TPCx-IoT for IoT data processing, TPC-DI for ETL workloads, and 4mbench [4], which is designed to evaluate decision-support queries in the manufacturing domain.

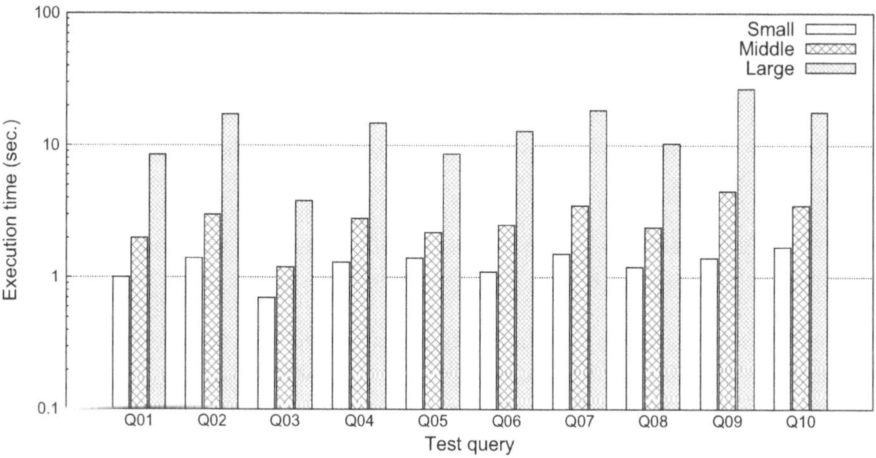

Fig. 5. Execution time of ten test queries across three data scales (small, middle, and large). This figure shows the execution time of each query run on synthetic data generated by the Hybrid approach. A trend of increasing execution time with larger data scales is observed. These results indicate that by adjusting the scale factor, it is possible to appropriately reproduce workloads to specific evaluation objectives.

However, as far as we know, standardized database benchmarks tailored to the healthcare domain have not been investigated in the existing literature. A database benchmark requires both a synthetic data generation method and a standardized workload definition. For instance, Synthea [23] provides a method for generating realistic synthetic electronic health records (EHRs), but it does not offer a standardized workload definition necessary for database performance evaluation.

6 Conclusion

This paper presented a GAN-based data augmentation method for tabular data, aiming to enable realistic and scalable database benchmarking under privacy and security constraints. This augmentation method enables the expansion of input tabular datasets to much larger scales while maintaining their original statistical characteristics and inter-table relationships.

Through experiments using sample data from medical insurance claims in Japan, we confirmed that synthetic data generated by RC-TGAN can effectively capture the inter-table relationships of the original data. To further improve the reproducibility of categorical variable distributions, we proposed a hybrid approach combining CTGAN, achieving both structural consistency and statistical fidelity. Additionally, we conducted scalability tests using the generated synthetic data on a commercial database engine, demonstrating that the data can be used as a practical benchmark in terms of capacity utilization and query performance.

However, several challenges remain. For example, the integration of data generated by RC-TGAN and CTGAN currently relies on manual processing, and there is room for improvement in terms of automation. The method of providing the data generator also requires further consideration. Moreover, while this study focused on generating datasets of up to 10 million claims, validation for even larger-scale data augmentation will be an important next step.

This study presents just one example of a realistic and reproducible data augmentation method for domains that handle sensitive information, such as healthcare. Future work includes tool development and automation for practical deployment, support for more diverse query patterns, and further refinement. We hope that the proposed method will contribute to the establishment of standardized database benchmarks in the healthcare domain.

Acknowledgments. This work has been in part supported by Cross-ministerial Strategic Innovation Promotion Program on Integrated Health Care System.

References

1. Borisov, V., Seßler, K., Leemann, T., Pawelczyk, M., Kasneci, G.: Language models are realistic tabular data generators. arXiv preprint arXiv:2210.06280 (2022)
2. Ceritli, T., Ghosheh, G.O., Chauhan, V.K., Zhu, T., Creagh, A.P., Clifton, D.A.: Synthesizing mixed-type electronic health records using diffusion models. arXiv preprint arXiv:2302.14679 (2023)
3. Croesus Lab: RC-TGAN GitHub Repository. https://github.com/croesuslab/RCTGAN (2023)
4. Goda, K., Hayamizu, Y., Nishikawa, N., Fujiwara, S.: 4mbench: performance benchmark of manufacturing business database. In: Proceedings of the TPCTC, pp. 94–109 (2022)
5. Goda, K., Hayamizu, Y., Yamada, H., Kitsuregawa, M.: Out-of-order execution of database queries. Proc. VLDB Endow. **13**(12), 3489–3501 (2020)
6. Gosain, A., Sardana, S.: Handling class imbalance problem using oversampling techniques: a review. In: Proceedings of the 2017 International Conference on Advances in Computing, Communications and Informatics (ICACCI), pp. 79–85 (2017)
7. Gueye, M., Attabi, Y., Dumas, M.: Row conditional-TGAN for generating synthetic relational databases. In: Proceedings of the ICASSP, pp. 1–5 (2023)
8. Han, H., Wang, W.-Y., Mao, B.-H.: Borderline-SMOTE: a new over-sampling method in imbalanced data sets learning. In: Huang, D.-S., Zhang, X.-P., Huang, G.-B. (eds.) ICIC 2005. LNCS, vol. 3644, pp. 878–887. Springer, Heidelberg (2005). https://doi.org/10.1007/11538059_91
9. Hashimoto, H., et al.: Indications and classes of outpatient antibiotic prescriptions in Japan: a descriptive study using the national database of electronic health insurance claims, 2012–2015. Int. J. Infect. Dis. **91**, 1–8 (2020)
10. Hitachi Ltd.: Manuals - Middleware - Hitachi Advanced Database (2011). https://itpfdoc.hitachi.co.jp/Pages/region/document_list/manuals/en/hadb.html
11. Japkowicz, N., Stephen, S.: The class imbalance problem: a systematic study. Intell. Data Anal. **6**(5), 429–449 (2002)

12. Kim, J., Kim, T., Choo, J.: EPIC: effective prompting for imbalanced-class data synthesis in tabular data classification via large language models. Adv. Neural. Inf. Process. Syst. **37**, 31504–31542 (2024)
13. Kotelnikov, A., Baranchuk, D., Rubachev, I., Babenko, A.: TabDDPM: modelling tabular data with diffusion models. In: Proceedings of the ICML, pp. 17564–17579 (2023)
14. Menéndez, M.L., Pardo, J.A., Pardo, L., Pardo, M.D.C.: The Jensen-Shannon divergence. J. Frankl. Inst. **334**(2), 307–318 (1997)
15. Ministry of Health, Labour and Welfare: NDB Open Data (2025). https://www.mhlw.go.jp/stf/seisakunitsuite/bunya/0000177182.html
16. Mukherjee, M., Khushi, M.: SMOTE-ENC: a novel SMOTE-based method to generate synthetic data for nominal and continuous features. Appl. Syst. Innov. **4**(1), 18 (2021)
17. O'Neil, P., O'Neil, E., Chen, X., Revilak, S.: The star schema benchmark and augmented fact table indexing. In: Nambiar, R., Poess, M. (eds.) TPCTC 2009. LNCS, vol. 5895, pp. 237–252. Springer, Heidelberg (2009). https://doi.org/10.1007/978-3-642-10424-4_17
18. Park, N., Mohammadi, M., Gorde, K., Jajodia, S., Park, H., Kim, Y.: Data synthesis based on generative adversarial networks. arXiv preprint arXiv:1806.03384 (2018)
19. Sato, J., Mitsutake, N., Yamada, H., Kitsuregawa, M., Goda, K.: Virtual patient identifier (vPID): improving patient traceability using anonymized identifiers in Japanese healthcare insurance claims database. Heliyon **9**(5) (2023)
20. SDV Dev Team: CTGAN GitHub repository (2019). https://github.com/sdv-dev/CTGAN
21. Shi, J., Xu, M., Hua, H., Zhang, H., Ermon, S., Leskovec, J.: TabDiff: a multimodal diffusion model for tabular data generation. arXiv preprint arXiv:2410.20626 (2024)
22. Shi, R., Wang, Y., Du, M., Shen, X., Wang, X.: A comprehensive survey of synthetic tabular data generation. arXiv preprint arXiv:2504.16506 (2025)
23. Walonoski, J., et al.: Synthea: an approach, method, and software mechanism for generating synthetic patients and the synthetic electronic health care record. J. Am. Med. Inform. Assoc. **25**(3), 230–238 (2018)
24. Wang, A.X., Chukova, S.S., Nguyen, B.P.: Synthetic minority oversampling using edited displacement-based k-nearest neighbors. Appl. Soft Comput. **148**, 110895 (2023)
25. Xu, L., Skoularidou, M., Cuesta-Infante, A., Veeramachaneni, K.: Modeling tabular data using conditional GAN. Adv. Neural Inf. Process. Syst. **32** (2019)
26. Zhao, Z., Kunar, A., Birke, R., Van der Scheer, H., Chen, L.Y.: CTAB-GAN+: enhancing tabular data synthesis. Front. Big Data **6**, 1296508 (2024)

Benchmarking Distilled Language Models: Performance and Efficiency in Resource-Constrained Settings

Sachin Gopal Wani(✉), Eric Page, Ajay Dholakia, and David Ellison

Lenovo, Infrastructure Solutions Group, Morrisville, NC, USA
{swani1,epage2,adholakia,dellison}@lenovo.com

Abstract. Knowledge distillation offers a transformative pathway to developing powerful, yet efficient, small language models (SLMs) suitable for resource-constrained environments. In this paper, we benchmark the performance and computational cost of distilled models against their vanilla and proprietary counterparts, providing a quantitative analysis of their efficiency.

Our results demonstrate that distillation creates a superior performance-to-compute curve. We find that creating a distilled 8B model is over 2,000 times more compute-efficient than training its vanilla counterpart, while achieving reasoning capabilities on par with, or even exceeding, standard models ten times its size. These findings validate distillation not just as a compression technique, but as a primary strategy for building state-of-the-art, accessible AI.

Keywords: Distillation · Small Language Models · Resource-Limited Settings · Computational Efficiency · Benchmarking · Model Evaluation · Large Language Models · Generative AI

1 Introduction

The advent of Large Language Models (LLMs) has marked a transformative era in artificial intelligence, demonstrating remarkable capabilities in natural language understanding, generation, and reasoning. The performance of these models has consistently scaled with their size, leading to the development of foundation models with hundreds of billions, or even trillions, of parameters. However, this relentless pursuit of scale comes at a staggering computational cost. The immense resources required for pre-training and fine-tuning are significant, but even deploying these massive models for inference demands substantial computational power. This creates significant barriers, limiting their use to a handful of well-resourced corporations and rendering them impractical for widespread adoption in real-world applications that require low latency and cost efficiency.

The challenge, therefore, is to create models that are not only compute-efficient but also possess the sophisticated capabilities required for specialized tasks. Standard training or fine-tuning approaches on smaller models often fail to replicate the nuanced reasoning and generalization abilities of their larger counterparts. This capability gap

R. Nambiar and M. Poess (Eds.): TPCTC 2025, LNCS 16261, pp. 186–202, 2026.
https://doi.org/10.1007/978-3-032-18070-4_12

underscores the need for more advanced techniques that can efficiently imbue smaller models with the deep knowledge learned by state-of-the-art foundation models, paving the way for a new generation of powerful, yet accessible, AI systems.

Knowledge distillation has emerged as a powerful and promising technique to achieve this goal [1]. The fundamental principle involves transferring the knowledge from a large, powerful "teacher" model to a smaller, more efficient "student" model. By training the student on the rich, soft-target outputs generated by the teacher, it can learn nuanced patterns and capabilities that are difficult to acquire through standard training on a dataset alone. This process allows for the creation of compact models that retain a significant portion of their larger counterparts' performance while drastically reducing computational overhead for inference and training (Fig. 1).

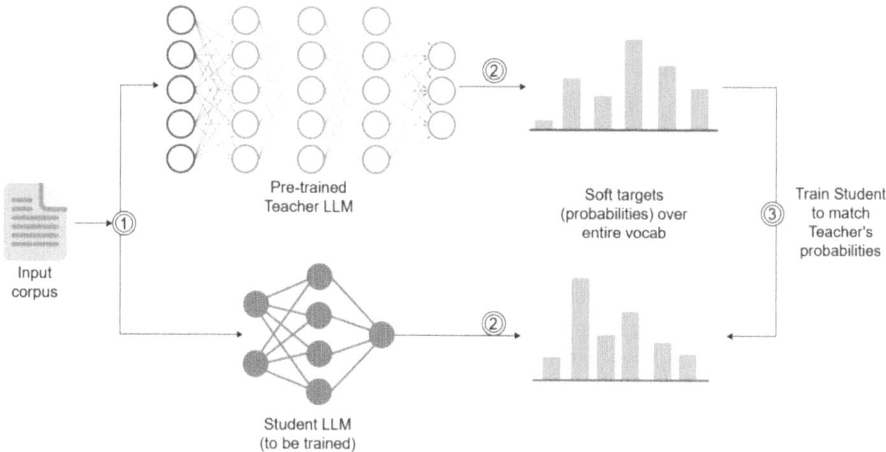

Fig. 1. Illustration of the Distillation process

In this paper, we conduct a comparative meta-benchmark[1] to quantify the trade-offs between knowledge distillation and other common model adaptation techniques. Through a rigorous analysis of published benchmarks and computational models, we evaluate the costs—measured in Floating Point Operations (FLOPs) and GPU-hours—alongside performance on standard tasks. We ground our analysis in concrete examples, such as the distillation of the DeepSeek-R1 model [2], to provide a clear, evidence-based framework for evaluating model efficiency. Our findings demonstrate that knowledge distillation offers a highly compute-efficient pathway for developing powerful models, positioning it as a preferred strategy for building and deploying generative AI systems within the operational and financial constraints of real-world environments.

[1] We run the benchmarks ourselves for three widely used vanilla models and their recent distilled counterparts. Other proprietary and large models have been added into comparison based on officially sourced data.

2 Related Work

2.1 LLM Evaluation and Benchmarking

The rapid advancement of LLMs has been accompanied by a parallel evolution in evaluation methodologies. Foundational efforts have focused on creating comprehensive, multi-task benchmarks to assess the broad capabilities and risks of language models. Notable examples include MMLU for measuring multitask accuracy [31], BIG-bench for diverse and challenging tasks [32], and HELM, which provides a holistic, multi-metric evaluation across a standardized set of scenarios [33]. Concurrently, domain-specific evaluations, such as the work on models trained on code, introduced critical metrics like pass@k, which have become standard for measuring complex reasoning and generation [19]. More recently, dynamic public leaderboards, such as the Open LLM Leaderboard [34], have emerged as a vital tool for real-time tracking of state-of-the-art model performance. Our work builds upon this landscape by focusing specifically on the intersection of performance and the computational cost of model creation, an area explored by recent studies on the efficiency spectrum of LLMs [35].

2.2 Fine-Tuning

Fine-tuning a LLM involves taking a pre-trained model and further training it on a smaller, more specialized dataset to improve its performance in a specific domain, such as question answering. Classical fine-tuning involves training a portion or the entire model, but due to the increasing size of LLMs, Parameter-Efficient Fine-Tuning (PEFT) methods have been developed to reduce memory and compute costs [3, 9, 10]. However, while fine-tuning has been shown to adjust a model's style, it doesn't imbue the model with new knowledge, especially outside of the fine-tuning dataset's domain [11]. This inherent limitation of fine-tuning—its inability to instill fundamentally new reasoning pathways—highlights the need for alternative methods like knowledge distillation to more effectively transfer capabilities from superior models.

2.3 Knowledge Distillation

Knowledge Distillation involves transferring the capabilities of a large "teacher" model into a smaller "student" one by having the student mimic the soft output distribution of the teacher instead of hard labels [1]. While originally applied to deep neural networks, this concept has been adapted to LLMs [12, 13]. In practice, distillation has been shown to be very effective as distilled models outperform their baseline counterparts across a variety of tasks. Most notably, distilling reasoning model outputs and Chain-of-Thought (CoT), particularly in a "distill step-by-step" manner [36], into smaller models significantly improves performance on reasoning tasks [2, 14]. This is because the student learns not just the correct answer, but also the nuanced, step-by-step reasoning process encoded in the teacher's soft probability distribution.

2.4 Estimating Computational Cost

A quantitative comparison of these adaptation techniques requires a standardized metric for computational cost. The most widely accepted metric is the number of total floating-point operations (FLOPs) required for training. A well-established formula for estimating the compute cost of training a standard transformer-based LLM is provided by Epoch AI [4]:

$$\text{Training}_{\text{FLOPs}} \approx 6 \times \text{N} \times \text{D}$$

where N is the number of parameters in the model and D is the number of tokens in the training dataset. The factor of 6 is a widely used approximation that accounts for both the forward pass (roughly 2 × N × D FLOPs) and the backward pass (roughly 4 × N × D FLOPs).

For knowledge distillation, we propose the computational cost can be decomposed into two distinct components: the cost of generating the training data using the teacher model and the cost of training the student model.

1. Teacher Inference Cost: This step only requires a forward pass of the teacher model over the distillation dataset.

$$\text{TeacherInference}_{\text{FLOPs}} \approx 2 \times \text{N}_{\text{teacher}} \times \text{D}_{\text{distill}}$$

2. Student Training Cost: This involves both forward and backward passes for the smaller student model.

$$\text{StudentTraining}_{\text{FLOPs}} \approx 6 \times \text{N}_{\text{student}} \times \text{D}_{\text{distill}}$$

The total cost of distillation is the sum of these two components. This decomposition is critical for understanding the trade-offs, as the cost is dominated by the size of the teacher model and the distillation dataset, while the student training itself is a relatively small portion of the overall compute. This framework provides the basis for our comparative analysis of compute efficiency. Furthermore, the seminal work on scaling laws by Hoffmann et al. [5] (the "Chinchilla" paper) provides an empirical foundation for these compute-performance trade-offs, demonstrating that for a fixed compute budget, an optimal balance between model size and the amount of training data is crucial. This supports the core premise of our work: that creating smaller, more data-efficient models through methods like distillation can be a superior strategy to simply scaling up model size.

3 Methodology

To conduct a robust comparative analysis, we established a systematic methodology for estimating and comparing the computational costs associated with distillation, fine-tuning, and retraining. Our approach is grounded in established computational formulas and accounts for real-world hardware performance characteristics to translate abstract FLOPs into tangible GPU-hours and CO_2 emissions.

3.1 Estimating Computational Cost in FLOPs

Our primary metric for computational cost is the total number of floating-point operations (FLOPs). We use the formulas outlined in Sect. 2.4 for our calculations. A key challenge in applying these formulas is determining the size of the training dataset (D) in tokens. Our approach varied depending on the model adaptation technique:

- **For Retraining and Fine-Tuning:** We relied on token counts reported directly in the source literature or associated with benchmark datasets. This includes large-scale pre-training datasets (e.g., 15.6 trillion tokens for Llama3 models) and smaller, instruction-tuning datasets (e.g., ~10 billion domain specific tokens). For models that do not report the training data, we directly use the provided compute FLOPs in supporting literature.
- **For Distillation:** In cases like the DeepSeek-R1 model, where the source paper reports the number of training samples rather than tokens, we estimated the total token count. The distillation data is composed of approximately 600,000 reasoning-focused samples featuring Chain-of-Thought trajectories and 200,000 non-reasoning samples. Given the token-intensive nature of CoT, we adopt a weighted average of 750 tokens per sample for our calculations. This estimate reflects the heavy skew towards complex reasoning data and is consistent with the token lengths of typical instruction-following datasets. This allows us to convert sample counts into the token counts required for our FLOPs calculations.

3.2 Converting FLOPs to GPU-Hours

While FLOPs provide a hardware-agnostic measure of computation, GPU-hours offer a more practical metric for real-world cost and time estimation. To bridge this gap, we use the concept of Model FLOPs Utilization (MFU), which measures the ratio of the actual achieved throughput of a training job against the theoretical peak performance of the underlying hardware. MFU accounts for real-world bottlenecks such as memory bandwidth, network latency, and software overhead, which prevent hardware from reaching its peak theoretical output. For instance, the recent training of Llama 3.1 reported achieving an MFU of 38–43% on clusters of NVIDIA H100 GPUs [15]. This provides a concrete, empirically-backed efficiency range for our estimations.

Our final formula for estimating GPU-hours is:

$$\text{GPUHours} = \frac{TotalFLOPs}{PeakFLOPs/s X\ MFU\ X\ 3600\, s/hr}$$

where PeakFLOPs is measured per second, the 3600 factors converting seconds to hours. This sophisticated approach allows us to generate credible time and cost estimates for running different training jobs on specific, real-world hardware. We analyze several leading data center GPUs, including NVIDIA's A100, H100, H200, and L40S, using their peak theoretical FP16/BF16 Tensor Core performance as a baseline [6].

3.3 Estimating CO_2 Emissions

Beyond computational time and cost, the environmental impact of training large models is a critical consideration. To quantify this, we estimate the carbon dioxide equivalent

(CO_2e) emissions for each training process. Our approach is based on the methodology outlined by Patterson et al. [16], which combines total energy consumption with the carbon intensity of the local power grid. We calculate the total emissions in metric tons of CO_2e (tCO_2e) using the following simplified formula:

$$tCO_2e = \text{GPUHours} \times \text{TDP}_{(MW)} \times \text{PUE} \times \text{CI}_{\text{Grid}}$$

where TDP is the Thermal Design Power of the GPU hardware in Megawatts, PUE is the Power Usage Effectiveness of the data center, and CIGrid is the carbon intensity of the power grid in tCO_2e/MWh. For our estimations, we assume a PUE of 1.1, consistent with modern hyperscale data centers, and a CIGrid of 0.429 tCO_2e/MWh, representing the average data center carbon emissions for 2020, as reported in the reference study [16]. This calculation allows us to translate the abstract cost of GPU-hours into a tangible measure of environmental impact, providing a more holistic view of the efficiency of different model adaptation strategies.

3.4 Benchmark Evaluation

Our evaluation framework, which plots performance against computational cost, is broadly applicable to any language model and performance metric. To demonstrate its utility in this study, we focus our analysis on two particularly challenging benchmarks: GPQA, a graduate-level question-answering dataset [17], and AIME 2024, a competition-level math problem-solving benchmark [18]. While many excellent evaluations exist, we specifically chose these two because they rigorously test the complex reasoning skills that efficiency techniques like distillation aim to preserve and enhance. Most importantly, their widespread adoption and the public availability of scores from top proprietary models allow for a direct and meaningful comparison across the entire LLM ecosystem, which is essential for contextualizing our findings.

For our evaluation metric, we adopt the pass@k methodology, as it provides a more stable and robust measure of performance than greedy decoding, especially for complex reasoning tasks [19]. Specifically, we report pass@1 scores and follow the evaluation setup detailed in the DeepSeek-R1 paper [2] for consistency. We generate k responses for each question using a sampling temperature of 0.6 and a top-p value of 0.95. The pass@1 score is then calculated as the average correctness across these k samples:

$$\text{pass@1} = \frac{1}{k}\sum_{i=1}^{k} p_i$$

where p_i denotes the binary correctness of the i-th response. This standardized approach ensures that our results are comparable to those published in other leading research.

3.5 Models and Assumptions

To ground our analysis, we center our case studies on widely recognized models and make our assumptions explicit:

- **Case Studies:** We compare vanilla (non-distilled) models directly with its distilled counterparts across benchmarks we ran locally. We also compare it with published results for larger open source and closed source models.
- **Data Precision:** All calculations assume training is performed using FP16/BF16 precision, which is standard for modern LLM training and leverages GPU Tensor Cores.
- **Efficiency Assumptions:** For our GPU-hour calculations, we use an MFU range consistent with published results, such as the 38–43% reported for Llama 3.1 on H-series GPUs [15]. For older hardware like the A-series, we assume a slightly lower MFU of 25–35%.
- **Epochs:** We assume a single epoch of training (E = 1) for large-scale retraining and distillation examples, and three epochs (E = 3) for common fine-tuning recipes, consistent with practices in the literature.

By clearly defining our methodology and assumptions, we provide a transparent and reproducible framework for evaluating the computational trade-offs of different model specialization strategies.

4 Case Studies

To demonstrate our methodology in practice, we present a series of case studies that walk through the cost estimation process for different types of models. The input parameters for these studies are taken directly from official technical reports unless explicitly specified otherwise. These examples serve to ground the abstract formulas from Sect. 3 in concrete numbers and illustrate the fundamental differences in resource requirements between standard training and knowledge distillation.

4.1 The Baseline: Training a Vanilla Foundation Model

We begin by establishing a baseline using a standard, non-distilled open-source model. For this, we analyze Qwen3-8B, an 8-billion parameter model trained on a large corpus of data. This case study demonstrates the standard calculation for the full pre-training cost of a modern LLM.

1. **Training Parameters:**
   - Model Size (N): 8 billion parameters
   - Training Dataset (D): 36 trillion tokens
2. **FLOPs Calculation:** Using the standard formula for from Sect. 2.4:

$$\text{Training}_{\text{FLOPs}} = 6 \times \left(8 \times 10^{9}\right) \times \left(36 \times 10^{12}\right) = 1.728 \times 10^{24}\text{FLOPs}$$

3. **GPU-Hours Calculation:** To convert FLOPs to a tangible training time, we estimate the required GPU-hours on a modern NVIDIA H100 SXM GPU. We assume an MFU of 38%, consistent with large-scale training runs.
   - Peak Theoretical Performance (H100 SXM, 16-bit non-sparse): ~1,000 TFLOPs

- Model FLOPs Utilization (MFU): 38%
- Effective Performance: 1,000 TFLOPs × 0.38 = 380 TFLOPs

$$\text{GPUHours} = \frac{1.728 \times 10^{24}\ \text{FLOPs}}{380\,x\,10^{12} FLOPs/s\,x\,3600\,s/hr} \approx 1{,}263{,}158\,\text{h}$$

4. **CO_2 Emissions Calculation:** Finally, we estimate the environmental impact using the GPU's Thermal Design Power (TDP) of 700W (0.0007 MW).
   - Total Energy: 1,263,158 h × 0.0007 MW × 1.1 PUE ≈ 972.6 MWh
   - Total Emissions: 972.6 MWh × 0.429 tCO_2e/MWh ≈ 417.25 tCO_2e

This baseline demonstrates that training even a relatively small 8B parameter model from scratch requires a staggering investment of over 1.2 million H100 GPU-hours and results in over 417 metric tons of CO_2 equivalent emissions.

4.2 The Challenger: Creating a Distilled Model

To contrast with the baseline, we now analyze the process of creating a distilled model of the same size: the 8B parameter DeepSeek-R1-0528-Qwen3-8B. This model inherits its capabilities from a much larger, 685B parameter "teacher" model. This case study highlights the dramatically different cost structure of distillation.

1. **Distillation Parameters:**
   - Teacher Model Size ($N_{teacher}$): 685 billion parameters
   - Student Model Size ($N_{student}$): 8 billion parameters
   - Distillation Dataset ($D_{distill}$): 800,000 samples, which we estimate ~600M tokens.
2. **FLOPs Calculation:** We use the two-part distillation formula from Sect. 2.4:
   - Teacher Inference: $2 \times (685 \times 10^9) \times (600 \times 10^6) = 8.22 \times 10^{20}$ FLOPs
   - Student Training: $6 \times (8 \times 10^9) \times (600 \times 10^6) = 2.88 \times 10^{19}$ FLOPs
   - Total Distillation FLOPs: $(8.22 \times 10^{20}) + (2.88 \times 10^{19}) \approx 8.5 \times 10^{20}$ FLOPs
3. **GPU-Hours Calculation:** Using the same H100 GPU and MFU as the baseline:

$$\text{GPUHours} = \frac{8.5 \times 10^{20}\ \text{FLOPs}}{380\,x\,10^{12} FLOPs/s\,x\,3600\,s/hr} \approx 621.9\,\text{h}$$

4. **CO_2 Emissions Calculation:**
   - Total Energy: 621.9 h × 0.0007 MW × 1.1 PUE ≈ 0.479 MWh
   - Total Emissions: 0.479 MWh × 0.429 tCO_2e/MWh ≈ 0.205 tCO_2e

The comparison is stark. Creating a highly capable 8B parameter model via distillation requires approximately 622 H100 GPU-hours, a reduction of over 2,000 times compared to training its vanilla counterpart from scratch. The corresponding carbon footprint is also reduced from over 400 metric tons to less than a single ton, illustrating the profound efficiency gains offered by this approach.

4.3 The Specialization Alternative: Fine-Tuning

We also analyze a third common scenario: specializing a pre-trained model for a particular domain via fine-tuning. This represents a highly compute-efficient path to task-specific performance, but with a different set of trade-offs compared to distillation.

1. **Fine-Tuning Parameters:**
   - Model Size (N): 8 billion parameters
   - Domain-Specific Dataset (D): 10 billion tokens (estimated data size as example)
   - Epochs (E): 3
2. **FLOPs Calculation:** Using the standard training formula, we account for the multiple epochs common in fine-tuning recipes.

$$\text{Training}_{\text{FLOPs}} = 6 \times \left(8 \times 10^9\right) \times \left(10 \times 10^9\right) \times 3 = 1.44 \times 10^{21}\text{FLOPs}$$

3. **GPU-Hours Calculation:** Using the same H100 GPU and MFU as the previous examples:

$$\text{GPUHours} = \frac{1.44 \times 10^{21}\ \text{FLOPs}}{380\,x\,10^{12} FLOPs/s\,x\,3600\,s/hr} \approx 1052.6\,\text{h}$$

4. **CO_2 Emissions Calculation:**
   - Total Energy: 1,052.6 h × 0.0007 MW × 1.1 PUE ≈ 0.81 MWh
   - Total Emissions: 0.81 MWh × 0.429 tCO_2e/MWh ≈ 0.347 tCO_2e

From a pure resource perspective, fine-tuning is also exceptionally efficient, requiring a fraction of the compute of full pre-training. However, its scope is inherently limited. This process adapts an existing model to a narrow domain, but it cannot impart the broad, generalizable reasoning capabilities that distillation can transfer from a much larger and more powerful teacher. Therefore, while fine-tuning is optimal for narrow task adaptation, distillation provides a superior path for creating smaller models that retain a high degree of general intelligence.

4.4 Estimating the Proprietary Frontier

To complete our comparative landscape, we analyze a state-of-the-art proprietary model, GPT-4o (0513 version). While exact architectural details remain undisclosed, external analyses provide credible estimates for the total training compute [20]. This allows us to apply our methodology to approximate the resources required to create a frontier model.

1. **Training Parameters:** Total Estimated Compute: 3.8×10^{25} FLOPs [20]
2. **GPU-Hours Calculation:** As the model size and training data are unknown, we directly use the estimated total FLOPs. Applying the same H100 hardware profile as in previous cases:

$$\text{GPUHours} = \frac{3.8 \times 10^{25}\ \text{FLOPs}}{380\,x\,10^{12} FLOPs/s\,x\,3600\,s/hr} \approx 27{,}777{,}778\,\text{h}$$

3. **CO_2 Emissions Calculation**

- Total Energy: 27,777,778 h $\times$ 0.0007 MW $\times$ 1.1 PUE $\approx$ 21,388.9 MWh
- Total Emissions: 21,388.9 MWh $\times$ 0.429 tCO_2e/MWh $\approx$ 9,175.83 tCO_2e

The scale of these figures is immense. The estimated cost to train a model like GPT-4o is over 27 million H100 GPU-hours, producing over 9,000 metric tons of CO_2e. This is more than 20 times the cost of training the 8B parameter Qwen3 model and underscores the astronomical resource barrier to entry for developing frontier models. It provides a powerful context for our results, reinforcing the critical importance of compute-efficient methods like distillation for enabling broader access to high-performance AI.

5 Results

This section presents the aggregated results of our analysis, consolidating the estimated costs and benchmark performance across a wide range of models. We first provide a comprehensive comparison of all models in our study, followed by a graphical analysis of performance versus compute, and conclude with a practical look at how hardware choice impacts training time.

5.1 Comprehensive Model Comparison

Table 1 provides a detailed breakdown of the models analyzed in this study. The performance data presented is a composite of our own local evaluations and publicly reported scores. For the first six models listed (vanilla and its distilled counterpart), we ran benchmarks locally using established evaluation frameworks such as LocalAIME [21], OpenAI's Simple Evals [22], and community-developed scripts [23]. For all other models, performance data was collected from official technical reports, model cards, leaderboards, and other reputable public sources [24–30].

For each model, we list its type—distinguished here as "Vanilla" for open-source models trained from scratch, "Distilled" for models created via knowledge distillation, and "Proprietary" for closed-source models. The table includes the total training compute in FLOPs, our estimated training time in H100 GPU-hours, the corresponding CO_2 emissions, and the model's performance on the GPQA and AIME 2024 benchmarks. Several key comparisons emerge directly from this data. For instance, the vanilla Llama 3.1 8B model required approximately 1.46 million H100 GPU-hours to train, whereas its distilled counterpart, DeepSeek-R1-Distill-Llama-8B, achieved superior performance on both benchmarks with only ~610 H100 GPU-hours—a reduction in compute of over 99.9%. This pattern of multi-order-of-magnitude efficiency gains for distilled models is consistent across all comparable pairs in our analysis.

5.2 Performance vs. Compute Analysis

To visualize the relationship between computational investment and reasoning performance, we plot the accuracy of each model against its total training compute. Figure 2

Table 1. Comprehensive model comparison and benchmarks evaluation

Model	Type	Training Compute	GPUHours (H100)	tCO_2e	GPQA Diamond	AIME 2024
Llama 3.1 8B	Vanilla	7.49E+23	1.46E+06	4.20E+02	30.4	10
DeepSeek-R1-Distill-Llama-8B	Distilled	8.34E+20	6.10E+02	2.01E−01	49	50.4
Llama 3.3 70B Instruct	Vanilla	6.55E+24	7.00E+06	2.04E+03	46.7	22.5
DeepSeek-R1-Distill-Llama-70B	Distilled	1.06E+21	7.73E+02	2.55E−01	65.2	70
Qwen 3 8B	Vanilla	1.73E+24	1.26E+06	4.17E+02	62	76
DeepSeek-R1-0528-Qwen3-8B	Distilled	8.51E+20	6.22E+02	2.05E−01	61.1	86
Phi-4 14B	Vanilla	9.30E+23	6.80E+05	2.25E+02	69.3	81.3
GPT-4o 0513	Proprietary	3.80E+25	2.78E+07	9.18E+03	53.6	9.3
Deepseek V3	Vanilla	3.40E+24	2.49E+06	8.21E+02	59.1	39.2
Grok 3	Proprietary	4.60E+26	3.36E+08	1.11E+05	75.4	52.2
Claude 3.7 Sonnet	Proprietary	3.30E+25	2.41E+07	7.97E+03	68	23.3
o3-mini	Proprietary	4.68E+23	3.80E+05	1.26E+02	76.8	79.6
Qwen3-235B-A22B	Vanilla	5.08E+25	3.71E+07	1.23E+04	71.1	85.7
Llama 3.1 405B	Vanilla	3.79E+25	3.08E+07	8.93E+03	50.7	23.3
Deepseek-R1	Teacher	5.20E+24	3.80E+06	1.26E+03	71.5	79.8
Deepseek-R1-0528	Teacher	5.20E+24	3.80E+06	1.26E+03	81	91.4

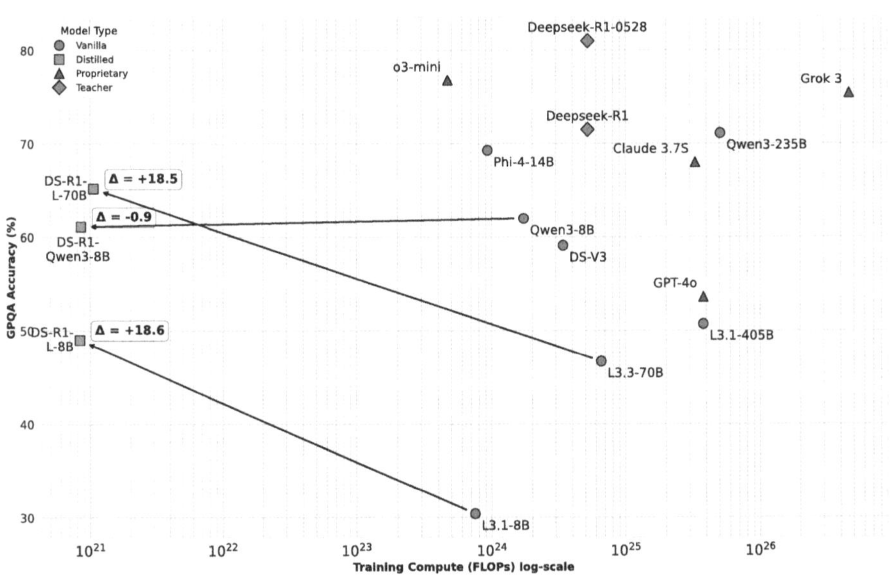

Fig. 2. GPQA accuracy v Training Compute (FLOPs) log-scale for models

and Fig. 3 show the results for the GPQA and AIME benchmarks, respectively, with the training compute axis on a logarithmic scale to accommodate the wide range of values.

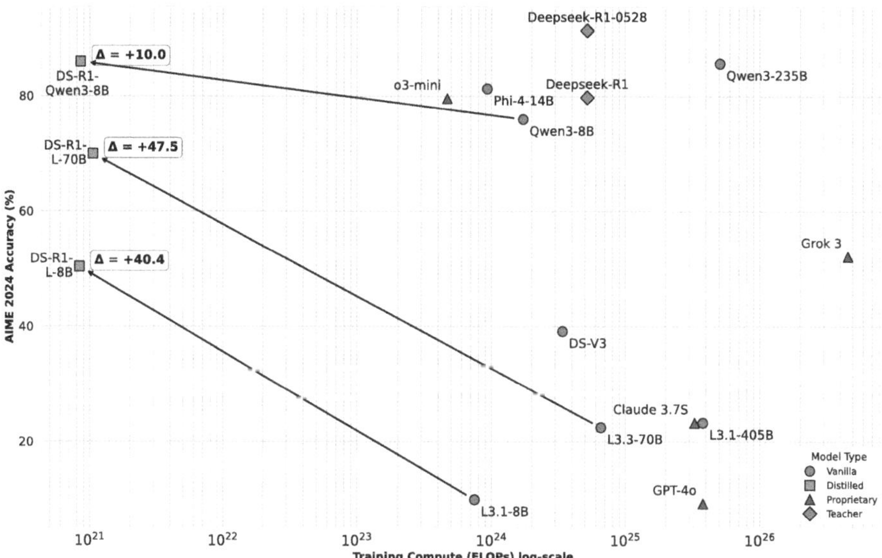

Fig. 3. AIME 24 accuracy v Training Compute (FLOPs) log-scale for models

The plots clearly reveal several key trends, with the AIME 2024 results in Fig. 2 providing a particularly stark illustration. While there is a general positive correlation between training compute and benchmark performance for vanilla models, the distilled models establish a new, far more efficient performance curve. For example, the distilled DeepSeek-R1-0528-Qwen3-8B model achieves a remarkable 86% accuracy. This not only dramatically exceeds its vanilla 8B counterpart but also surpasses the performance of the massive Qwen3-235B model (85.7%), which required nearly 60,000 times more training compute to develop. This trend demonstrates that for complex reasoning tasks, distillation is not merely an optimization but a method for achieving a step-change in performance per FLOP, challenging the notion that frontier performance is exclusively tied to frontier-scale compute.

5.3 Hardware Impact on Training Time

While H100 GPUs were used as the baseline for our primary calculations, the choice of hardware has a significant practical impact on project timelines and costs. Table 2 provides a focused comparison of estimated training times and CO2 footprints for a selection of models across different generations of NVIDIA data center GPUs. This table illustrates that for a fixed computational workload (FLOPs), newer hardware like the H100 can reduce training time and associated emissions compared to previous generation A100 GPUs, highlighting the role of hardware efficiency in the overall cost equation.

The collective results from our tables and plots provide strong, quantitative evidence that knowledge distillation represents a paradigm shift in creating compute-efficient, high-performance language models.

Table 2. Comparison of performance and CO_2e across GPUs

Workload	Training Compute	A100 (80GB)	L40S (48GB)	H100 SXM (80GB)
		Hours I tCO_2e	Hours I tCO_2e	Hours I tCO_2e
Qwen3-8B Training (Vanilla)	1.73E+24	4.67M I 881.3	4.42M I 730.0	1.26M I 417.3
8B Model Distillation (Challenger)	8.50E+20	2297 I 0.43	2174 I 0.36	622 I 0.21
8B Model Fine-Tuning (Specialization)	1.44E+21	3890 I 0.73	3683 I 0.61	1053 I 0.35

6 Discussion

Our analysis of the computational costs and performance benchmarks associated with various model creation strategies provides a clear, quantitative basis for decision-making. The results from Sect. 5, particularly the comprehensive data in Table 1 and the performance-compute relationships visualized in Figs. 2 and 3, surface critical insights into the trade-offs between these methods.

6.1 Deconstructing the Cost-Performance Trade-Off

The case studies in Sect. 4 established the vast differences in computational cost between model creation methods, a finding that is reinforced across the entire landscape of models in Table 1. Training a vanilla foundation model from scratch, even a relatively small 8B parameter model, requires over a million GPU-hours and hundreds of tons of CO_2e. In stark contrast, creating a distilled model of the same size, as shown in our case study, requires less than 0.1% of that compute budget.

However, the most crucial finding of this paper is not just that distillation is cheaper, but that it redefines the efficiency frontier. As visualized in Figs. 2 and 3, distilled models do not simply follow the same scaling curve as vanilla models. Instead, they establish a new, superior curve. A distilled 8B model, for example, can achieve reasoning performance on par with, or even exceeding, a vanilla 70B model, but with a computational cost that is orders of magnitude lower. This demonstrates that distillation is not merely a cost-saving measure; it is a method for achieving a step-change in performance per FLOP. Fine-tuning, while also computationally inexpensive, does not exhibit this trait, as its performance is fundamentally capped by the capabilities of its base model. Distillation breaks this ceiling by directly transferring knowledge from a far more capable teacher.

6.2 The Strategic Imperative for Distillation

Based on these results, the strategic context for employing distillation becomes clear. It is the optimal choice when the goal is to create a deployable model that maximizes reasoning capability within a constrained computational budget. The key prerequisites are the existence of a powerful teacher model—whether proprietary or a large internal model—and a well-curated distillation dataset.

Our findings suggest that for tasks demanding high-level reasoning, investing a small fraction of a compute budget into a distillation process can yield a significantly higher return on investment than spending the same budget on further pre-training or fine-tuning a vanilla model. This holds true across the model size spectrum, from creating small, on-device models to developing highly capable mid-size models for enterprise use. Furthermore, as noted in our methodology, the high initial cost of the teacher's inference pass is a one-time, amortizable expense. Organizations can reuse the resulting dataset to distill multiple specialized student models, further driving down the effective cost per model and enabling the creation of a diverse suite of efficient, high-performing AI agents.

6.3 Deployment Scenarios and Workload Characteristics

The benefits of distillation extend far beyond the training phase and directly address critical deployment constraints in real-world applications. The smaller model size achieved through distillation is not just a matter of storage; it is a fundamental enabler for a wider range of deployment targets and workloads.

Inference latency and cost are directly proportional to a model's size. A distilled 8B model is inherently faster and cheaper to run than a 70B vanilla model. This advantage is amplified by quantization, a technique that reduces the precision of the model's weights. Smaller models are more amenable to aggressive quantization with less performance degradation. For example, an INT4 quantized 8B distilled model can have its memory footprint reduced to under 5GB [37], making it feasible to run on consumer-grade PCs, edge devices, and systems with limited VRAM—a feat impossible for larger models.

This opens three critical deployment tiers that are often inaccessible to large vanilla or proprietary models:

- **Edge and On-Device Deployment:** For applications in manufacturing (e.g., real-time quality control analysis on a factory floor) or retail (e.g., AI-powered kiosks), data privacy and low latency are paramount. Distilled models can run directly on local hardware, ensuring instantaneous responses and that sensitive data never leaves the premises.
- **PCs and Workstations:** In sectors like healthcare, professionals such as radiologists or researchers need powerful AI assistants that can analyze confidential patient data locally. A compact, distilled model can run on a standard workstation, providing sophisticated analysis without relying on a cloud connection, thus preserving patient privacy.
- **Cost-Effective Data Center Deployment:** Even in the cloud, smaller models are more efficient. They can be served on less expensive GPUs, and more instances

can be run on a single server, significantly lowering the operational cost for any AI-powered service.

By creating models that are not only powerful but also compact, distillation directly addresses the practical hardware, latency, and power efficiency constraints that often dictate the viability of real-world AI applications.

6.4 Broader Implications for the AI Ecosystem

The practical implications of these findings are significant. The extreme resource requirements for training frontier models, as estimated for GPT-4o in Sect. 4.4, create a landscape dominated by a few large players. Knowledge distillation is a powerful democratizing force. It provides a viable pathway for startups, academic institutions, and enterprises without access to massive GPU clusters to create models with competitive, state-of-the-art reasoning abilities.

This has profound effects on several fronts:

- **Economic Accessibility:** By drastically lowering the barrier to entry for creating high-performance models, distillation fosters innovation and competition. The estimated 1.2M GPU-hours for training a vanilla 8B model represents a significant financial and environmental cost, whereas the ~622 GPU-hours for its distilled counterpart are orders of magnitude more accessible.
- **Deployment Flexibility:** The smaller footprint of distilled models makes them ideal for a wider range of deployment scenarios, from latency-sensitive cloud applications to privacy-centric on-premise or edge deployments.
- **Sustainable and Energy-Efficient AI:** As the environmental cost of AI becomes a greater concern, methods that reduce the carbon footprint of training are critical. Furthermore, the lower power draw of smaller, distilled models during inference contributes to significant energy savings over the model's operational lifecycle, a crucial factor for large-scale and edge deployments.

In essence, our results quantitatively demonstrate that distillation is not just an optimization technique but a strategic necessity for any organization looking to balance performance, cost, and accessibility in the development of advanced AI systems.

7 Conclusion

This paper set out to benchmark the performance and efficiency of distilled language models in resource-constrained settings. Our comprehensive analysis, spanning computational cost estimation, local benchmarking, and synthesis of public data, confirms that knowledge distillation offers a transformative approach to model creation. The findings presented in our results demonstrate that distilled models consistently outperform their vanilla counterparts, achieving superior reasoning capabilities for a fraction of the training cost.

For practitioners operating under computational constraints, this trade-off is paramount. The dual benefits of distillation—drastically reduced training compute and the creation of smaller, more performant models—directly address the primary challenges of real-world deployment. Crucially, the efficiency gains extend beyond the training phase. Since inference latency is fundamentally linked to the size of a model and its active parameters, the smaller student models produced through distillation are inherently faster and cheaper to run. This enables the deployment of powerful AI in latency-sensitive applications where larger models would be impractical. Ultimately, by providing a pathway to elite performance without demanding elite resources, distillation is the definitive strategy for developing and deploying advanced, efficient, and accessible language models.

References

1. Hinton, G., Vinyals, O., Dean, J.: Distilling the knowledge in a neural network. In: NIPS Deep Learning and Representation Learning Workshop (2015)
2. Guo, D., Yang, D., Zhang, H., et al.: DeepSeek-R1: incentivizing reasoning capability in LLMs via reinforcement learning. arXiv:2501.12948 (2025)
3. Parthasarathy, V.B., Zafar, A., Khan, A., Shahid, A.: The ultimate guide to fine-tuning LLMs from basics to breakthroughs: an exhaustive review of technologies, research, best practices, applied research challenges and opportunities. arXiv:2408.13296 (2024)
4. Epoch AI: Estimating Training Compute of Deep Learning Models. https://epoch.ai/blog/estimating-training-compute. Accessed 08 June 2025
5. Hoffmann, J., Borgeaud, S., Mensch, A., et al.: Training compute-optimal large language models. In: Proceedings of the 36th Conference on Neural Information Processing Systems (NeurIPS 2022). Curran Associates, Red Hook (2022)
6. Gcore Team: A Comparative Analysis of NVIDIA Data Center GPUs. https://gcore.com/blog/nvidia-gpu-comparison/. Accessed 08 June 2025
7. Xu, X., et al.: A survey on knowledge distillation of large language models. arXiv:2402.13116 (2024)
8. Strubell, E., Ganesh, A., McCallum, A.: Energy and policy considerations for deep learning in NLP. In: Korhonen, A., Traum, D., Màrquez, L. (eds.) Proceedings of the 57th Annual Meeting of the Association for Computational Linguistics, pp. 3645–3650. Association for Computational Linguistics, Florence, Italy (2019)
9. Hu, E.J., et al.: LoRA: low-rank adaptation of large language models. arXiv:2106.09685 (2021)
10. Dettmers, T., Pagnoni, A., Holtzman, A., Zettlemoyer, L.: QLoRA: efficient finetuning of quantized LLMs. In: Advances in Neural Information Processing Systems, vol. 36, pp. 10088–10115. Curran Associates, Inc. (2023)
11. Gudibande, A., Wallace, E., Snell, C., et al.: The false promise of imitating proprietary LLMs. In: Krause, A., Ranzato, M., Beygelzimer, A., Dauphin, Y., Liang, P., Vaughan, J.W. (eds.) Proceedings of the 40th International Conference on Machine Learning, PMLR, vol. 202, pp. 11956–11984. PMLR (2023)
12. Gu, Y., Dong, L., Wei, F., Huang, M.: MiniLLM: knowledge distillation of large language models. In: Proceedings of the Twelfth International Conference on Learning Representations (ICLR). OpenReview.net (2024)
13. Agarwal, R., Vieillard, N., Zhou, Y., et al.: On-policy distillation of language models: learning from self-generated mistakes. In: Proceedings of the Twelfth International Conference on Learning Representations (ICLR). OpenReview.net (2024)
14. Liu, A., Feng, B., Xue, B., et al.: DeepSeek-V3 technical report. arXiv:2412.19437 (2024)

15. Grattafiori, A., et al.: The llama 3 herd of models. arXiv preprint arXiv:2407.21783 (2024)
16. Patterson, D., et al.: The carbon footprint of machine learning training will plateau, then shrink. Commun. ACM **65**(10), 43–52 (2022)
17. Rein, D., et al.: GPQA: a graduate-level google-proof Q&A benchmark. In: Oh, A., Naumann, T., Globerson, A., Saenko, K., Hardt, M., Levine, S. (eds.) Advances in Neural Information Processing Systems, vol. 36. Curran Associates, Inc. (2023)
18. Zhang, Z., Yao, Y., Ding, M., et al.: AIME: a meticulously curated benchmark for large language model evaluation. In: Advances in Neural Information Processing Systems, vol. 38. Curran Associates, Inc. (2024)
19. Chen, M., Tworek, J., Jun, H., et al.: Evaluating large language models trained on code. arXiv preprint arXiv:2107.03374 (2021)
20. Epoch AI: AI Benchmarking Hub. https://epoch.ai/data/ai-benchmarking-dashboard. Accessed 18 June 2025
21. LocalAIME. https://github.com/Belluxx/LocalAIME. Accessed 20 June 2025
22. OpenAI: simple-evals. https://github.com/openai/simple-evals. Accessed 20 June 2025
23. DeepSeek-V2-Ollama-Simple-Evals. https://github.com/kennethleungty/DeepSeek-V2-Ollama-Simple-Evals. Accessed 20 June 2025
24. Yang, A., et al.: Qwen3 technical report. arXiv:2505.09388 (2025)
25. Yang, A., Yang, B., Zhang, B., et al.: Qwen2.5 technical report. arXiv:2412.15115 (2024)
26. DeepSeek AI: DeepSeek-R1-0528-Qwen3-8B. https://huggingface.co/deepseek-ai/DeepSeek-R1-0528-Qwen3-8B. Accessed 20 June 2025
27. xAI: Grok 3 Beta—The Age of Reasoning Agents. https://x.ai/news/grok-3. Accessed 20 June 2025
28. Prithiv ML Mods: o3-mini & Deepseek-R1. https://huggingface.co/blog/prithivMLmods/o3-mini-deepseek-and-r1. Accessed 20 June 2025
29. Microsoft: microsoft/phi-4. https://huggingface.co/microsoft/phi-4. Accessed 20 June 2025
30. Vellum: LLM Leaderboard 2025. https://www.vellum.ai/llm-leaderboard. Accessed 20 June 2025
31. Hendrycks, D., et al.: Measuring massive multitask language understanding. In: Proceedings of the International Conference on Learning Representations (ICLR) (2021)
32. Srivastava, A., et al.: Beyond the imitation game: quantifying and extrapolating the capabilities of language models. arXiv preprint arXiv:2206.04615 (2022)
33. Liang, P., et al.: Holistic evaluation of language models. arXiv preprint arXiv:2211.09110 (2022)
34. Gasanov, E., et al.: Hugging face open LLM leaderboard. https://huggingface.co/spaces/HuggingFaceH4/open_llm_leaderboard. Accessed 01 Aug 2025
35. Poretschkin, M., et al.: Efficiency spectrum of large language models. arXiv preprint arXiv:2404.18560 (2024)
36. Hsieh, C.Y., et al.: Distilling step-by-step! outperforming larger language models with less training data and smaller model sizes. arXiv preprint arXiv:2305.02301 (2023)
37. Wani, S., Ellison, D., Page, E., Dholakia, A.: Lenovo LLM Sizing Guide. Lenovo Press. https://lenovopress.lenovo.com/lp2130-lenovo-llm-sizing-guide. Accessed 01 Aug 2025

Next Generative AI Benchmark Development

Hamesh Patel[1(✉)], Nirmala Sundararajan[2], Nicholas Wakou[2], Paul Cao[3], and David Schmidt[4]

[1] Intel Corporation, Hillsboro, OR, USA
hamesh.s.patel@intel.com
[2] Dell Technologies, Austin, TX, USA
{nirmala.sundararajan,nicholas.wakou}@dell.com
[3] HPE, Spring, TX, USA
paul.cao@hpe.com
[4] Red Hat, Raleigh, NC, USA
daschmid@redhat.com

Abstract. The Transaction Processing Performance Council (TPC) is initiating the development of a new benchmark standard to address the emerging demands of Generative AI (GenAI) workloads. Building on the success of TPCx-AI, which established a comprehensive framework for evaluating end-to-end machine learning pipelines, this new benchmark aims to capture the unique computational and data-centric characteristics of GenAI systems. Generative AI models, including large language models (LLMs), diffusion models, and multimodal architectures, introduce novel challenges in data processing, model evaluation, and system scalability. The new benchmark is being designed to reflect real-world, production-scale GenAI scenarios. The benchmark will represent relevant end to end scenarios and full-stack evaluation pipeline, including data ingestion, inference, post-processing, and quality assessment. The TPC consortium is actively engaging with industry stakeholders to define representative workloads, including text summarization, code generation, image synthesis, and multimodal reasoning. The benchmark may incorporate a range of performance metrics critical to GenAI, including throughput, latency, model quality and price performance. Emphasis will also be placed on reproducibility, transparency, and auditability, in line with TPC's established benchmarking principles. This paper outlines the challenges, design goals, methodologies and early architectural considerations for a new GenAI benchmark.

Keywords: Generative AI · AI · AI benchmark · LLMs · RAG

1 Introduction

Generative AI models are evolving rapidly, and large language models (LLMs) have captured the public interest. Unlike traditional machine learning models, LLMs are non-deterministic, context-sensitive, and multi-modal. Benchmarking LLMs using static metrics is difficult because their outputs vary with the hyperparameters such as prompt phrasing, context length, and even temperature settings. LLMs power chatbots, agents,

R. Nambiar and M. Poess (Eds.): TPCTC 2025, LNCS 16261, pp. 203–220, 2026.
https://doi.org/10.1007/978-3-032-18070-4_13

copilots, summarizers, translators, and more. Each use case has different performance expectations. For example, latency is important for a chatbot use case, whereas factuality is more important for summarization tasks or creative writing. The new TPC Generative AI (GenAI) benchmark will focus on generative tasks such as text generation/summarization, code generation, multi-modal tasks etc., and will not focus on object detection, classification or recommendation.

Many current benchmarks primarily focus on result quality and performance and do not consider factors like cost efficiency, availability, and commercial support. A real-world performance measurement involves mixed workloads, concurrency, and resource management that existing benchmarks ignore.

The need for a new TPC GenAI benchmark arises from the unique characteristics and demands of generative AI workloads, which differ significantly from traditional inference tasks. Newer models like multi-modal transformers, agentic systems, and chain-of-thought reasoning require computing patterns and latency profiles. Despite the robustness of the existing benchmarks, there is a need for a new GenAI benchmark to reflect these emerging workloads. The benchmarks will be extensible and continuously updated to accommodate rapidly evolving models. Inference workloads are highly variable with seasonal spikes and real time demands and benchmarks should account for burst handling, latency under load, and resource elasticity.

The Transaction Processing Council (TPC) benchmarks are industry standard for database, analytics, and system performance evaluation. They focus on throughput, latency, scalability, concurrency, and cost efficiency which are critical in production and is underrepresented in the existing AI benchmarks. Any TPC benchmark requires the following three primary metrics:

- Performance Metrics
- Price/Performance Metrics
- Hardware and Software Availability

and the new GenAI benchmark is no exception to this. In addition to real-world metrics like time-to-accuracy and cost-to-accuracy rather than just throughput or accuracy alone, the GenAI benchmark will also provide inference latency and cost. By integrating the TPC benchmarking principles, the GenAI benchmark will measure tokens/sec per dollar and efficiency under multi-user workloads. Like TPC's OLTP/OLAP (Online Transaction Processing/Online Analytical Processing) benchmarks, the GenAI benchmark handles workloads that involve batch inference, real-time streaming and retrieval augmented generation (RAG). The enterprise-workloads mix tasks such as summarization, retrieval and reasoning rather than a targeted single specific task.

The new TPC GenAI benchmark will strive to extend beyond measuring quantitative metrics such as latency and throughput and focuses on end-to-end pipeline benchmarking from data processing, fine-tuning all the way to inferencing. It is architecture-neutral and reproducible. It tests a wide range of models across various hardware and software stacks. The existing benchmarks use latency or throughput as the target. As a result, the systems might be tuned and optimized to get a good score rather than to genuinely improve performance. The GenAI benchmark will be resistant to Goodhart's Law that states that "when a measure becomes a target, it ceases to be a good measure". To avoid falling into the Goodhart trap, the next-gen AI benchmark includes task-specific metrics for alignment with production criteria. The GenAI benchmark is open-ended, subjective and measures end-to-end utilization. The standardized benchmarking suite will allow for cross-model comparisons.

2 LLM Inference Workloads and Performance Metrics

LLM inference workloads are characterized by distinct computational and system level requirements. Key performance metrics for evaluating LLM inference include Time-to-first-token (TTFT), Request latency and tokens/second. Request concurrency and overall throughput can also be used as metrics to assess the performance of these workloads.

Optimizations for LLM inference systems encompass areas such as efficient memory management, including techniques like PagedAttention [10], and distributed inference across multiple accelerators. Other significant techniques include speculative decoding and optimized transformer engines. The components of parallel inference engines typically involve inputs (prompts, reasoning context, and replies from earlier conversation turns), outputs, model weights, model layers, and accelerators.

Generative AI workloads span a wide array of real-world applications; we will review some of these in the remainder of this section.

2.1 Text Generation and Summarization

This category includes generating single-sentence summaries of articles, creating headlines, engaging in creative writing (e.g., creating a children's story with a particular setting), and document summarization. It also extends to translating text between pairs of natural languages. These tasks generally involve medium length prompts, exhibit moderate latency sensitivity, and are highly quality sensitive in their outputs. Quality is assessed using metrics like BLEU, ROUGE, or through human preference scoring.

2.2 Code Generation and Completion

Examples include autocompletion of code, bug fixing, and synthesizing code from natural language descriptions. A specific task mentioned is completing a function body given source code in a directory.

These tasks necessitate high precision in their generated outputs. Evaluation predominantly focuses on functional correctness or the successful execution of unit tests, using metrics such as Pass@k and exact match, along with other execution-based metrics.

2.3 Retrieval-Augmented Generation (RAG)

RAG applications are widely used in enterprise search, knowledge-grounded question-answering, and document-based chat systems. Examples of Multimodal RAG with PDF extraction could involve finding and extracting specific contract terms from documents and citing sources. RAG critically combines vector search with LLM inference. RAG performance is highly sensitive to both retrieval latency and the context window size.

Benchmarking prioritizes answer accuracy, retrieval precision, and latency. Examples of Multimodal RAG with PDF extraction involves an ingestion pipeline that processes diverse content types (e.g., charts, pages, tables as images, and text) to extract content and metadata, feeding into a retrieval pipeline that integrates components like NeMo Retriever Embedding (NVIDIA), NeMo Retriever Reranking (NVIDIA), a Vector Database, and an LLM to generate responses to user queries. User feedback on responses can also be incorporated.

2.4 Multimodal Reasoning

This category encompasses tasks such as image captioning, visual question answering, and extracting text or charts from PDFs. These applications usually demand the integration of vision and language models, leading to high memory and compute requirements. Evaluation employs task-specific metrics such as CIDEr (Consensus-based Image Description Evaluation) and METEOR (Metric for Evaluation of Translation with Explicit Ordering), in addition to human evaluation.

2.5 Feedback-Driven Learning and PEFT (Parameter-Efficient Fine-Tuning)

This represents a workflow for LLM customization. Techniques include traditional fine-tuning and Parameter-Efficient Fine-Tuning (PEFT) methods like LoRA (Low-Rank Adaptation) and QLoRA (Quantized Low-Rank Adaptation). These customization approaches are gaining increasing prevalence.

3 Benchmarking Methodologies and Challenges

Benchmarking LLMs and their inference workloads is a complex and multifaceted challenge. The rapidly growing popularity of LLMs necessitates representative benchmarks for accurate comparisons across various use cases. Beyond traditional accuracy and throughput, new metrics like energy efficiency, bias, trust, and sustainability are emerging as important considerations.

3.1 Challenges in Quality Evaluation

No single metric can fully capture the complex behavior of an LLM, especially for open-ended tasks. In addition, while task-based accuracy approaches (e.g. MMLU-Massive Multitask Language Understanding or HELM-Holistic Evaluation of Language Models) and probability-based metrics (e.g., perplexity, K-L divergence) are used, probability-based metrics do not always correlate with user satisfaction. Evaluation often involves subjective comparisons, head-to-head competitions, rubric-based scoring, and human-in-the-loop assessments.

3.2 Broader Benchmarking Challenges

There is a critical need for standardized, reproducible benchmarks for inference workloads. Variability in prompt design, model versions, and system configurations can lead to inconsistent results. In addition, performance depends not solely on the model but on the entire inference stack, including model layout and sharding, KV cache and speculative decoding, vector databases, and document stores. Benchmarks must account for end-to-end latency, throughput, and resource usage under realistic workloads. Rapid Ecosystem Evolution where new models, frameworks, and optimization techniques are introduced frequently pose an additional challenge in benchmark development. This requires benchmarks to be modular and extensible to adapt to evolving best practices and hardware capabilities. Finally, the lack of diversity across data types (textual, numerical, audio, image), problem classes (supervised, unsupervised), and methods (classification, clustering, regression, Deep Learning vs. Machine Learning) are a few of the additional dimensions that make representative benchmark development challenging.

4 Benchmarking Metrics

The rapid evolution of Generative AI (GenAI) technologies—spanning large language models (LLMs), diffusion models, and multimodal architecture has introduced unprecedented demands on system performance, scalability, and evaluation methodologies. As models like Google's Gemini 1.0 Ultra demonstrate, the computational demands and associated costs underscore the importance of optimizing performance metrics [2]. This section explores the foundational metrics necessary for evaluating GenAI systems, aligning with the benchmark's goals of capturing real-world, production-scale scenarios and ensuring reproducibility, transparency, and auditability.

4.1 Performance

Understanding the responsiveness and scalability of GenAI systems is critical for real-world deployment. As models grow in complexity and size, their computational demands increase significantly. For example, Google's Gemini 1.0 Ultra reportedly cost $192 million to train, reflecting the scale of infrastructure needed to support state-of-the-art performance [2]. Key performance metrics include:

- Time-to-First-Token (TTFT) measures the latency from request initiation to the generation of the first token. This metric is vital for interactive applications, where user experience depends on perceived responsiveness. In our Llama-3.1-8b test case, TTFT averaged 277.65ms, with a p99 value of 282.13ms. Table 1 presents results from a default, unoptimized configuration. These figures are illustrative only and do not reflect the system's actual performance.
- Request Latency captures the end-to-end response time, including data ingestion, inference, and post-processing. The Llama-3.1-8b benchmark showed an average latency of 6,497.01ms, with extreme values (p99) reaching 10,270.61ms for long-form summarization tasks.

- Inter-token latency measures the time between the generation of consecutive tokens for a given request. In this example, inter-token latency averaged 9.97ms, with a p99 value of 10.02ms.
- Tokens per Second: This metric quantifies generation speed and reflects overall system throughput. The tested model achieved 95.96 tokens per second in this example scenario.
- Throughput Under Concurrency: Assesses system scalability under simultaneous requests, reflecting real world deployment conditions.

Table 1. Llama-3.1-8b Inference Performance Metrics

	avg	min	max	p99	p90	p75
Time to First Token (ms)	277.65	267.23	283.57	282.13	280.78	279.82
Time to Second Token (ms)	9.26	8.71	11.05	9.59	9.44	9.37
Request Latency (ms)	6,497.01	358.41	10,286.83	10,270.61	10,257.37	10,247.42
Inter-token Latency (ms)	9.97	9.86	10.07	10.02	9.99	9.99
Output Sequence Length (tokens)	1000					
Input Sequence Length (tokens)	7000					
Output Token Throughput (per sec)	95.96					
Request Throughput (per sec)	0.15					

The example charts below present token throughput results across varying concurrency levels. This data highlights how system performance scales with increased parallel requests, providing insight into the efficiency and responsiveness of typical GenAI workloads under load.

The configurations as shown in the legends of Fig. 1 and Fig. 2 are explained in Table 2.

Figure 2 demonstrates that tokens/sec increases with concurrency across all configurations. This behavior is expected, as higher concurrency allows the system to process more requests in parallel, thereby increasing overall throughput. Depending on the resources of the underlying infrastructure, configurations with larger input sequence lengths (e.g.,config1 to config4) show superior scaling, indicating better utilization of hardware resources under high load but as sequence lengths grow (e.g.,config6 7000–1000), the throughput saturation point is achieved at a lower concurrency level, beyond which, adding more requests yield diminishing returns.

Conversely, Fig. 1 reveals that tokens/sec/request decreases as concurrency increases. This indicates a decline in per-core efficiency, likely due to increased contention for shared resources such as memory bandwidth, cache, and compute cycles. As concurrency rises, the overhead associated with managing parallel workloads begins to offset the gains in throughput.

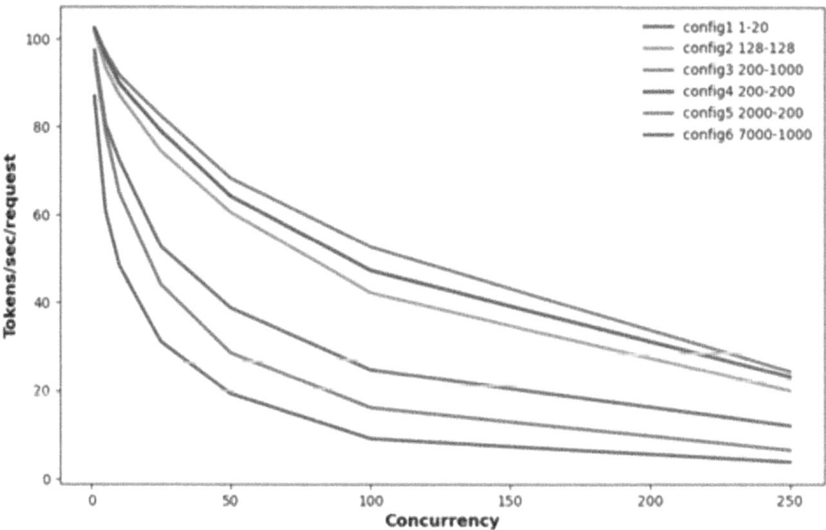

Fig. 1. Tokens/sec/request vs Concurrency for various configurations

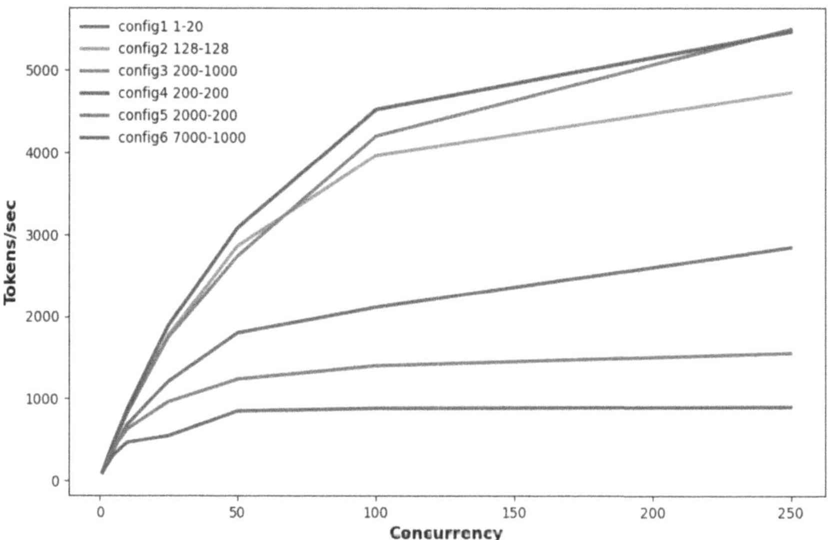

Fig. 2. Tokens/sec vs Concurrency for various configurations

Table 2. Token Configuration Matrix for Gen AI Use Cases

Configuration	Use Case	Scenario
1-20	Token-Level Prediction	Token-by-Token Autocomplete
128-128	Real-Time Interaction	Real-Time Assistive AI
200-200	Conversational Generation	Response Chatbots and Virtual Assistants
200-1000	Prompted Content Generation	Creative Writing or Story generation
2000-200	Response analysis	Customer Support or Knowledge Base
7000-1000	Long-Form Summarization	Long-Context Document Analysis and Summarization

4.2 Performance, Concurrency and Efficiency Trade-Off Analysis

The interplay between concurrency, performance, and efficiency in Generative AI inference workloads reveals a nuanced and often non-linear relationship. As concurrency increases, systems can process more requests in parallel, resulting in higher aggregate throughput—typically measured in tokens per second. This scaling behavior is advantageous for batch-oriented tasks such as large-scale document generation or pipeline-based inference, where maximizing output volume is the primary goal.

However, increased concurrency introduces resource contention, particularly across CPU cores and memory bandwidth. This leads to a decline in per-core efficiency, measured as tokens per core per request. The degradation stems from factors such as scheduling overhead, cache contention, and diminished locality, which intensify under high concurrency. Consequently, while total throughput improves, the system performs less work per unit of resource.

This trade-off is workload-dependent. Latency-sensitive applications—like real-time summarization or interactive chat—benefit from lower concurrency, preserving responsiveness and resource efficiency. In contrast, throughput-driven applications can tolerate longer latencies in exchange for better utilization. Configuration choices, such as batch size, further influence this balance: larger batches may improve utilization, while smaller batches maintain responsiveness but limit throughput.

The trade-off between performance and efficiency in GenAI inference is a balancing act shaped by concurrency. Understanding and tuning this interplay is critical for designing inference systems that align with specific operational goals, whether optimizing for latency, throughput, or cost-efficiency.

4.3 Quality Evaluation Metrics

The rapid advancement of GenAI technologies has necessitated equally sophisticated evaluation frameworks. Traditional metrics like perplexity and KL divergence provide foundational and statistical insights but fail to capture the full spectrum of model capabilities and limitations in applied settings. Task-based evaluations and human-in-the-loop scoring provide context-sensitive assessments. Evaluating the output quality of GenAI models requires both objective and subjective measures.

Recent benchmarks such as MMLU and HELM as models are increasingly used in creative and decision-making contexts, rubric-based scoring and expert reviews are essential to capture nuances that automated metrics may miss [19].

4.3.1 Task-Based Benchmarks

Task-based benchmarks are designed to simulate real-world use cases, offering a contextualized and domain-specific lens through which model capabilities can be assessed. These benchmarks are particularly valuable for evaluating generalization, reasoning, and factual accuracy across diverse subject areas.

- MMLU

The Massive Multitask Language Understanding (MMLU) benchmark is one of the most widely adopted tools for evaluating cross-domain generalization in LLMs. It comprises multiple-choice questions drawn from 57 academic disciplines, including mathematics, history, law, and medicine. Each question is designed to test not only factual recall but also reasoning and comprehension. MMLU is especially useful for identifying gaps in a model's knowledge base and for comparing performance across different model architectures [6]. Its structure allows for fine-grained analysis of subject-specific strengths and weaknesses, making it a cornerstone in academic and enterprise evaluations.

- HELM

The Holistic Evaluation of Language Models (HELM) framework extends the scope of evaluation beyond task accuracy. It incorporates multiple dimensions such as calibration, robustness, fairness, and efficiency across diverse scenarios. HELM evaluates models in tasks like question answering, summarization, and dialogue generation, enabling stakeholders to assess not just performance but also reliability and ethical behavior [12]. HELM is particularly valuable for organizations deploying models in production environments where operational stability and ethical considerations are paramount.

4.3.2 Probability-Based Metrics

Probability-based metrics are foundational to model training and optimization. They provide statistical insights into how well a model predicts language sequences, but they often fail to capture semantic correctness or contextual appropriateness—especially in tasks requiring creativity or nuanced understanding. While useful for optimization, these metrics show limited correlation with human-perceived quality in creative tasks [12].

- Perplexity

Perplexity measures a model's uncertainty in predicting the next token in a sequence. It is calculated as the exponentiation of the average negative log-likelihood of predicted tokens. Lower perplexity values indicate higher confidence and predictive accuracy. However, perplexity does not necessarily correlate with human-perceived quality, as grammatically correct but semantically irrelevant text may still yield low perplexity [14].

- KL Divergence

Kullback-Leibler (KL) divergence quantifies the difference between the probability distribution of generated outputs and a reference distribution often derived from ground truth data. It is useful in tasks involving distributional alignment, such as imitation learning or style transfer. KL divergence can reveal whether a model is overconfident or underconfident, but it does not assess qualitative aspects like coherence or creativity [1]. However, like perplexity, KL divergence is limited in its ability to assess qualitative aspects such as coherence, creativity, or factual correctness.

4.3.3 Human-in-the-Loop Assessment

Given the limitations of automated metrics, human-in-the-loop (HITL) evaluation has become a critical component of GenAI assessment pipelines. Human-in-the-loop evaluation incorporates expert judgment to assess dimensions of quality that are difficult to quantify algorithmically. These methods are essential for evaluating creativity, coherence, and factual accuracy in high-stakes or subjective applications.

- *Rubric-Based Scoring* Rubric-based scoring frameworks involve structured evaluation by domain experts using predefined criteria. These rubrics assess creativity, coherence, factual accuracy, and relevance, providing consistent and reproducible assessments [15].
- *Creativity and Coherence* Creativity scoring evaluates the novelty, originality, and aesthetic appeal of generated content. This is particularly important in applications such as advertising, storytelling, and design, where the value of output is inherently subjective. Coherence analysis, on the other hand, assesses the logical structure and internal consistency of text. It ensures that generated outputs follow a clear narrative or argumentative flow, which is essential for tasks like essay writing, legal drafting, or technical documentation.
- *Factual Accuracy Verification* Factual accuracy is a critical metric in domains where misinformation can have serious consequences. Human reviewers verify the correctness of model outputs against trusted sources, identifying hallucinations, outdated information, or biased interpretations. This process is especially important in healthcare, legal, and financial applications, where even minor inaccuracies can lead to significant risks. HITL verification often involves cross-referencing with databases, literature, or expert knowledge, making it a resource-intensive but indispensable component of quality assurance.

Recent research has shown that hybrid evaluation strategies—combining automated metrics with human review—yield the most reliable assessments. These approaches leverage the scalability of automated tools while preserving the depth and nuance of expert judgment, enabling more accurate and context-aware evaluations [13].

4.4 Cost and Efficiency Metrics

As GenAI models scale in size and complexity, their operational costs— both financial and environmental—have become central concerns. Evaluating these costs is essential for sustainable deployment, especially in enterprise and cloud environments.

4.4.1 Energy Consumption

Training and inference for large models require substantial computational resources, leading to high energy consumption. For instance, the training of GPT-4 reportedly consumed energy equivalent to that used by 33,000 U.S. households [4]. Inference workloads also contribute to increased water usage in data centers, primarily for cooling purposes [7]. These environmental impacts have prompted calls for energy-aware model design, including the use of more efficient architectures, quantization techniques, and hardware accelerators. Tracking energy consumption across training and deployment phases is now a key metric for organizations committed to sustainability.

4.4.2 Cost per Query

Cost per query quantifies the financial overhead associated with each model invocation. It includes compute time, memory usage, storage, and infrastructure costs such as cloud provisioning and network bandwidth. This metric is particularly relevant for high-volume applications like customer support, search engines, and recommendation systems, where even small inefficiencies can scale into significant expenses [17]. Cost per query also enables comparative analysis across models and configurations, supporting decisions about model selection, deployment strategies, and pricing models for API-based services.

4.4.3 Model Size vs. Performance Trade-Offs

Larger models generally offer superior performance in tasks requiring deep contextual understanding, multi-step reasoning, or domain-specific expertise. However, this performance gain comes at the cost of increased resource consumption, longer inference times, and higher operational expenses. Evaluating the trade-off between model size and performance involves analyzing the marginal utility of additional parameters relative to their computational cost. Techniques such as model distillation, pruning, and low-rank adaptation (LoRA) have emerged as effective strategies for reducing model size while preserving performance [20]. These methods enable the deployment of lightweight models tailored to specific tasks, offering a more efficient alternative to monolithic architectures.

5 System and Framework Considerations

We now turn our attention to system-level optimizations that apply both to LLM inference itself (i.e., text generation) and to applications and systems built atop language models. In the context of a TPC benchmark submission, these are the sorts of changes that a test sponsor might vary to differentiate their solution. We will provide a high-level overview of the concrete demands of LLM inference, introduce several important software and hardware-specific optimization strategies, and conclude by discussing some higher-level concerns and workflows that LLM systems must address.

5.1 Inference Fundamentals and Performance Demands

A detailed description of transformer-based inference is outside the scope of this paper[1]; the brief explanation that follows is intended to provide context for the scale of performance challenges involved in LLM applications.

LLM inference has two phases: *prefill*, in which the model builds up context for a prompt input, and *decoding*, in which the model generates new text one token at a time. While prefill can be compute-bound, since it is possible in general to process an entire prompt in parallel given sufficient arithmetic capacity, decoding is often memory- (or communication-)bound, largely because it is *autoregressive* and thus cannot exploit as much parallelism: the conditional probability of generating a token t_{i+1} following a sequence of tokens t_0, ..., t_i transitively depends on the conditional probabilities of generating every prior token given the sequence preceding them. Put another way, the prefill phase for a sufficiently-large request can saturate the arithmetic capacity of an accelerator (GPU, TPU, ASIC, or SIMD CPU), but multiple decode requests must be batched together in order to maximize utilization.

At a high level, the arithmetic demands of LLM are dominated by matrix multiplications and projections. (As a rule of thumb, a standard "dense" LLM will require roughly $2N$ floating-point operations to generate a token in the forward pass, where N is the number of parameters in the model; [8] other LLM architectures will use fewer operations.) The memory demands of LLM inference arise from multiple factors:

- the model weights themselves, which must remain resident in memory during inference. These weights are static and can easily consume tens or hundreds of gigabytes of memory; for example, a 70 billion parameter model using 16-bit floating point weights would require over 130 GiB of memory for the weights alone.
- the key-value (KV) cache, which caches intermediate activations to support autoregressive inference and must also remain resident in memory; the amount of memory consumed per token in a model's context is a function of the model's architecture. As an example, Meta's Llama 3 model with 70 billion parameters and 16-bit arithmetic requires 320 KiB per token for KV cache entries, or 10 GiB for the context necessary to support a request with a 32k token context window.

Since LLM inference is so memory-intensive, it is often necessary to shard model weights or KV cache blocks across multiple accelerators or nodes. There are several strategies for doing this, including *tensor parallelism*, which tiles matrices across multiple accelerators, i.e., dividing individual layers of the model into smaller tensors that can be processed independently, and *pipeline parallelism*, which distributes the model layers across multiple devices. Tensor parallelism requires finer-grained communication but can be easier to schedule than pipeline parallelism (Fig. 3).

[1] Vaswani et al. [18] is the essential reference in this space.

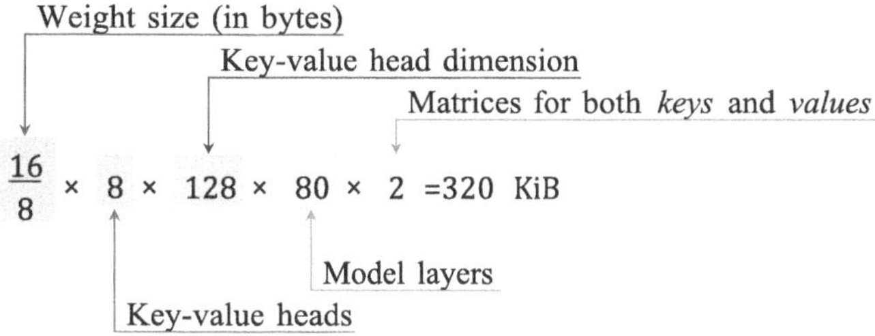

Fig. 3. KV cache memory usage per token for Llama 3 with 70 billion parameters.

5.2 Optimizations

Because many real workloads are dominated by decoding time, many common optimizations aim to increase the compute-to-communication ratio of decoding. This can take several forms, including:

- quantizing weights using smaller numeric data types in order to increase the computation possible per bit read from memory or via accelerator-to-accelerator communication,
- virtualizing KV-cache tensor memory in fixed-size blocks in order to improve spatial locality, reduce fragmentation, and enable sharing, as in PagedAttention, [10] and
- fusing multiple logically distinct operations and using I/O-aware tiling in order to limit unnecessary memory accesses, as in FlashAttention [5].

Another important class of optimizations focuses on exposing additional parallelism in decoding. The most notable such family of techniques are referred to as *speculative decoding* [3, 11]. In the most basic form of speculative decoding, a small *draft model* generates candidate output that is checked by the prefill mechanism of the larger *target model*. If the first n tokens of the draft model's output are accepted by the target model, then the target model will return n tokens in the decoding pass instead of one. Even a very small acceptance rate can thus dramatically improve response latency without materially affecting output quality.

5.3 Application Considerations

Simply generating text in response to prompts is a nontrivial capability, but it is only a small part of the responsibilities of a production system. Real systems are more complex and require additional capabilities and coordination, including:

- routing requests to one of several models or configurations (e.g., in order to place a long-running conversation on the replica with its context cached or to select the appropriate model for a given compute budget and application SLA),
- orchestrating pipelines incorporating the results of several models (e.g., to summarize a very long document by summarizing sections and then summarizing the aggregated summaries),
- orchestrating application logic that depends on the output of LLM inference requests (i.e., in agent-based applications),

- locating and supplying additional context related to the user's request (e.g., for personalization, enterprise search, office or coding assistants, or "talk to your data" applications),
- constraining overall output generation (e.g., to implement guardrails preventing unsafe or offensive replies), and
- constraining token sampling to satisfy a particular grammar (e.g., to produce structured output for API calls, code generation, or data generation).

Some of these capabilities can be implemented using application frameworks that encode common LLM system workflows. Some require additional components (e.g., vector databases or search engines for retrieval-augmented generation). Finally, capabilities like structured output generation can impact inference optimization strategies.

5.4 Customizing Models

Many organizations are currently using LLMs, but—in contrast to other machine learning techniques—most organizations are not training their own foundation models. Rather, most organizations are typically starting with another model and customizing it to meet application-specific needs. There are a spectrum of customization techniques for existing models, which generally offer increased control over the system's behavior in exchange for greater effort:

- The simplest form of customization is *prompt engineering*, in which users explore model-specific techniques and templates that cause an unmodified model to produce the best results
- A more systematic approach to prompt engineering involves automatically optimizing basic prompts into ones that are more suitable given user-specified fitness criteria, as in the DSPy system [9], and
- Fine-tuning a model involves optimizing some of its layers so that its outputs better match a corpus of application-specific examples.

6 Evaluation Challenges

Despite the growing maturity of LLM systems and inference infrastructure, evaluating their performance and quality remains a complex, multi-dimensional challenge. This section outlines the key difficulties that any standardized benchmark– such as the one proposed by the TPC Council–must address.

6.1 Subjectivity in Quality Assessment

In Sect. 4, task-based benchmarks like MMLU (a big test of knowledge across school subjects) and HELM (a framework that looks at fairness and reliability) are introduced as ways to measure how good GenAI is. It also talks about humanin-the-loop (HITL) evaluation, where people judge the AI's answers.

The problem is that "quality" often depends on who you ask. For example, one person might want a short, direct answer, while another might prefer a long and detailed explanation. Similarly, some people like very literal translations, while others want translations that sound natural in their language. Even politeness and tone can be judged differently in cultures.

Because of this, our judgment is subjective. HITL can help, but it is expensive, slow, and not always fair because different reviewers may disagree. So while Sect. 4 shows these tools are necessary, we would like to note that they are far from perfect.

6.2 Diverse Quality Metrics

In Sect. 4, we also see probability-based metrics like Perplexity (measures how surprised the model is when predicting text) and KL Divergence (measures how different the AI's predictions are from real examples). These are mathematical scores that provide insights into how the model "thinks."

But these numbers don't always line up with what people consider "good." For example, a piece of text can be grammatically correct (so it gets a good score) but still can be irrelevant, or boring. Similarly task-based metrics, often used in translation and summarization, may spuriously give low scores to perfectly good answers.

We suggest combining automated scores with human review to cover these gaps. In areas like medicine or law, you need actual experts to check if the answers are correct, because the AI might sound confident but still be wrong.

6.3 Reproducibility and Fairness

In general, benchmarks must be reproducible (you should get the same result if you test the same system again) and transparent (the testing process should be clear and open). But in this section, we show why this is so hard:

- Small changes in the prompt wording or the length of the conversation history can change the answer.
- Updates to the software or tokenizer (the tool that breaks text into chunks) can also shift results.
- Cloud-based models may change in the background without anyone being told, so yesterday's result might not match today's.
- Running the same model on different hardware (like a powerful H200 GPU vs. a smaller Jetson device) can produce very different outcomes.

This means the performance metrics can lose their meaning if the testing environment isn't carefully standardized.

6.4 System-Level Complexity

Performance is measured using metrics like Time-to-First-Token (TTFT), request latency, and throughput (how many tokens or requests the model can handle). However, these metrics don't tell the full story because the entire system matters. The AI's speed and quality are affected by:

- Hardware setup (e.g., using different accelerators or interconnects).

- Prefill and cache management (whether the system can efficiently handle long prompts and avoid repeated work for shared context).
- Inference software stack and specialized optimizations.

As a result, two companies running the same model report different performance numbers just because of differences in their infrastructure. The metrics in Sect. 4 are thus only meaningful in the context of a full disclosure report indicating how they were achieved.

6.5 Rapid Ecosystem Evolution

AI benchmarks need to adapt quickly to keep up with new models, frameworks, and use cases. New models like GPT-5, Claude Opus, Gemini 2.5, Llama 4, and Mistral 24 are being released every few months. As soon as benchmarks are set up, they may already be outdated. Community benchmarks sometimes "fork" into different versions, making it harder to compare published results.

On top of that, GenAI is moving beyond just text. Models are now handling images, audio, and video at the same time (multimodal AI). Benchmarks that only test text won't be enough in the future. This means benchmarks need to be flexible and expandable to stay useful.

In summary, the Generative AI Benchmark kit will be a system for fairly and clearly testing AI inference performance. We will initially focus on execution performance for large language models and evaluate response quality against reference implementations and by using LLM-as-a-judge techniques that will incorporate new modalities and evaluation techniques as they emerge.

Together, we need to build a fair and lasting benchmark that has clear rules that can also adapt to an evolving workload landscape.

7 Conclusion and Future Work

As we have seen, the field of generative AI is changing rapidly and designing a fair, robust, and useful GenAI benchmark is quite complex. There are many metrics that can be gathered, both objective and subjective, and they can vary considerably from use case to use case. The TPCx-AI committee is in the process of creating an industry-standard GenAI benchmark to address these challenges. It is working to address a few key questions:

- What cases should be included? The selection should include representative LLM use cases which are current. Care should be taken not to duplicate other benchmarks within the field. Some use cases under consideration are multimodal, multilingual, and streaming inference.
- What metrics should be gathered? What variables will contribute to the final benchmark "score" and what will be used to determine the quality of the score need to be defined.
- What should be fixed? To ensure reproducibility and cross-platform comparability, certain workload aspects need to be constrained, e.g. pre-defined prompt sets, evaluation rubric, scoring logic, accuracy/latency thresholds.

- What can be varied? The degrees of freedom that are allowed to the benchmark user or test sponsor need to be defined. Examples of what can be varied may include model layout, inference engine, vector database, document store.
- What needs to be disclosed? To ensure reproducibility and auditing purposes, the details of the system under test that must be disclosed need to be detailed. Such items may include system specifications, optimization flags (HW and SW), cost metrics.

The TPCx-AI subcommittee invites anyone who is interested in collaborating with this effort to reach us at tpc-ai@tpc.org.

Acknowledgments. The authors thank William C. Benton for helpful discussions within the TPCx-AI subcommittee about the mechanics of LLM inference and evaluation and for assistance in drafting and revising this manuscript. Benton is not an author and bears no responsibility for the final content.

References

1. Amini, A., Vieira, T., Cotterell, R.: Better estimation of the kl divergence between language models (2025). https://arxiv.org/abs/2504.10637
2. Anil, R., et al.: Gemini: a family of highly capable multimodal models (2025). https://arxiv.org/abs/2312.11805
3. Chen, C., Borgeaud, S., Irving, G., Lespiau, J.B., Sifre, L., Jumper, J.: Accelerating large language model decoding with speculative sampling (2023). https://arxiv.org/abs/2302.01318
4. Chen, S.: How much energy will AI really consume? the good, the bad and the unknown. Nature **639**(8053), 22–24 (2025)
5. Dao, T., Fu, D., Ermon, S., Rudra, A., Ré, C.: Flashattention: fast and memoryefficient exact attention with IO-awareness. Adv. Neural. Inf. Process. Syst. **35**, 16344–16359 (2022)
6. Hendrycks, D., et al.: Measuring massive multitask language understanding (2021). https://arxiv.org/abs/2009.03300
7. Jegham, N., Abdelatti, M., Elmoubarki, L., Hendawi, A.: How hungry is AI? benchmarking energy, water, and carbon footprint of LLM inference (2025). https://arxiv.org/abs/2505.09598
8. Kaplan, J., et al.: Scaling laws for neural language models (2020). https://arxiv.org/abs/2001.08361
9. Khattab, O., et al.: Dspy: compiling declarative language model calls into self-improving pipelines (2024)
10. Kwon, W., et al.: Efficient memory management for large language model serving with paged attention. In: Proceedings of the 29th Symposium on Operating Systems Principles, SOSP 2023, p. 611626. Association for Computing Machinery, New York (2023). https://doi.org/10.1145/3600006.3613165
11. Leviathan, Y., Kalman, M., Matias, Y.: Fast inference from transformers via speculative decoding. In: Krause, A., Brunskill, E., Cho, K., Engelhardt, B., Sabato, S., Scarlett, J. (eds.) Proceedings of the 40th International Conference on Machine Learning. Proceedings of Machine Learning Research, vol. 202, pp. 19274–19286. PMLR (2023). https://proceedings.mlr.press/v202/leviathan23a.html
12. Liang, P., et al.: Holistic evaluation of language models (2023). https://arxiv.org/abs/2211.09110
13. Mai, Y., Liang, P.: Massive multitask language understanding (mmlu) on helm (2024). https://crfm.stanford.edu/2024/02/15/mmlu.html

14. Otten, N.V.: Perplexity in NLP: understand how to evaluate LLMs (2024). https://spotintelligence.com/2024/08/19/perplexity-in-nlp/
15. Pangakis, N., Wolken, S.: Keeping humans in the loop: human-centered automated annotation with generative AI (2024). https://arxiv.org/abs/2409.09467
16. Pope, R., et al.: Efficiently scaling transformer inference (2022). https://arxiv.org/abs/2211.05102
17. Tunguz, T.: AI pricing: How much does AI cost in 2025? (2025). https://www.getmonetizely.com/blogs/ai-pricing-how-much-does-ai-cost-in-2025
18. Vaswani, A., et al.: Attention is all you need. In: Proceedings of the 31st International Conference on Neural Information Processing Systems, NIPS 2017, p. 60006010. Curran Associates Inc., Red Hook (2017)
19. Williams, A.: Comparison of generative AI performance on undergraduate and postgraduate written assessments in the biomedical sciences. Int. J. Educ. Technol. High. Educ. **21** (2024). https://doi.org/10.1186/s41239-024-00485-y
20. Zellinger, M.J., Thomson, M.: Economic evaluation of LLMs (2025). https://arxiv.org/abs/2507.03834

Author Index

R. Nambiar and M. Poess (Eds.): TPCTC 2025, LNCS 16261, pp. 221–222, 2026.
https://doi.org/10.1007/978-3-032-18070-4

The manufacturer's authorised representative in the EU is Springer Nature Customer Service Centre GmbH, Europaplatz 3, 69115 Heidelberg, Germany. If you have any concerns regarding our products, please contact ProductSafety@springernature.com

Printed and bound by CPI Group (UK) Ltd, Croydon, CR0 4YY
07/07/2026
02160917-0003